Collins

MW01152792

CAMBRIDGE
IGCSE®
PHYSICAL EDUCATION

Leon Fraser, Gareth Norman and Matthew Brown

William Collins' dream of knowledge for all began with the publication of his first book in 1819.
A self-educated mill worker, he not only enriched millions of lives, but also founded a flourishing publishing house.
Today, staying true to this spirit, Collins books are packed with inspiration, innovation and practical expertise. They place you at the centre of a world of possibility and give you exactly what you need to explore it.

Collins. Freedom to teach.

An imprint of HarperCollins*Publishers*
The News Building
1 London Bridge Street
London
SE1 9GF

Browse the complete Collins catalogue at
www.collins.co.uk

10 9 8 7 6 5 4 3 2 1

ISBN 978-0-00-820216-3

British Library Cataloguing in Publication Data
A catalogue record for this publication is available from the British Library.

Commissioned by Karen Jamieson
Project managed by Caroline Green and Sadique Basha
Developed by Hugh Hillyard-Parker
Edited by Jan Schubert
Proofread by Anna Carroll
Indexed by Jouve India Private Limited
Text permission research by Rachel Thorne
Photo research by Alison Prior
Cover design by Angela English
Cover photo © Stefan Schurr/Shutterstock
Typeset by Jouve India Private Limited
Illustrations by Jouve India Private Limited
Production by Lauren Crisp
Printed and bound by Grafica Veneta in Italy

IGCSE® is the registered trademark of Cambridge International Examinations.

MIX
Paper from
responsible sources

FSC www.fsc.org   **FSC™ C007454**

Contents

Introduction

Getting the most from the book

This Student Book is part of a rich and focused set of resources designed to help you fulfil your potential when studying for the Cambridge IGCSE® Physical Education course.

Through a series of 11 chapters (sub-divided into 53 topics) you will:

- deepen your knowledge and understanding of key Physical Education topics
- explore how theoretical topics relate to practical performance
- find out more about sports that are familiar to you, as well as some you have not tried yourself
- learn a range of skills by reflecting on your own performance
- monitor your progress with handy checklists.

The aim of the book is to be stimulating and enjoyable, whilst at the same time helping you build, develop and apply the skills listed above. Each topic does this through a straightforward structure of smaller tasks which end with a chance for you to apply what you have learned in a more challenging way. To help you, there are many useful features such as **clear learning objectives** for each topic, **explanations of key terms**, the opportunity to keep a **reflective log** (a sort of journal) of your thoughts and experiences, **checklists for success** in particular tasks, and **check-your-progress statements** so you can evaluate how you are doing, and go back over topics if you need to spend more time on them.

Throughout the book, clear diagrams, graphs, charts and up-to-date photographs will support you in your learning (particularly with the anatomy and physiology topics), and will help deepen your understanding and enable you to commit key information to long-term memory.

Although the book focuses primarily on preparation for the theoretical part of your course, many of the activities you complete will also encourage you to think about the theory in a practical setting. In addition, you will be asked to think about what you already know about a topic and draw on that knowledge as you learn more about the topic and undertake the tasks. This active approach will be very engaging, and you will feel like you are participating in the learning process in a positive and constructive way, building your knowledge and understanding of the topics covered in the course. General **study tips** are included to help you remember key information, and you can even use some of these tips in your study of other subjects too.

We hope this book gives you the support you need as you prepare for your Physical Education IGCSE qualification. In addition, it is our hope that by deepening your understanding of the impact and effects of physical activity on body and mind, you will develop a life-long enjoyment of sport which will have enormous benefits for your lifestyle and well-being.

Leon Fraser, Gareth Norman, and Matthew Brown

Getting the best from the book

The *Collins Cambridge IGCSE® Physical Education* Student Book contains four units, to match the syllabus: Anatomy and physiology; Health, fitness and training; Skill acquisition and psychology; Social, cultural and ethical influences.

Units are broken down into subject chapters, each chapter covering the key topics in manageable sections so that you can progress through at a comfortable pace, fully supported through the 'Explore, Develop, Apply' approach within every topic.

The pages are carefully designed and laid out, with diagrams and illustrations, to enable you to build confidence, and apply your learning in a practical way to your own performance.

Chapter openers give an overview of what the chapter will cover, and a comprehensive list showing the detailed learning points.

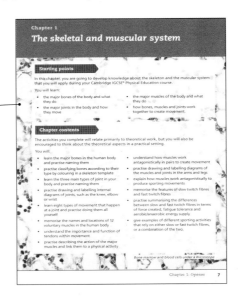

Clear topic headings and Learning Objectives show you what you will be covering.

The 'Starting point' section introduces the topic and helps you to think about what you may know already.

The 'Exploring the skills' section presents the key ideas within the topic.

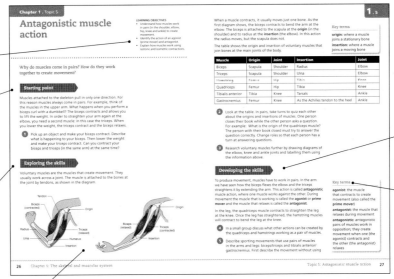

Clear and colourful illustrations and diagrams support learning.

The 'Developing the skills' section takes the key ideas to a deeper level. Activities in this section start to challenge you to think more deeply about the topic.

The 'Key terms' boxes give you clear definitions of important words you need to understand.

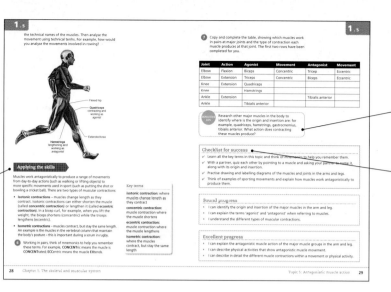

The 'Applying the skills' section at the end of the topic, contains activities which will prompt you to think further about the ideas you have learned and how they apply in a practical way.

The 'Reflective log' feature in every topic encourages you to keep notes on how the learning may apply to you directly.

The 'Checklist for success' at the end of every topic enables you to keep track of what you have covered in the topic.

The final page of the chapter includes a 'Check your progress' feature so you can see how well you are progressing and identify where you may need to go back and review some of the more challenging topics.

At the end of the book is an Index with page numbers, so you can quickly find key words (which are on the pages shown in bold) and topics you want to go back to.

Chapter 1

The skeletal and muscular system

Starting points

In this chapter, you are going to develop knowledge about the skeleton and the muscular system that you will apply during your Cambridge IGCSE® Physical Education course.

You will learn:

- the major bones of the body and what they do
- the major joints in the body and how they move
- the major muscles of the body and what they do
- how bones, muscles and joints work together to create movement.

Chapter contents

The activities you complete will relate primarily to theoretical work, but you will also be encouraged to think about the theoretical aspects in a practical setting.

You will:

- learn the major bones in the human body and practise naming them
- practise classifying bones according to their type by colouring in a skeleton template
- learn the three main types of joint in your body and practise naming them
- practise drawing and labelling internal diagrams of joints, such as the knee, elbow or wrist
- learn eight types of movement that happen at a joint and practise doing them all yourself
- memorise the names and locations of 12 voluntary muscles in the human body
- understand the importance and function of tendons within movement
- practise describing the action of the major muscles and link them to a physical activity
- understand how muscles work antagonistically in pairs to create movement
- practise drawing and labelling diagrams of the muscles and joints in the arms and legs
- explain how muscles work antagonistically to produce sporting movements
- memorise the features of slow twitch fibres and fast twitch fibres
- practise summarising the differences between slow and fast twitch fibres in terms of force created, fatigue tolerance and aerobic/anaerobic energy supply
- give examples of different sporting activities that rely on either slow or fast twitch fibres, or a combination of the two.

Bone marrow and blood cells under a microscope

The skeleton and its functions

How does our skeleton work? What bones make it up and what roles do they play in ensuring our bodies work and perform to their potential?

Starting point

The human **skeleton** is made up of 206 **bones** held together at the joints by ligaments. They vary in size from the longest (the femur) in your leg to the smallest found in the ear. The diagram shows the main bones in the human skeleton.

Key terms

skeleton: the internal framework of the body made up of 206 bones

bone: a hard, whitish, living tissue that makes up the skeleton; bones are lightweight but strong and perform many functions

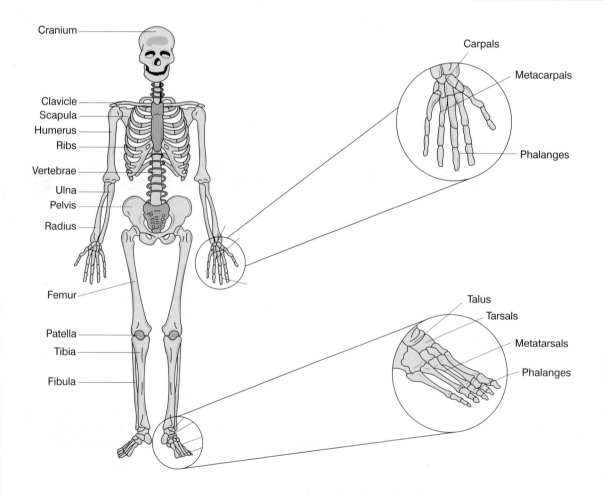

Cranium

Clavicle
Scapula
Humerus
Ribs
Vertebrae
Ulna
Pelvis
Radius

Femur

Patella
Tibia
Fibula

Carpals
Metacarpals
Phalanges

Talus
Tarsals
Metatarsals
Phalanges

1 For your first task use a copy of this diagram with the labels removed (or a blank template provided by your teacher). Close this book and label each of the bones identified above. Label as many of the bones as you can remember. Compare your version with the one here and take care to add in (and learn) all the ones you didn't include. (Keep your annotated diagram – you will need it for other tasks in this chapter.)

2 Many of the bones in our body have more common, everyday names. For example, the cranium is commonly called the skull. What are the proper names of the bones commonly known as:

  a) the kneecap   **b)** the shoulder blade

  c) the collarbone   **d)** the anklebone?

Exploring the skills

The skeleton has four functions.

- It gives the human body shape and support.
- It allows the body to create movement.
- It produces blood.
- It protects vital organs, such as the brain, heart and lungs.

Each of these functions relies on different bones located in the skeleton. The table below summarises how they perform these functions.

Function	How it does this	Example
Shape and support	The skeleton provides shape and support for the body. It forms the frame to which our muscles can attach and in which our organs can sit.	The backbone enables us to stay upright.
Muscle attachment for movement	Muscles are attached to the skeleton. Movement occurs when muscles contract and pull on bones making them move about a joint.	The biceps muscle connects the shoulder and elbow and helps with lifting.
Protection for vital organs	Internal organs are soft, delicate and easily damaged. These vital organs are protected by the skeleton.	The cranium protects the brain. The ribs help protect the heart and lungs.
Blood production	The centre of some large bones contains red bone marrow, which creates red blood cells.	The pelvis and femur are both important in blood production.

3 Add more notes to your skeleton diagram indicating the key functions of the bones mentioned in the table above.

Developing the skills

You can now connect the functions of the skeleton with some specific bones located within in it. In fact, bones come in many different shapes and sizes. The table below identifies the four different types of bone and the roles each type plays.

Types of bone	Function	Examples
Long bones *Femur*	These act as levers to produce a large range of movement.	Femur, tibia, fibula Humerus, ulna, radius Phalanges Clavicle
Short bones *Tarsal*	These are small and squat bones that enable movement. They can provide movement in lots of directions and also give strength.	Carpals Tarsals
Flat bones *Scapula*	These provide a large surface area for muscles to attach to. They also provide protection for organs.	Pelvis Cranium Scapula
Irregular bones *Vertebra*	These bones provide protection and support. They are shaped to suit the specific job they have to do.	Vertebrae

4 Shade the bones on your skeletal template using the colours shown in this table. Create a key to identify which type of bone each colour indicates.

5 Look at the picture of the skeleton and discuss with a partner which bones protect:

a) the heart

b) the brain

c) the lungs

d) the spinal column.

6 Then copy and complete this table.

Bone	Type	Function
Phalange		
Radius		
Scapula		
Pelvis		
Patella		
Metatarsal		

Applying the skills

During different sports or activities the skeleton is put under pressure to ensure that all of its various functions can operate. The different bones help our body during sport: for example, long bones act as levers to help you move fast, while short bones take impact and bear the body's weight.

7 Look at the photo on the previous page of a triple jumper in action. Which bones are involved in this sport?

> **REFLECTIVE LOG**
> Identify a sport or activity that you have participated in and make notes to answer the following questions: Which bones are involved? What types of bones are these? How do they protect the body during the activity?

Checklist for success

✔ Learn the different bones in your body and practise naming them.

✔ With a partner, quiz each other by pointing to a bone and asking your partner to name the bone and describe its function.

✔ Makes notes about bones in different parts of the body: for example, how many bones are there in the hand, what are they called and what are their functions?

✔ Practise classifying bones according to their type by colouring in a blank skeleton template several times.

Sound progress

• I can identify each of the skeleton's four functions.

• I can locate and name the main bones in the skeleton.

• I can describe the four different bone types (short, long, flat, irregular).

Excellent progress

• I can explain the four functions of the skeleton, giving an example of each function.

• I can locate and name the main bones in the skeleton, giving examples of how different bones are involved in various sporting activities.

• I can describe the four different bone types (short, long, flat, irregular) and explain the function of each type.

Joint types, structure and formation

LEARNING OBJECTIVES
- Identify the three different types of joint.
- Describe two types of freely moveable joints.

What are joints? How are they made up and why are they so important in movement?

Starting point

A **joint** is the point where two or more bones meet which allows a different range of movement or rotation for the body.

1 Identify with your partner the different locations of joints in your body. Use sticky notes to label them. If you know the anatomical name of the joint, write that on the note.

Key term

joint: a point in the body where two or more bones are joined in a way that permits movement

Exploring the skills

There are three main types of joint and each has a different freedom of movement. To ensure they can be supported, joints have ligaments that provide the elastic fibres joining bone to bone. It is common to hear a sportsperson talking about a torn or ruptured ligament, a type of injury that can take a long time to heal.

Type of joint	Description	Example
Fixed or immoveable joints (fibrous joints)	These bones cannot move at all and are found in the skull (cranium). These joints are also known as 'fibrous joints' as the bones are joined via fibrous connective tissue.	Fibrous joints
Slightly moveable joints (cartilaginous joints)	The bones in these joints can move a small amount as they are linked together by ligaments and cartilage (which absorbs the movement). They are found in the vertebral column (spine) and the ribs.	Body of vertebra Articular cartilage Intervertebral discs

Type of joint	Description	Example
Freely moveable joints (synovial joints)	Synovial joints have a greater amount of movement and include the elbow, shoulder, knee and hip. These joints have a number of parts, illustrated in the diagram and described in the table below.	Muscle / Synovial membrane / Bone / Synovial fluid / Joint capsule / Tendon / Cartilage

Part of the joint	Description and role
Synovial membrane	Surrounds the joint capsule with a synovial fluid
Synovial fluid	Acts a lubricant that reduces friction in the joint; allows for smoother movement and reduces wear and tear
Joint capsule	The structure that surrounds and protects the joint, holding the bones together; made up of an outer fibrous membrane and an inner synovial membrane
Ligament	The strong, elastic fibres that hold the bones together and keep them in place
Cartilage	A strong but flexible material found at the end of the bones that acts as a cushion to stop bones knocking together
Tendon	A tough band of fibrous tissue that connects muscle to bone and enables joints to withstand tension

2 Look at the table. In pairs, take turns to quiz each other about the parts of a joint. One person closes their book and listens while the other person reads a definition aloud. The person with their book closed must try to remember what part of a joint the definition relates to, and say it aloud.

3 Copy this diagram of the side view of a synovial joint (the knee) and label it. Practise until you can draw the joint and label it confidently from memory.

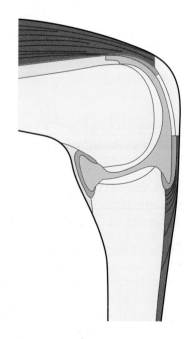

Developing the skills

There are several types of synovial joints (freely moveable joints) located in the body that provide a variety of movement within sports and activities. Two of the most important are ball and socket joints and hinge joints.

Type of synovial joint	Description	Example
Ball and socket joints	These are found at the shoulders and hips. They provide a large range of movement in every direction. One bone has a bulge or ball that fits into a socket in the other bone. Ball and socket joints allow actions such as an overhead clear in badminton or bowling in cricket.	Acetabulum of hip bone Head of femur
Hinge joints	These are located in the elbow and the knee and are like the hinges on a door, allowing movement in one direction. Your elbows and knees allow you to bend or straighten your arms and legs when performing a jump shot in basketball.	

Due to the wider range of movement and complexity, a ball and socket joint is less stable than a hinge joint, which moves in just one direction. A ball and socket joint is therefore less stable and more prone to injury than a hinge joint.

Generally speaking the following can be said to be true:

more motion = less stability = more wear and tear = more susceptibility to injury

4 Think of six more sporting movements you perform using each of these different joints. Draw an image and write a brief description of the movement: for example, punching in boxing needs extension at the elbow.

5 Create a PowerPoint or a verbal presentation to explain these two synovial joints, showing how the body relies on them to perform particular sporting movements. Remember to link in your understanding of the bones that are associated with the joint.

Applying the skills

Movements can be more complex than just moving one joint. For example, throwing a ball involves several joints: the shoulder to lift the ball, the elbow to bend the arm, and the fingers to let the ball go.

Less stable joints depend more on surrounding structures like muscles and ligaments to protect and stabilise them, and these joints are particularly susceptible to ligament and muscle injuries. Joints can be especially prone to injury when playing sport. This is because a lot of stress is placed on them during

physical exercise. It is important, therefore, to identify how easily injuries can occur and what you can do to prevent ligament damage. One of the most common types of injury is a sprain. This happens when one or more of the ligaments are stretched, twisted or torn.

 Working with a partner, carry out some research (for example, on the internet) on how to prevent sprains. Write a short leaflet giving advice to fellow students on steps they can take to prevent sprains.

REFLECTIVE LOG

Thinking of a sport that you regularly play, identify another example of a movement that involves using several joints. What are the joints and how do they work together to help you perform the movement?

Checklist for success

✔ Learn the three main types of joint in your body and practise naming them.

✔ Learn two types of freely moving (synovial) joints in your body.

✔ With a partner, quiz each other by pointing to a joint and asking your partner to name the joint and its type.

✔ Practise drawing and labelling internal diagrams of joints, such as the knee, elbow or wrist.

Sound progress

• I can identify and describe the different types of joints used in the body.

• I know the different parts of a synovial joint and examples of it.

Excellent progress

• I know where the different types of joint occur in the body and can provide examples.

• I can explain how a specific sporting action is performed by a range of joints in the body.

Movement at joints

LEARNING OBJECTIVES
By the end of this section you will:
- Know the four main pairs of movement around a joint.
- Understand that each movement can go in at least two directions and know the names of each of these directions.
- Provide sporting examples for each of these types of movement.

What different kinds of movements are created at joints when we move or perform?

Starting point

Movement is made possible by the various joints we have in our bodies. The joints in the upper part of the body are focused on movements that help us function (for example, using our arms to feed ourselves), while joints in the lower part are more focused on stability to ensure we stay balanced.

1 Recap the different types of joints and mime some physical activities, such as serving in tennis or kicking a football, and identify the movement that is happening within the type of joint.

2 Think about how joints in the lower body help you to maintain stability. Give three examples of situations where you use these joints (e.g. knee, ankle, toes) to help keep yourself stable (e.g. to stop you falling over).

Exploring the skills

There are eight directions of movements that can happen at joints. We use these joint movements to move the parts of our body and perform physical activities. These eight movements can be grouped into four pairs, as the movements are linked, one often being the reverse of the other.

Whilst running, you repeatedly flex and extend your hip, knee and shoulder joints. The knee flexes the leg as it swings backwards and extends as it swings forwards.

Flexion / extension

Flexion involves *bending* a part of the body: for example, bending your arm at the elbow.

Extension means *straightening* a part of the body: for example, straightening your arm at the elbow.

Flexion Extension Flexion Extension

Abduction / adduction

Abduction is a sideways movement *away from* the centre of the body: for example, lifting your arm from your side.

Adduction is a sideways movement *towards* the centre of the body.

Rotation and circumduction

Rotation is a turning point around an imaginary line. Turning your head from left to right is one example, with the imaginary line running vertically through your skull.

When you turn your leg to point your feet and toes out to the side, you are rotating your leg.

Circumduction occurs when the end of a bone moves in a circle. An example is swinging your arms in a circle at your shoulder.

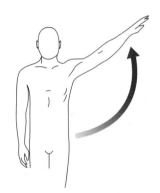 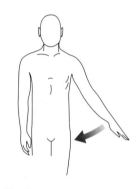

Shoulder abduction Shoulder adduction

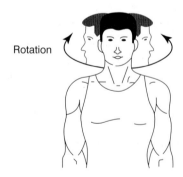

Rotation

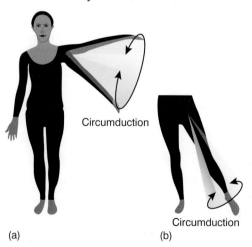

Circumduction

Circumduction

(a) (b)

Plantar flexion and dorsiflection

These are two types of movement in the ankle and foot. Plantar flexion is the movement in the ankle joint that points the foot away from the leg: for example, when you plant your foot to the ground whilst running.

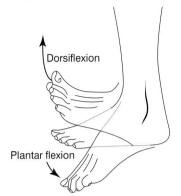

Dorsiflexion

Plantar flexion

Dorsiflexion is the movement in the ankle where the toes are brought closer to the shin: for example, when you lift your foot off the ground whilst running.

3 In pairs, practise making each of these movements with your own body. One person calls out a type of movement and the other shows an example of that movement. Swap roles so that both have a chance to practise.

4 Copy and complete the table:

Movement type	Joint	Sporting example
Flexion		Biceps curl
Extension		
Adduction	Shoulder	
Abduction		Pitcher spinning a baseball
Rotation		Tennis serve
Circumduction	Shoulder	
Dorsiflexion		Sprinters feet in the starting blocks
Plantar flexion	Ankle	Gymnast pointing their toes

REFLECTIVE LOG Think of mnemonics (memory aids) to help you remember these terms and, in particular, the difference between similar terms, such as adduction, abduction and circumduction. Make a note of these in your reflective log to help you learn and remember these terms. For example:

ADDuction = **ADD**ing a limb to the centre line of the body.

ABduction = the limb is **AB**sent from the centre line.

CIRCUMduction = the limb draws the **CIRCUM**ference of a circle.

Developing the skills

Joints allow and provide a range of different movements. For example, the shoulder can perform flexion, extension, adduction, abduction and rotation, all of which are essential in different sports and allow the performer to compete in their sport to the highest level.

5 In a practical lesson, explore a variety of activities such as running, jumping, throwing and kicking. Working as a class, discuss and identify the movement, joints and bones involved in each activity. Record your findings in a table.

6 Compare the range of movement and the stability of two types of synovial joint: the ball and socket joint and hinge joint.

> **REFLECTIVE LOG** For each type of movement, act it out and then think of other sporting examples that rely on that movement. For example, what other sports use circumduction at the shoulder? (Hint: think of athletics field events.)

Applying the skills

Analysis of performance is becoming an important factor in improving sporting technique and success. Sports coaches watch and feed back on their athletes' movements and are able to identify ways of preventing problems or improving their athletes' performance.

7 Look at the three photographs. For each number, name the joint and the type of movement that will occur next in the joint.

Checklist for success

✔ Learn the eight types of movement that happen at a joint and practise doing them all yourself.

✔ Remember that movement can go in different directions and learn the linked movements.

✔ With a partner, quiz each other by naming a type of movement and asking your partner to describe the movement and give a sporting example.

✔ Analyse how different sporting movements are performed and the types of movement involved.

Sound progress

• I can identify the joints that can create each type of movement.

• I can describe how to perform a sporting movement by identifying the movement.

Excellent progress

• I can describe the sequence of a movement linking it to movement, joints and bones.

• I can explain sporting examples for each of the eight types of movement.

Muscles

LEARNING OBJECTIVES
- Know the location and role of the major muscles in the body.
- Understand the importance and role of tendons.
- Provide sporting examples for each of these types of movement.

What are the main skeletal muscles of the body and what actions do they produce?

Starting point

Muscles are used in every movement of your body. Without them all aspects of daily living would be extremely difficult – in fact, you would not be able to move at all! Muscles work by shortening or contracting, thereby producing movement at a joint.

Key term

muscle: a band of fibrous tissue that has the ability to contract, producing movement in the body

Exploring the skills

The main muscles in your body that move your bones are called voluntary muscles. They are called 'voluntary' because you move them at will – that is, you choose to move them. The diagram below shows the location of the main muscles.

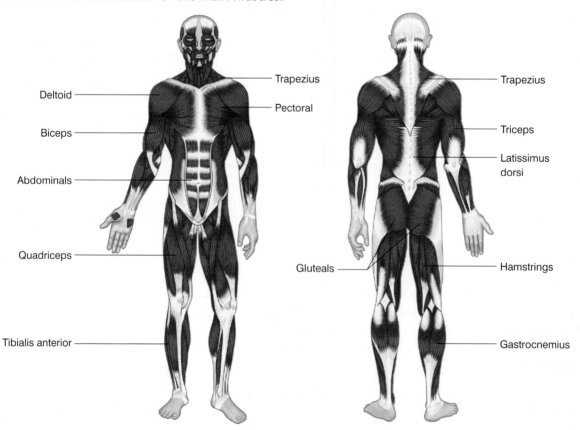

- Deltoid
- Biceps
- Abdominals
- Quadriceps
- Tibialis anterior
- Trapezius
- Pectoral
- Trapezius
- Triceps
- Latissimus dorsi
- Gluteals
- Hamstrings
- Gastrocnemius

This table describes the action of the main voluntary muscles, starting from the top of your body.

Muscle	Main action(s)	Sporting action
Trapezius	Holds and rotates your shoulders. Moves your head back and sideways.	A swimmer turning their head to breathe
Deltoids	Raises each arm forwards, backwards and sideways at the shoulder.	Overhead clear in badminton
Pectorals	Moves the arm at the shoulder through adduction.	Forehand drive in tennis
Biceps	Bends your arm at the elbow.	Drawing back a bow in archery
Triceps	Straightens your arm at the elbow.	Releasing a javelin or a ball
Latissimus dorsi (often just called 'lats')	Pulls your arm down at the shoulder. Draws it behind your back.	Swimming strokes
Abdominals	Flexes your spine so that you can bend forwards. Create a pull in the abdomen.	Rowing
Hip flexors	Supports movement of the leg and knee upwards.	Lifting the knees during a sprint
Gluteals	Pulls your leg back at the hip. Raises it sideways at the hip. The biggest of the gluteal muscles is the gluteus maximus.	Moving the leading leg and trail leg when hurdling
Quadriceps (often just called 'quads')	Straightens the leg at the knee. Keeps the leg straight to stand up.	Getting elevation in a high jump
Hamstrings	Bends the leg at the knee.	Pulling back of the knee before kicking ball
Gastrocnemius (the largest of the calf muscles)	Straightens the ankle joint so you can stand on your tiptoes.	Take-off for a lay-up in basketball
Tibialis anterior	Helps with dorsiflexion, the action of pulling the foot toward the shin.	Walking, running or toe-kicking a ball

1   For the following task use a copy of the diagram on the previous page with the labels removed (or a blank template provided by your teacher). Copy the names of the muscles onto sticky notes or small pieces of paper/card. Practise placing the labels in the correct place to identify the muscle groups. Keep practising until you are able to place all the labels correctly.

2   Think of other examples of sporting actions that involve each of the muscles in the table.

Developing the skills

In Topic 1.2, you learnt about ligaments and tendons and their function as part of joints. Ligaments are strong elastic tissues that provide stability for joints by holding the bones together. **Tendons**, on the other hand, join muscle to bone. They are very strong, able to withstand the tension created when muscles contract. This means they play a vital part in movement. They have limited elasticity, making the muscles absorb the impact.

3 The tendon most people have heard of is the Achilles tendon in the lower leg. This joins the calf muscle to the heel bone. Locate your own Achilles tendon: first touch your heel bone and then run your fingers slowly up the back of your leg. The Achilles tendon is the hard ridge that runs up to your calf muscles.

4 Make notes summarising what tendons are and what their role is.

> **Key term**
>
> **tendon:** tough band of fibrous tissue that anchors muscles to a bone and allows movement to happen

Applying the skills

Regular exercise provides your muscular system with long-term benefits. Your muscles increase in size and strength, which promotes stability and good posture. Analysing the way muscles work is also vital in sport for improving movement and performance.

5 Create a video of the following physical activities, identifying the major muscles, joints and bones that are being used.

  a) bending your arm at the elbow

  b) straightening your arm at the elbow

  c) starting with your arms at your side and lifting them outwards and up high

  d) folding your arms across your chest

  e) unfolding your arms from across your chest

  f) lifting your heel to your bottom

  g) straightening your leg.

Injuries to ligaments and tendons are among the most common injuries suffered by people playing sport. This is because of the pressure sport can place on muscles and joints. Under pressure the ligament can tear and result in dislocation in the joint. Extreme pressure can result in a torn tendon, a very serious sporting injury.

 REFLECTIVE LOG Identify specific muscular and tendon injuries that occur in sports you play or are particularly interested in. Write a blog on the ways to avoid them and treat them.

Checklist for success

✔ Memorise the names and locations of the 12 main voluntary muscles in the human body.

✔ With a partner, quiz each other by pointing to a muscle and asking your partner to name it.

✔ Remember the importance and function of tendons within movement, and learn the difference between ligaments and tendons.

✔ Practise describing the action of the major muscles and link them to a physical activity.

Sound progress

• I can identify the location and action of all the major muscles in the body.

• I can describe the function of tendons.

Excellent progress

• I can explain which muscles are contracting whilst performing specific sports movements.

• I can explain how a muscle produces movement in a physical activity.

Antagonistic muscle action

Why do muscles come in pairs? How do they work together to create movement?

Starting point

Muscles attached to the skeleton pull in only one direction. For this reason muscles always come in pairs. For example, think of the muscles in the upper arm. What happens when you perform a biceps curl with a dumbbell? The biceps contracts and allows you to lift the weight. In order to straighten your arm again at the elbow, you need a second muscle: in this case the triceps. When you lower the weight, the triceps contract and the biceps relaxes.

1. Pick up an object and make your biceps contract. Describe what is happening to your biceps. Then lower the weight and make your triceps contract. Can you contract your biceps and triceps (in the same arm) at the same time?

Exploring the skills

Voluntary muscles are the muscles that create movement. They usually work across a joint. The muscle is attached to the bones at the joint by tendons, as shown in the diagram.

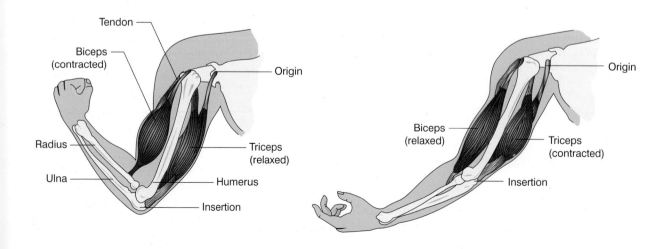

When a muscle contracts, it usually moves just one bone. As the first diagram shows, the biceps contracts to bend the arm at the elbow. The biceps is attached to the scapula at the **origin** (in the shoulder) and to radius at the **insertion** (the elbow). In this action the radius moves, but the scapula does not.

The table shows the origin and insertion of voluntary muscles that join bones at the main joints of the body.

Key terms

origin: where a muscle joins a stationary bone

insertion: where a muscle joins a moving bone

Muscle	Origin	Joint	Insertion	Joint
Biceps	Scapula	Shoulder	Radius	Elbow
Triceps	Scapula	Shoulder	Ulna	Elbow
Hamstring	Femur	Hip	Tibia	Knee
Quadriceps	Femur	Hip	Tibia	Knee
Tibialis anterior	Tibia	Knee	Tarsals	Ankle
Gastrocnemius	Femur	Knee	As the Achilles tendon to the heel	Ankle

2. Look at the table. In pairs, take turns to quiz each other about the origins and insertions of muscles. One person closes their book while the other person asks a question. For example: What is the origin of the quadriceps muscle? The person with their book closed must try to answer the question correctly. Change roles so that each person has a turn at answering questions.

3. Research voluntary muscles further by drawing diagrams of the elbow, knee and ankle joints and labelling them using the information above.

Developing the skills

To produce movement, muscles have to work in pairs. In the arm we have seen how the biceps flexes the elbow and the triceps straightens it by extending the arm. This action is called **antagonistic** muscle action, where one muscle works against the other. During movement the muscle that is working is called the **agonist** or **prime mover** and the muscle that relaxes is called the **antagonist**.

In the leg, the quadriceps muscle contracts to straighten the leg at the knee. Once the leg has straightened, the hamstring muscles will contract to bend the leg at the knee.

4. In a small group discuss what other actions can be created by the quadriceps and hamstrings working as a pair of muscles.

5. Describe sporting movements that use pairs of muscles in the arms and legs: biceps/triceps and tibialis anterior/gastrocnemius. First describe the movement without using

Key terms

agonist: the muscle that contracts to create movement (also called the **prime mover**)

antagonist: the muscle that relaxes during movement

antagonistic: antagonistic pairs of muscles work in opposition; they create movement when one (the agonist) contracts and the other (the antagonist) relaxes

the technical names of the muscles. Then analyse the movement using technical terms. For example, how would you analyse the movements involved in rowing?

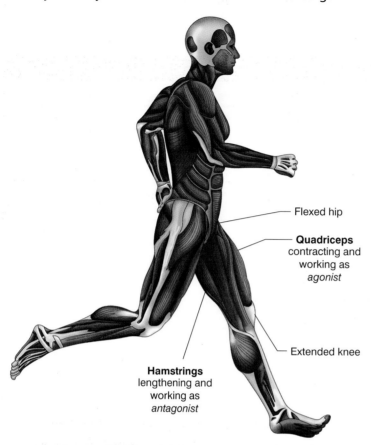

- Flexed hip
- **Quadriceps** contracting and working as *agonist*
- Extended knee
- **Hamstrings** lengthening and working as *antagonist*

Applying the skills

Muscles work antagonistically to produce a range of movements from day-to-day actions (such as walking or lifting objects) to more specific movements used in sport (such as putting the shot or bowling a cricket ball). There are two types of muscular contractions:

- **Isotonic contractions** – muscles change length as they contract. Isotonic contractions can either shorten the muscle (called **concentric contraction**) or lengthen it (called **eccentric contraction**). In a bicep curl, for example, when you lift the weight, the biceps shortens (concentric) while the triceps lengthens (eccentric).

- **Isometric contractions** – muscles contract, but stay the same length. An example is the muscles in the vertebral column that maintain the body's posture – this is important during a scrum in rugby.

6 Working in pairs, think of mnemonics to help you remember these terms. For example, **CONCENT**ric means the muscle is **CONCENT**rated; **ECC**entric means the muscle **EX**tends.

Key terms

isotonic contraction: where muscles change length as they contract

concentric contraction: muscle contraction where the muscle shortens

eccentric contraction: muscle contraction where the muscle lengthens

isometric contraction: where the muscles contract, but stay the same length

7 Copy and complete the table, showing which muscles work in pairs at major joints and the type of contraction each muscle produces at that joint. The first two rows have been completed for you.

Joint	Action	Agonist	Movement	Antagonist	Movement
Elbow	Flexion	Biceps	Concentric	Tricep	Eccentric
Elbow	Extension	Triceps	Concentric	Biceps	Eccentric
Knee	Extension	Quadriceps			
Knee		Hamstrings			
Ankle	Extension			Tibialis anterior	
Ankle		Tibialis anterior			

REFLECTIVE LOG Research other major muscles in the body to identify where is the origin and insertion are: for example, quadriceps, hamstrings, gastrocnemius, tibialis anterior. What action does contracting these muscles produce?

Checklist for success

✔ Learn all the key terms in this topic and think of mnemonics to help you remember them.

✔ With a partner, quiz each other by pointing to a muscle and asking your partner to name it, along with its origin and insertion.

✔ Practise drawing and labelling diagrams of the muscles and joints in the arms and legs.

✔ Think of examples of sporting movements and explain how muscles work antagonistically to produce them.

Sound progress

• I can identify the origin and insertion of the major muscles in the arm and leg.

• I can explain the terms 'agonist' and 'antagonist' when referring to muscles.

• I understand the different types of muscular contractions.

Excellent progress

• I can explain the antagonistic muscle action of the major muscle groups in the arm and leg.

• I can describe physical activities that show antagonistic muscle movement.

• I can describe in detail the different muscle contractions within a movement or physical activity.

Muscle fibre types

What are slow twitch and fast twitch muscle fibres, and how does our body use these in different types of activity?

Starting point

What are you better at: sprinting or long-distance running? The answer to this question may be found in your muscles. There are a few different types of **muscle fibre**, each designed for a specific type of muscle activity. Some muscle fibres are good for endurance exercises; others work best for the short bursts of strength exercises.

Some people naturally have more of one type than the other – partly a result of what you inherit from your parents. This would explain why people who are good at sprinting often struggle with running over longer distances.

Key term

muscle fibres: the cells or basic building block of the muscle; they contract when a message from the brain tell them to, enabling movement

Exploring the skills

There are two main different types of muscle fibre:

- **Slow twitch fibres** use oxygen to fire; they take longer to get going, but they can work for longer without getting tired.

- **Fast twitch fibres** are thicker and quicker to contract, but they wear out more quickly. They are more powerful and lower in endurance, and they are activated when the body nears maximum exertion.

The table summarises the differences between these two types.

Slow twitch fibres (Type I)	Fast twitch fibres (Type II)
Contract slowly	Contract quickly
Produce a little force	Produce a large amount of force
Higher fatigue tolerance – do not tire easily	Lower fatigue tolerance – tire quickly
Good for endurance	Good for strength and power

 1 Think about the following activities. Which type of muscle fibre is being used in each case?

a) walking to school

b) running 800 m

c) throwing a punch in boxing

d) swimming 1500 m.

Developing the skills

The type of muscle fibre used in a physical activity is also linked to the muscle's need for energy. Different types of exercise supply energy in different ways:

- In **aerobic exercise** (often called 'cardio') your heart rate increases to supply oxygenated blood to the muscles so they can keep performing at moderate levels over an extended period of time (e.g. walking, swimming).

- **Anaerobic exercise** is a short period of high-intensity activity, where your body's demand for oxygen is greater than the supply available. Oxygenated blood cannot be supplied to the muscles quickly enough. The body uses up energy sources stored in the muscles with a possible build-up of lactic acid in the muscles.

Aerobic exercise is associated with slow twitch fibres, whereas anaerobic exercise involves fast twitch fibres. People with a higher proportion of fast twitch fibres will be suited to sprinting and power activities. Those with slower twitch fibres can maintain a higher supply of oxygen to their muscles for a longer period. They are more suited to endurance events like marathons.

> **REFLECTIVE LOG**
>
> Think of three sports or activities you are particularly interested in. Which type of muscle fibre is more important in that sport? Make notes, referring to the points discussed in this topic (force created, fatigue tolerance, energy supply).

2 Create a poster presentation of the two types of muscle fibre, summarising the key points. Illustrate it with examples of sportsmen and women that you would assume to have a higher proportion of the different types.

Applying the skills

In many sporting activities the muscle fibres work in combination. During aerobic exercises such as running or swimming, slow twitch fibres are the first to contract. If there were a need to add an explosive action such as a sprint, then the fast twitch fibres would take over.

Although you may inherit muscle types from your parents, you can train each type of fibre to work better.

- Aerobic exercises using slow twitch fibres can increase the oxygen capacity of your muscles, allowing the body to burn energy for longer periods of time.

- Increasing muscle mass and improving strength using the fast twitch fibres, is the focus point of anaerobic exercise. These types of training include resistance training with heavy weights and performing explosive, power-based movements.

Athletes and coaches are interested in analysing how to improve performance by combining the aerobic and anaerobic energy systems and developing different muscle fibres using different exercises and a varied training programme.

3 Read the following example, which explains what happens in the body of a running during a long-distance event:

A 10 000 m runner (such as Mo Farah) would be using aerobic energy supply. The main muscular focus would be on the quadriceps and hamstrings muscles working efficiently and antagonistically. They would depend on large numbers of slow twitch fibres maintaining a constant of oxygen.

Continue this example, describing what happens in the final stages of the race as the runners near the finishing line.

4 Using the above structured example, can you provide a similar answer for a sprinter such as Usain Bolt.

Checklist for success

✔ Memorise the features of slow twitch fibres and fast twitch fibres.

✔ Practise summarising the differences between slow and fast twitch fibres in terms of force created, fatigue tolerance and aerobic/anaerobic energy supply.

✔ Think of examples of different sporting activities that rely on either slow or fast twitch fibres, or a combination of the two.

Sound progress

- I know the difference between fast twitch and slow twitch muscle fibres.
- I can identify movements that require fast twitch or slow twitch fibres.

Excellent progress

- I can explain clearly how fast and slow twitch muscle fibres differ in terms of force created, fatigue tolerance and aerobic/anaerobic energy supply.
- I can explain why certain movements or actions require fast twitch or slow twitch fibres.

Check your progress

Use these statements as a way of evaluating your progress throughout this chapter.

Sound progress

- I can identify each of the skeleton's four functions.
- I can locate and name the main bones in the skeleton.
- I can describe the four different bone types (short, long, flat, irregular).
- I can identify and describe the different types of joints used in the body.
- I know the different parts of a synovial joint and examples of it.
- I can identify the joints that can create each type of movement.
- I can describe how to perform a sporting movement by identifying the movement.
- I can identify the location and action of all the major muscles in the body.
- I can describe the function of tendons.
- I can identify the origin and insertion of the major muscles in the arm and leg.
- I can explain the terms 'agonist' and 'antagonist' when referring to muscles.
- I understand the different types of muscular contractions.
- I know the difference between fast twitch and slow twitch muscle fibres.
- I can identify movements that require fast twitch or slow twitch fibres.

Excellent progress

- I can explain the four functions of the skeleton, giving an example of each function.
- I can locate and name the main bones in the skeleton, giving examples of how different bones are involved in various sporting activities.
- I can describe the four different bone types (short, long, flat, irregular) and explain the function of each type.
- I know where the different types of joint occur in the body and can provide examples.
- I can explain how a specific sporting action is performed by a range of joints in the body.
- I can describe the sequence of a movement, linking it to movement, joints and bones.
- I can explain sporting examples for each of the eight types of movement.
- I can explain which muscles are contracting whilst performing specific sports movements.
- I can explain how a muscle produces movement in a physical activity.
- I can explain the antagonistic muscle action of the major muscle groups in the arm and leg.
- I can describe physical activities that show antagonistic muscle movement.
- I can describe in detail the different muscle contractions within a movement or physical activity.
- I can explain clearly how fast and slow twitch muscle fibres differ in terms of force created, fatigue tolerance and aerobic/anaerobic energy supply.
- I can explain why certain movements or actions require fast twitch or slow twitch fibres.

Chapter 2

Respiratory system

In this topic, you will investigate the key components and functions of the respiratory system. Its main role is to transfer oxygen into the bloodstream, providing the cells of the muscles with oxygen to produce energy. At the same time, it also removes the waste product carbon dioxide from the body. The respiratory system depends on the mechanics of breathing and you will explore these, looking at the role of the diaphragm and ribcage. Finally you will learn about breathing volumes and how to measure them.

You will learn how to:

- identify the functions of each component of the respiratory system
- explore the important role alveoli have in the exchange of gases
- describe the structure and function of the breathing mechanism
- explain the terms of tidal volume, vital capacity, residual value and minute ventilation.

Chapter contents

The activities you complete will primarily relate to the respiratory system, but you will also be able to identify links to other topics to help reinforce your learning as a whole.

You will:

- complete and label a diagram of the respiratory system that identifies the different parts of the system and their functions
- draw flow diagrams that show the pathway of air as it enters and leaves the body
- sketch a diagram showing the mechanics of breathing, naming the different parts involved and their functions
- draw up a table summarising what happens during inhalation and exhalation, and how gaseous exchange occurs
- write definitions of four different breathing volumes and explain why it is useful to measure these
- identify sports that require an efficient respiratory system and discuss the reasons why they require an efficient respiratory system to perform at a high level
- investigate the short-term and long-term effects of exercise on the respiratory system
- explore the benefits of exercise and training for the respiratory system.

Cross-section of lung tissue under a microscope

The pathway of air and gaseous exchange

How does air travel through the body? How does the respiratory system supply oxygen to the blood while removing carbon dioxide from it?

Starting point

Breathing is one of those automatic processes that the body carries out and that we take for granted. As you are reading this, you are breathing in and out without really thinking about it.

Breathing, otherwise known as respiration, is a complex process whereby air travels into and out of the lungs. This is essential for our survival and functioning.

1 Sometimes you can become more aware of your breathing – perhaps because you are feeling breathless or out of breath, or are consciously 'deep breathing'. In what sort of situations does this occur? Discuss this with other students.

Exploring the skills

The diagram on the right shows the breathing system.

When we breathe in (inhale), we take into our lungs air that includes oxygen. This oxygen is then transported to the working muscles and used to create energy. The pathway that oxygen follows is described here:

- Oxygen (one of several gases that are present in air) enters the respiratory system through the nasal passages (nose) and mouth.

- It travels down the trachea (windpipe), which divides into left and right bronchi, the main pathways into the lungs.

- The airways begin to narrow and branch off into smaller airways called bronchioles.

- Finally, oxygen reaches the **alveoli** (a broccoli-shaped collection of airways covered in capillaries), where **gaseous exchange** occurs.

> **Key term**
>
> **respiratory system:** in humans, the series of organs responsible for taking in oxygen and expelling carbon dioxide

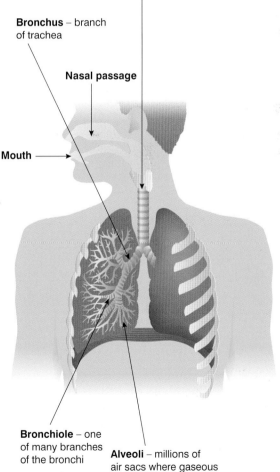

Trachea (windpipe) – has rings of cartilage to prevent it from collapsing

Bronchus – branch of trachea

Nasal passage

Mouth

Bronchiole – one of many branches of the bronchi

Alveoli – millions of air sacs where gaseous exchange takes place

2 Create a flow diagram that shows the pathway of air as it enters the body and continues into the bloodstream.

Developing the skills

When you breathe out, the air you are expelling contains more carbon dioxide and less oxygen than the air you breathe in. This is because of the gaseous exchange that has taken place in the alveoli. Carbon dioxide is a waste product because it is of no use to the body.

The alveoli are well designed to allow the exchange of carbon dioxide and oxygen. Exchange is maximised because:

- there are millions of alveoli in each lung, presenting a large, moist surface area for exchange to take place

- each individual **alveolus** is surrounded by blood capillaries which ensure a good blood supply

- the walls of the capillaries (tiny blood vessels – see Topic 3.1) supplying the blood are only one cell thick, allowing the gases to pass through easily

- the alveoli are well ventilated – air can reach them easily.

The diagrams below show how gaseous exchange occurs.

Key terms

alveoli: small air sacks in the lungs where gaseous exchange takes place

gaseous exchange: the process in the lungs whereby oxygen is delivered to the bloodstream, while carbon dioxide is removed from it; takes places in the alveoli

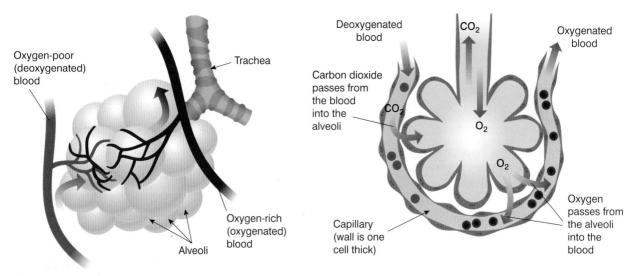

Oxygen-poor (deoxygenated) blood

Trachea

Oxygen-rich (oxygenated) blood

Alveoli

Deoxygenated blood

CO_2

Oxygenated blood

Carbon dioxide passes from the blood into the alveoli

CO_2

O_2

O_2

Capillary (wall is one cell thick)

Oxygen passes from the alveoli into the blood

3 Create a second flow diagram that shows the pathway of carbon dioxide as it leaves the lungs and is expelled from the body.

Applying the skills

When you are doing strenuous physical activity or exercise, your body needs more oxygen in order to supply the muscles with the energy they need. For that reason, an efficient respiratory system is particularly important for anyone involved in sport.

4 Think back to the first question in 'Starting point', where you thought about occasions when you become 'out of breath'. With a partner discuss what is happening in the respiratory system when you experience this. Try to explain this feeling in terms of gaseous exchange and your body's need for oxygen.

5 To check your understanding of the respiratory system, make a copy of the diagram in Topic 2.1 with the labels removed (or a blank template provided by your teacher). Practise naming all the parts of the system, with notes about the features and functions of each. Keep practising until you are able to describe the complete system accurately.

 REFLECTIVE LOG Take 5 minutes to reflect or test yourself on the components of the respiratory system, their order in the system and their roles in transporting oxygen into the bloodstream. Make a note of any parts of the system that you are not fully clear about and need to study further.

Checklist for success

✔ Learn the different parts of the respiratory system and practise naming each part.

✔ Practise drawing a sketch of the respiratory system, naming the different parts and their features.

✔ Add notes about the function of each part of the respiratory system to your diagram.

✔ Practise drawing flow diagrams of the pathway of air into and out of the body.

✔ Memorise the list of features of alveoli and practise drawing a diagram of how they work.

Sound progress

• I can identify the components of respiratory system and their roles in supporting the body's functioning.

• I can describe what happens to the oxygen and carbon dioxide during breathing.

Excellent progress

• I understand the importance of alveoli and can describe how they allow both oxygen and carbon dioxide to pass into and out of the circulatory system.

• I can explain the importance of an efficient respiratory system during physical activities.

The mechanics of breathing

What are the functions of the diaphragm and intercostal muscles in normal breathing?

Starting point

In Topic 2.1, you learned about the body's ability to transfer oxygen into the bloodstream during breathing, while also expelling carbon dioxide. In this topic you will learn about the mechanics of breathing. Breathing is a process created by the movement of the ribcage and the **diaphragm**. The ribcage is made up of the ribs and the muscles between them, called the **intercostal muscles**.

1 The diaphragm, ribs and intercostal muscles are shown on the diagram in Topic 2.1. Identify those features now. Add labels to your own diagrams of the respiratory system to show these parts of the respiratory system.

Key terms

diaphragm: muscular 'sheet' at the base of the chest cavity dividing it from the abdomen

intercostal muscles: the muscles between the ribs that raise and lower the ribs

Exploring the skills

Breathing in (inhaling) is known as inspiration and breathing out (exhaling) is known as expiration. During the process of inhaling and exhaling, the ribcage and diaphragm move as shown in the diagram and following table.

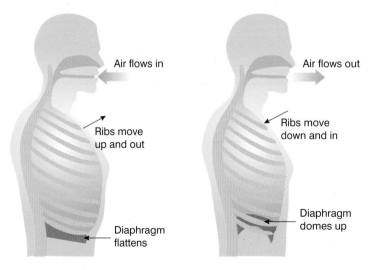

Air flows in

Ribs move up and out

Diaphragm flattens

Air flows out

Ribs move down and in

Diaphragm domes up

	Inhalation (breathing in)	Exhalation (breathing out)
Ribcage	Moves outwards and upwards as the intercostal muscles contract and lengthen.	Moves inwards and downwards as intercostal muscles relax.
Diaphragm	Contracts to become flatter.	Relaxes and domes upwards.
Effect	The lungs draw in air containing oxygen.	Air containing carbon dioxide is forced out of the body.

2 Draw and label your own diagram of the mechanics of breathing like the one pictured above.

3 Locate your own diaphragm. Place your hands below your ribcage with the fingers touching just below the bottom of the breastbone. Breathe in and out slowly and feel for the strong muscle that tightens as you breathe in and relaxes as you breathe out.

4 Look back at Topic 1.5, where you learned about muscle action and different types of muscle contraction. With a partner discuss the following questions:

a) What kind of contractions do the intercostal muscles have: isometric or isotonic?

b) When do the intercostal muscles have concentric contractions? And when do they have eccentric contractions?

Developing the skills

When you breathe in and out, the volume and pressure inside your lungs also change, as shown in the table.

	Inhalation (breathing in)	Exhalation (breathing out)
Volume of lungs	Increases	Reduces
Pressure in lungs	Reduces	Increases
Effect	The lungs draw in air containing oxygen.	Air containing carbon dioxide is forced out of the body.

5 Draw up your own table, summarising all the information about inhalation and exhalation from the two tables above.

REFLECTIVE LOG

Think of a mnemonic to help you remember the mechanics of breathing. Here is an acronym to help remember the mechanics of breathing in:

IVF = ribs Increase Volume, diaphragm Flattens.

Can you devise a mnemonic for breathing out?

Applying the skills

The respiratory system can be improved through exercise by using the system to its limits. The muscles responsible for the mechanics of breathing can be trained to be more effective. For example:

- When breathing in, you can help increase the volume of the chest cavity by lifting your ribcage further using the pectorals and the neck muscles. Try to keep your shoulders relaxed, however – lifting the shoulders doesn't help with the mechanics of breathing.

- When we breathe out during exercise, we can remove more air by using our abdominals to pull the ribs down, forcing even more air out of the lungs.

Over a sustained period of time, exercise will help increase the strength of the muscles involved in breathing (intercostal and diaphragm). This enables them to expand further, increasing the volume of the lungs and letting more oxygen to be drawn into them. It means athletes can compete at a higher intensity for longer.

6 The next activity will help you to investigate the short-term effects of exercise on the respiratory system.

- First make a copy of the table. Then, sitting still, record the number of breaths you take in one minute. This is your resting breathing rate. In the right-hand column, make notes about the way you are breathing – for example, are they short or long breaths, shallow or deep, noisy or silent?

- Then complete a **submaximal** exercise, such as a 12-minute run. At the end of the run, again count the number of breaths in one minute. Record this in the table along with comments about the way you are breathing.

- Finally, complete a **maximal** form of exercise such as a 100 m sprint. Once again, take your breathing rate for one minute after you have completed the exercise and comment on the way you are breathing. Record all this in the table.

Key terms

submaximal exercise: an activity with a steady increase in workload or intensity, working at 85% of the maximum heart rate

maximal exercise: an activity where the intensity is constant throughout a short period of time

	Breathing rate	Comments on characteristics of breathing
At rest		
Submaximal		
Maximal		

REFLECTIVE LOG Using the knowledge you have gained in this chapter so far, think about the effects of exercise and how your breathing has been affected. Can you analyse the results from your exercise and explain what has occurred? Why has your respiratory system reacted to these different situations in the way it has?

Checklist for success

✔ Practise drawing sketches showing the mechanics of breathing, naming the different parts involved and their functions.

✔ Draw up a table summarising what happens during inhalation and exhalation, and the effects of each.

✔ Devise mnemonics to help you remember the key points of the mechanics of breathing.

✔ Remember the effects that exercise has on breathing and the body's need for oxygen.

Sound progress

• I can identify the mechanics of breathing and the functions of the different parts of the system.

• I can outline the effects of breathing on the lungs and intake of oxygen.

Excellent progress

• I can explain the entire process of the mechanics of breathing in detail.

• I can demonstrate my understanding of the short-term and long-term effects of exercise on the respiratory system and breathing.

Breathing volumes and minute ventilation

LEARNING OBJECTIVES
- Explain what is meant by the terms 'tidal volume', 'vital capacity', 'residual volume', 'minute ventilation'.
- Outline the role and importance of each of these during the mechanics of breathing.
- Describe the effect of exercise for the volumes of tidal volume, vital capacity, residual volume, minute ventilation.

What is meant by 'breathing volumes' and how can we measure them? What effect does exercise have on breathing volumes?

Starting point

The ability to hold our breath for a long time is not always encouraged, unless you are a free diver like Aleix Segura Vendrell (from Spain), who in 2016 set a new world record for holding his breath under water ... How long for? An amazing 24 minutes and 3.45 seconds! He is clearly able to take in and efficiently use a huge volume of breath.

You have learnt about the mechanics of breathing and how exercise can improve the volume of air the lungs take in as more oxygen is supplied to the muscles. This is an important factor for people carrying out sports and exercise.

1. Do all activities affect or use breathing in the same way? Look at the following activities and describe what happens to the breathing:

   a) an archer drawing back their arrow

   b) a gymnast performing a floor routine

   c) a runner running a marathon.

Exploring the skills

There are a number of measurements that can be taken to assess how well the respiratory system is functioning. The **tidal volume** provides an indication of how much air you can inhale in each breath. It can be measured using a spirometer, a small machine attached by a cable to a mouthpiece, and is usually given in millilitres (ml).

Key term

tidal volume: the volume of air you inhale with each breath during normal breathing

When the tidal volume is multiplied by the number of breaths you take in one minute (respiratory rate), it gives a result known as the **minute ventilation**. This is usually expressed in litres per minute (l/min).

Tidal volume × **Number of breaths** = **Minute ventilation**
(ml)   per minute   (l/min)
For example: 500 (0.5 l)   ×   15   =   7.5 l/min

This knowledge provides coaches and physiologists with information that can be used to improve athletes' performance as they can identify how breathing can affect movement. For example, they can encourage their athletes to use deep breathing by their diaphragm instead of the chest. Further to improving performance, the diffusion of oxygen into the blood through the alveoli and capillaries is more efficient.

2 A coach has measured an athlete's tidal volume and drawn up this table. Fill in the missing information.

	Tidal volume (ml)	Number of breaths per minute	Minute ventilation (l/min)
a)	500 (0.5 litres)		8
b)	3 000 (3 litres)	35	

3 What can you tell from the figures in question **2** about what activities the athlete is doing?

Developing the skills

Another measurement that can be taken to measure breathing volume is your **vital capacity**. This is the maximum volume of air that you can breathe out after breathing in as much as you can. This can be up to ten times more than you would normally exhale. Vital capacity can also be measured using a type of spirometer and is normally expressed in litres.

There is always some air left in the lungs after breathing out, to prevent the lungs from collapsing. The amount left is called the **residual volume**. This small volume of air cannot be breathed out.

By adding the vital capacity and residual volume together, you get your total lung capacity.

4 Look at the following test to measure vital capacity and see if whether you and your classmates can complete it.

a) Each student should have a balloon ready for inflation.

b) Inhale as much air as you can and then exhale forcefully into your own balloon.

c) Pinch the end of the balloon and measure its diameter (see the diagram below).

d) Record your results.

e) Compare your results with those of the rest of the class.

f) Use the graph to read off your lung capacity from the diameter measurement.

5 Explore this further by looking at:

a) the difference between male and female

b) whether height affects the vital capacity

c) whether athletes in different sports have variations in vital capacity.

> Sports coaches can use these volumes with athletes as a baseline to see how far vital capacity increases through training.

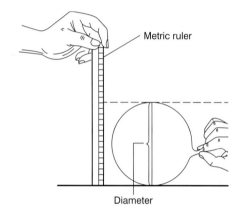

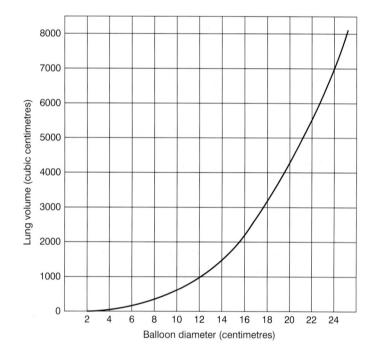

REFLECTIVE LOG Another instrument used to measure breathing volumes is the peak flow meter. Carry out some research to find out what this is and why is it used.

Applying the skills

During exercise, your lung volume can increase by as much as 15 per cent. To meet the demands of your heart and muscles during exertion, your breathing becomes deeper and much more rapid, delivering more oxygen to your bloodstream.

As your rate of breathing increases, so does your tidal volume. It can go from the normal half litre per breath toward your vital capacity. Minute ventilation also increases: a normal adult at rest breathes about 7.5 litres of oxygen every minute. During strenuous exercise, the amount can increase to 120 litres per minute.

Exercise has numerous benefits for the respiratory system. Increasing the body's respiratory capacity improves the efficiency of the system. Research into sports performance has shown that the (intercostal) muscles can be trained and strengthened to improve sports performance in elite athletes.

This is especially true for physical activities such as swimming, long-distance (marathon) running, rowing and cycling.

6   Make notes summarising what happens to the respiratory system during strenuous exercise. What increased demands are placed on the body and how does the respiratory system help to meet those demands?

Checklist for success

✔ Write definitions of the different breathing volumes – tidal volume, vital capacity, residual volume and minute ventilation – stating why it is useful to measure these.

✔ Practise calculations involving tidal volume and minute ventilation.

✔ Make notes summarising the effects of exercise on lung volumes.

Sound progress

• I can define tidal volume, minute ventilation, vital capacity and residual volume.

• I can describe what effects exercise has on breathing volume.

Excellent progress

• I can explain how the mechanism of breathing works in terms of tidal volume, minute ventilation, vital capacity and residual volume.

• I can demonstrate my understanding of all measurements of breathing volume and how they affect the performance in a sport or physical activity.

Check your progress

Use these statements as a way of evaluating your progress throughout this chapter.

Sound progress

- I can identify the components of the respiratory system and their roles in supporting the body's functioning.
- I can describe what happens to the oxygen and carbon dioxide during breathing.
- I can identify the mechanics of breathing and the functions of the different parts of the system.
- I can outline the effects of breathing on the lungs and intake of oxygen.
- I can define tidal volume, minute ventilation, vital capacity and residual volume.
- I can describe what effects exercise has on breathing volume.

Excellent progress

- I understand the importance of alveoli and can describe how they allow both oxygen and carbon dioxide to pass into and out of the circulatory system.
- I can explain the importance of an efficient respiratory system during physical activities.
- I can explain the entire process of the mechanics of breathing in detail.
- I can demonstrate my understanding of the short-term and long-term effects of exercise on the respiratory system and breathing.
- I can explain how the mechanism of breathing works in terms of tidal volume, minute ventilation, vital capacity and residual volume.
- I can demonstrate my understanding of all measurements of breathing volume and how they affect the performance in a sport or physical activity.

Chapter 3

Circulatory system

Starting points

In this chapter, you are going to explore the components of blood and the important role blood plays in transporting oxygen and nutrients around the different parts of the circulatory system.

You will learn how to:

- identify the functions of each component of blood
- explore the important role haemoglobin has in the circulatory system
- describe the structure and function of the heart and blood vessels
- explain the terms 'cardiac output', 'heart rate' and 'stroke volume'.

Chapter contents

The activities you complete will primarily relate to the circulatory system, but you will also be able to identify links to other topics to help reinforce your learning as a whole.

In this chapter, you will:

- create a mind map for the components of blood and their link to the circulatory system
- create a flow diagram that shows the pathway from the lungs around the circulatory system
- use a drawing style activity to reinforce your understanding and your ability to explain the circuits/sides/blood type
- complete a heart template that identifies specific locations and their functions
- use an acronym to remember the sides of the heart: *LORD*
- design a circuit training session using the structure of the heart with eight stations
- identify six different sports that require cardiovascular fitness to perform at a high level
- investigate the effects of exercise on the heart rate, stroke volume and cardiac output
- create an information map to collate the information from this section.

Red blood cells carry oxygen around our bodies.

Components of blood

LEARNING OBJECTIVES
- Identify the different components of blood.
- Understand the role of haemoglobin.
- Describe the structure of the blood vessels and their functions.

What are the components of blood, and what role does blood play in the circulatory system?

Starting point

The body relies upon the **circulatory system** to transport oxygen and nutrients (substances providing nourishment) to the cells in the body (via **oxygenated blood**), whilst also extracting waste and carbon dioxide via **deoxygenated blood** away from the cells.

The heart pumps red, oxygen-rich **blood** to each part of the body. Blue, oxygen-poor blood returns from the body to the heart. It then travels through the lungs where carbon dioxide (CO_2) is exchanged for new oxygen.

1 Copy the diagram of the circulatory system adding labels and using specific colours to show the transportation of blood.

Key terms

circulatory system: the body's transport system that consists of the lungs, heart, blood vessels and blood

blood: a liquid containing four components: plasma, red blood cells, white blood cells and platelets, each with a specific function

haemoglobin: a dark red chemical responsible for transporting oxygen in the blood

oxyhaemoglobin: a bright red chemical formed when haemoglobin combines with oxygen, resulting in oxygenated blood

Exploring the skills

As well as transportation, the blood has an important role in protecting the body from infection and disease. The image opposite of blood in the test tube identifies the components that form the structure of our blood. Each of these has an important function:

- Plasma consists mainly of water to allow substances to dissolve and be transported easily.
- Red blood cells contain **haemoglobin**, which reacts with oxygen from the lungs to form **oxyhaemoglobin**.
- White blood cells (part of the immune system) defend the body against pathogens (disease-causing organisms) by engulfing them or creating antibodies to attack them.
- Platelets contain an enzyme that causes blood to clot when there is damage to **blood vessels** or they are exposed to air.

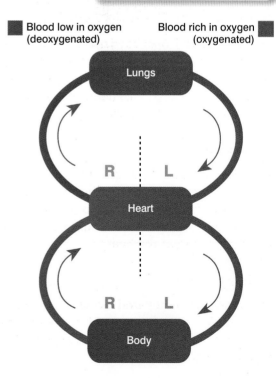

Blood low in oxygen (deoxygenated)   Blood rich in oxygen (oxygenated)

Lungs

R | L

Heart

R | L

Body

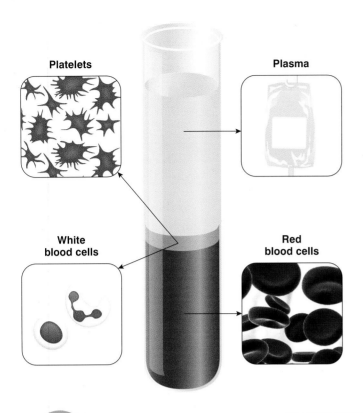

Platelets

Plasma

White blood cells

Red blood cells

Key term

blood vessels: three different types of vessels that carry blood: arteries, veins and capillaries

> **REFLECTIVE LOG** Create a mind map that includes all the components of blood, their functions and how they link to the circulatory system and the body as a whole.

Developing the skills

The transportation of oxygenated blood (oxyhaemoglobin) to the cells and the removal of carbon dioxide (waste product) is made possible through a series of blood vessels. They are divided into three groups (identified in the following images), each with a distinct function.

Arteries

Arteries are muscular, elastic tubes that transport oxygenated blood away from the heart. They have a small internal lumen (the name given to the passageway inside the tube). Arterial blood is pumped at high pressure because of the strong pumping action of the heart.

Veins

Veins carry deoxygenated blood to the heart. They contain blood under low pressure, and so have thinner walls and a larger internal lumen. Veins also have valves that prevent blood flowing backwards.

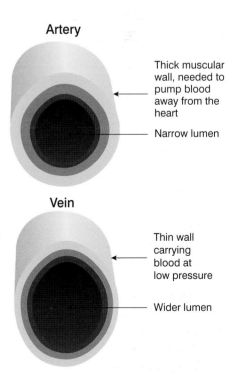

Artery

Thick muscular wall, needed to pump blood away from the heart

Narrow lumen

Vein

Thin wall carrying blood at low pressure

Wider lumen

Capillaries

Capillaries are tiny blood vessels that form networks throughout the body's tissues. Blood from the arteries flows into the capillaries, where oxygen and nutrients are extracted. The blood then flows back into the veins carrying wastes (such as CO_2). Capillaries have thin walls – only one cell thick – that allow them to perform their function effectively.

Capillary

Walls a single cell in thickness, allowing substances to pass into and out of cells (e.g. oxygen and CO_2)

2 Bleeding is much more severe when an artery is cut compared with when a vein is cut. From what you have read, why do you think this is so?

To help remember the difference between arteries and veins, note the following: **a** is for **a**rtery that travels **a**way from the heart. Ve**in**s carry blood **in**to the heart, and contain **v**alves (to stop blood flowing backwards).

What is the function of capillaries?

The function of capillaries is to allow food and oxygen to diffuse *to* cells while waste is diffused *from* cells. Capillaries have thin walls – only one cell thick – that allow them to perform their function effectively.

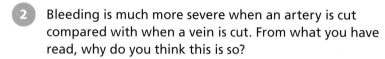
Applying the skills

3 Where in your body can you feel your pulse most strongly? Press the skin there to feel the pumping action – you have located an artery! The pulse is the regular expansion and contraction of the arterial wall as the beating heart forces blood through the artery.

4 The pulse is an indication of the rate at which your heat is beating. With a partner, discuss why this is can be a useful measurement to take. Think of applications in sport and medicine, for example.

5 To reflect upon this learning, create a flow diagram with illustrations, that starts at the lungs and travels around the circulatory system. Include the following key terms and think about how you can explain your choices to others: 1) lungs, 2) oxyhaemoglobin, 3) veins, 4) heart, 5) capillaries, 6) CO_2, 7) arteries.

Checklist for success
. . . .
- ✔ Practise summarising the functions of blood and the ways in which each helps the body.
- ✔ Memorise the four components of blood and the functions of each one.
- ✔ Practise drawing sketches of the structure of each type of blood vessel and adding notes about the importance of their role.

Sound progress

- I know what haemoglobin is and what role it plays in the body.
- I can identify the four components of blood and their roles in supporting the body.
- I can name the three types of blood vessel and describe their part in the circulatory system.

Excellent progress

- I know the importance of haemoglobin and can describe how it transports both oxygen and waste products around the circulatory system.
- I can clearly describe the different types of blood vessel and explain how their structures support their functions.
- I can summarise the main features of the circulatory system and explain the role of its various components.

Heart structure and function

LEARNING OBJECTIVES
- Identify the location of each section of the heart.
- Describe the functions of atria, ventricles and valves.
- Describe the pathway of blood through the heart.

What is the structure of the heart, and what pathway does blood follow through the heart?

Starting point

Topic 3.1 introduced the circulatory system as the transport system of the body. In this topic we look in greater detail at how **oxygenated blood** and **deoxygenated blood** are pumped around the body by the heart through the arteries, veins and capillaries, to their destinations.

1. To help you understand and learn this **double circulation** system, draw your own version of the diagram. Then copy the labels onto small cards or cut up pieces of paper and practise placing them in the correct position. You could work with a partner to test each other's knowledge.

Key terms

double circulation: the heart has a double pump and circulation: the **pulmonary circuit (right side)** pumps blood to the lungs and back to the heart. The **systemic circuit (left side)** pumps blood to the body and back to the heart

Exploring the skills

The **heart** consists of four chambers. The two at the top are atria (singular form is atrium) and the two at the bottom are ventricles. The two sides of the heart are separated by a thick muscular wall called the septum, which ensures that the blood in the two sides of the heart doesn't mix and that the blood always flows in one direction. The heart also has several valves positioned where the blood enters and leaves the heart. These valves prevent the blood flowing backwards.

Note that in the diagram on the next page, the heart is seen from the front, so the right side of the heart is shown on the left of the diagram, and vice versa.

2. Using a heart template, label the specific locations and summarise their functions: atria/ventricles/valves/ pulmonary artery/aorta/pulmonary vein/vena cava. Colour the sections to identify whether each location is dealing with **oxygenated** (red) or **deoxygenated** (blue) blood. Include arrows to indicate the direction in which the blood will flow.

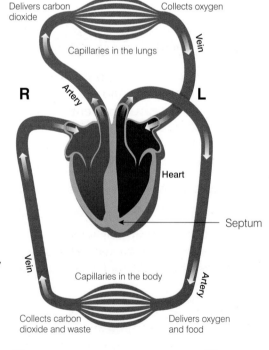

Delivers carbon dioxide

Collects oxygen

Capillaries in the lungs

R

Artery

Vein

L

Heart

Septum

Vein

Artery

Capillaries in the body

Collects carbon dioxide and waste

Delivers oxygen and food

■ Blood low in oxygen (deoxygenated)

Blood rich in oxygen (oxygenated) ■

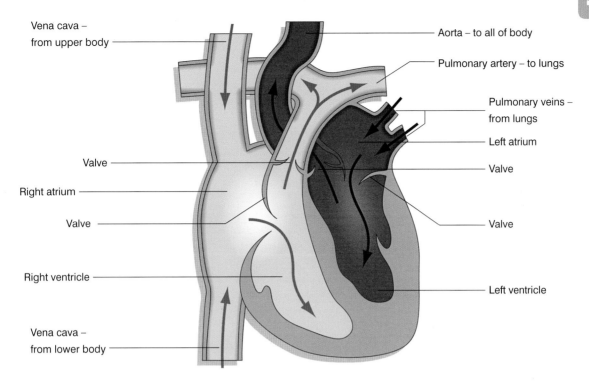

Vena cava – from upper body

Aorta – to all of body

Pulmonary artery – to lungs

Pulmonary veins – from lungs

Left atrium

Valve

Right atrium

Valve

Valve

Valve

Right ventricle

Left ventricle

Vena cava – from lower body

REFLECTIVE LOG

Here is an acronym to remember the sides of the heart: <u>LORD</u> – <u>L</u>eft <u>O</u>xygenated, <u>R</u>ight <u>D</u>eoxygenated. Can you devise other helpful acronyms for the sections of the heart?

Key term

heart: a muscular organ that expands as it fills with blood and contracts to force blood away through the arteries; the blood returns through the veins to the heart

Developing the skills

The heart has a particular sequence that allows the blood to follow its pathway around the body. First the atria both contract at the same time; then the ventricles both contract at the same time to move the blood through the heart. This double circulation sees blood passing through the heart twice in each circuit at a high pressure to flow faster to the body.

The heart pumps blood in two stages:

Stage 1: **Deoxygenated** blood from the body enters via the vena cava into the right atrium, which contracts forcing the blood past the valve into the right ventricle. The right ventricle contracts forcing the blood through the pulmonary artery to the lungs.

Stage 2: **Oxygenated** blood from the lungs enters via the pulmonary vein into the left atrium, which contracts forcing the blood past the valve into the left ventricle. The left ventricle contracts forcing the blood through the aorta to the body.

Applying the skills

3 Working with your classmates, devise a training circuit game based on the structure of the heart and the circulatory system. Set up various training stations to represent the atria, ventricles, veins, arteries, aorta and lungs. Then divide the group into two halves, with one half wearing blue bibs to start (representing **deoxygenated blood**) and the other half wearing red bibs (representing **oxygenated blood**).

4 The blue-bibbed people start by entering through the vena cava, while the red-bibbed people enter via the pulmonary veins. Work out the circuit that each person will need to take through the system. At some point everyone will need to change the colour of their bib. When does that happen? And why?

Checklist for success

✔ Summarise the stages connected to the double circulation of oxygenated and deoxygenated blood around the body.

✔ Practise drawing and labelling diagrams showing the structure of the heart and the flow of blood around the body.

Sound progress

• I can describe the sections of the heart and the importance of their functions.

• I can describe in broad terms the way in which blood circulates through the heart.

Excellent progress

• I can demonstrate my understanding of the pathway that blood follows through a verbal or diagrammatic explanation.

• I can explain the double circulatory system identifying the sections that contain oxygenated and deoxygenated blood.

Cardiac output

LEARNING OBJECTIVES
- Explain the terms 'heart rate', 'stroke volume' and 'cardiac output'.
- Identify how cardiac output can be calculated.

What happens to the heart during exercise and how can you measure your cardiovascular fitness?

Starting point

Anyone who does regular exercise or sport will be aware of the desire to improve their **cardiovascular fitness**. Your level of cardiovascular fitness depends on the amount of oxygen that your body can transport to the working muscles via the lungs and blood system, as well as the ability of your muscles to use that oxygen.

To understand – and improve – cardiovascular fitness, you need to know what happens inside your heart during exercise. In this topic we will explore three main features: heart rate, stroke volume and cardiac output. Of these, **heart rate** is the one that most people are aware of as it is something you can experience directly. For example, we all know that our heart rate increases after exercise.

We can take measurements of our heart rate by feeling for the pulse point, which is where the blood flows through an artery near to the skin, such as the carotid (neck) or radial (wrist) arteries. The diagram on the right shows the location of the body's main arteries.

An elite athlete may have a resting heart rate (RHR) as low as 40 beats per minute (bpm), whereas a person of the same age with an average level of fitness might have an RHR of 70 bpm. Heart rate can be affected by various factors, including a person's age, gender and size.

1 For this activity you will need to work with a partner. Look at the picture on the right, locate a pulse and count the time you feel your pulse 'bump' while your partner counts to 10 seconds. Multiply this number by 6 to work out your beats per minute (6 x 10 seconds = 1 minute). This provides an estimate of your resting heart rate (RHR). Keep a note of this figure.

Key terms

cardiovascular fitness: the ability to exercise continuously for extended periods without tiring, often referred to as *stamina*

heart rate: measures the heart beats per minute (bpm) when the ventricles are contracting. Resting heart rate is generally 50–90 bpm (teenager) and 60–80 bpm (adult)

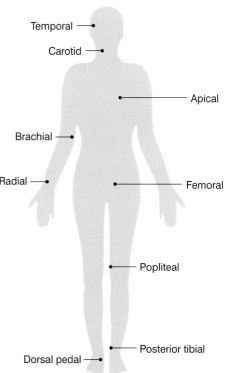

Temporal

Carotid

Apical

Brachial

Radial

Femoral

Popliteal

Posterior tibial

Dorsal pedal

Exploring the skills

During intensive exercise the heart rate can reach a maximum of 220 minus your age. So, for a 15 year old:

maximum bpm will be 220 – 15 = 205 bpm.

Having a high level of cardiovascular fitness benefits the entire body and it is recommended that you work at 55–85 per cent of your maximum heart rate to improve your fitness. For a 15 year old, therefore, this would be:

> maximum bpm = 205 bpm at 55–85% = 113–174 bpm

The fitness of a person is determined by how fast their heart rate can recover to normal (resting) after exercise. A faster recovery time is another long-term benefit of exercising.

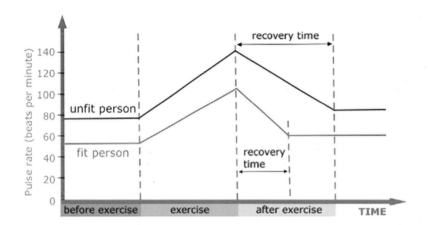

2. Recovery times can be explored further using the Harvard step test either in your practical lesson or as conditioned activity in the classroom.

   a) Identify your RHR from the previous question.

   b) March on the spot for 1 minute (your teacher will time this).

   c) Take your pulse for a second time and record that score.

   d) Sit down and rest.

   e) After 30 seconds take your pulse again and record the score – has it reached your RHR? If yes, then stop checking; if no, rest for a further 30 seconds.

   f) Continue until your RHR has been reached.

   g) You can now work out how long it takes to recover after 1 minute's activity.

As well as heart rate, another important aspect of fitness is the volume of blood that the heart pumps out with every beat. This is called the **stroke volume** and is measured in millilitres (ml).

Regular exercise will increase a person's stroke volume as a result of the heart growing in size through hypertrophy (increase in muscle size) and being able to retain blood in the chambers so they fill more and empty more. The heart becomes more efficient and each contraction is stronger, forcing more blood out into the body.

Key term

stroke volume: the volume of blood pumped out of the heart by each ventricle in one beat; a person of average fitness has a stroke volume of around 70 ml, while for an athlete it is around 90 ml

REFLECTIVE LOG Identify six different sports that require a high level of cardiovascular fitness to perform at a high level.

Developing the skills

Measuring a person's heart rate and stroke volume allows you to calculate their **cardiac output**. For athletes, having a clear understanding of their cardiac output will benefit their training. By monitoring their heart rate as exercise increases, they can establish different levels of training intensity. This provides additional information about cardiac output, as more blood will result in an increased oxygen supply.

The cardiac output is determined by the stroke volume and the heart rate of an individual and will change over a long period of exercise. For example, someone at rest with a heart rate of 70 bpm and a stroke volume of 70 ml/beat will have a cardiac output of just under 5 litres/minute, as shown in this calculation:

> **Key term**
>
> **cardiac output:** the amount of blood expelled from the heart each minute; it is usually expressed in litres per minute

Heart rate (HR) × Stroke volume (SV) = Cardiac output (CO)

(HR) 70 (bmp) × (SV) 70 (ml) = (CO) 4.9 litres/minute

The fitter a person is, the stronger their stroke volume will be, allowing more blood to be pumped and oxygen delivered and resulting in a higher cardiac output. A fit athlete with a stroke volume of 120 ml doing intensive exercise will have a much higher cardiac output:

Heart rate (HR) × Stroke volume (SV) = Cardiac output (CO)

(HR) 150 (bmp) × (SV) 120 (ml) = (CO) 18 litres/minute

A world-class athlete in an endurance sport might have a maximum cardiac output as high as 35 litres/minute!

3 Calculate the cardiac output of the following people:

a) a person resting with a heart rate of 60 bpm and a stroke volume of 80 ml

b) someone doing gentle exercise with a heart rate of 105 bpm and a stroke volume of 70 bpm

c) an athlete running a marathon with a heart rate of 160 bpm and a stroke volume of 90 bpm.

Applying the skills

4 Investigate the following effects of exercise on the heart rate and cardiac output. As a class' divide into three

groups to complete a 400 m race whilst wearing heart
rate monitors (if possible) or otherwise taking your pulse
rate before and after. Select four people from each of the
groups to record their resting heart rates and their final
heart rates after the following sequence:

- Group 1 will run as fast as possible.
- Group 2 will jog at a rate at which they can still talk to
  each other.
- Group 3 will jog for 50 m, then sprint for 50 m until they
  complete 400 m.

Present your findings as a graph and discuss the difference in the
heart rates and why this was. Which group returned to resting
heart rate the quickest?

5 Now calculate the output before and after their exercise
for a student from each group. To do this you will need to
estimate their stroke volume. Search on the internet to find
the typical stroke volume of people their age.

> **REFLECTIVE LOG**
>
> Create an information map to summarise all of the
> information from this topic. Include notes on how
> this fits into the topic of the circulatory system,
> covered in this chapter. Include the following
> sections: key words/useful definitions/diagrams/
> examples of exercise/sport.

Checklist for success

✔ Memorise the definitions or key features of the following terms: heart rate, stroke volume,
cardiac output.

✔ Practise the calculations for working out cardiac output and maximum heart rate.

Sound progress

- I can locate where a pulse is and identify my resting and active heart rates.
- I understand the terms 'stroke volume' and 'cardiac output' and know what topics they are
  measured in.

Excellent progress

- I can explain how changes in levels of activity affect heart rate, stroke volume and cardiac
  output, and the importance to athletes of monitoring these aspects.
- I can use data about my heart rate and stroke volume to calculate my cardiac output.

Check your progress

Use these statements as a way of evaluating your progress throughout this chapter.

Sound progress

- I know what haemoglobin is and what role it plays in the body.
- I can identify the four components of blood and their roles in supporting the body.
- I can name the three types of blood vessel and describe their part in the circulatory system.
- I can describe the sections of the heart and the importance of their functions.
- I can describe in broad terms the way in which blood circulates through the heart.
- I can locate where a pulse is and identify my resting and active heart rates.
- I understand the terms 'stroke volume' and 'cardiac output' and know what topics they are measured in.

Excellent progress

- I know the importance of haemoglobin and can describe how it transports both oxygen and waste products around the circulatory system.
- I can clearly describe the different types of blood vessel and explain how their structures support their functions.
- I can summarise the main features of the circulatory system and explain the role of its various components.
- I can demonstrate my understanding of the pathway that blood follows through a verbal or diagrammatic explanation.
- I can explain the double circulatory system identifying the sections that contain oxygenated and deoxygenated blood.
- I can explain how changes in levels of activity affect heart rate, stroke volume and cardiac output, and the importance to athletes of monitoring these aspects.
- I can use data about my heart rate and stroke volume to calculate my cardiac output.

Chapter 4

Energy supply and the effects of exercise on the body

Starting points

In this topic, you will explore how energy is supplied to the body, looking at two different types of respiration: aerobic and anaerobic. You will investigate factors that affect your ability to recover from strenuous activity. You will also study the effects that exercise can have on your body, both immediately and in the longer term.

You will learn how to:

- explain what aerobic and anaerobic respiration are
- identify how we recovery after exercise
- explain the short-term and long-term effects of exercise on the body.

Chapter contents

The activities you complete will primarily relate to the aerobic and anaerobic systems, but you will also be able to identify links to other topics to help reinforce your learning as a whole.

You will:

- discover ways to recall the word equations for aerobic and anaerobic respiration
- draw a flowchart to show where glucose comes from, how it is produced and where it is stored
- make lists of sports and physical activities that depend on different types of respiration
- think of a mnemonic to help you remember the definitions of oxygen debt and EPOC, and the difference between them
- create a poster or leaflet illustrating the lactic acid word equation
- draw up a table summarising the factors affecting recovery time
- interpret graphs showing the effect of short-term exercise on heart rate and breathing rate
- create a poster or wall chart to illustrate the short-term effects of exercise
- sketch a diagram of the heart showing the benefits of long-term exercise
- outline a training programme to increase the body's tolerance of lactic acid.

Marathon running is a form of aerobic exercise.

Aerobic and anaerobic respiration

LEARNING OBJECTIVES
- Describe the processes involved in converting food to energy.
- State the equations for both aerobic and anaerobic respiration.
- Link the use of aerobic and anaerobic respiration to different types of physical activity.

How does my body provide energy to my muscles? What is the difference between aerobic and anaerobic respiration, and when do we need each type?

Starting point

In Chapter 1 you learnt how movement is created by muscles contracting, but in order to do this, the muscles need energy. Energy comes from food, which is a mixture of different substances: carbohydrates, fats, proteins, minerals, vitamins and fibre. Food is broken down in your gut into a liquid in a process known as **digestion**. The components within this liquid can pass through into your blood and be carried to your cells for energy, growth and repair.

Key term

digestion: the process of breaking food down in the gut

Exploring the skills

During digestion, carbohydrates are broken down into **glucose**.

Some glucose gets stored in the liver. It is released when glucose levels in the blood fall too low. Some glucose gets stored in the muscles as **glycogen**, and the rest is carried to other cells in the body.

1. The body is able to break down carbohydrates easily into glucose. Research what carbohydrates are and why they are important. List some types of food that are high in carbohydrates. Have you eaten any of them this morning? Why would you eat them at the start of your day?

Key terms

glucose: an important energy source needed by all the cells and organs of our bodies; commonly called sugar

glycogen: a form of glucose stored in liver and muscles; it is a form of energy that muscles can use immediately

Developing the skills

Aerobic respiration

Aerobic respiration is respiration that takes place in the presence of oxygen. Oxygen is transported to the muscle cell through red blood cells (see Topic 3.1). The oxygen combines with glucose inside living cells to release energy. This allows the muscle to contract and create movement.

The process of converting glucose can be summarised as an equation:

$$glucose + oxygen \rightarrow water + carbon\ dioxide\ (+ energy)$$

During this process several things happen:

- Heat is produced. In normal respiration this heat is used to maintain our high body temperature.
- Water molecules are created and transported by the blood, either to be used by the body or expelled from the body as urine.
- Carbon dioxide is created and removed by the blood and exhaled though the lungs.

2 Write out the word equation for aerobic respiration. Annotate it and show where the glucose comes from and where the oxygen comes from. Show what happens to the water and carbon dioxide and the energy.

Anaerobic respiration

Anaerobic respiration is the process of converting glucose into energy *without* oxygen. It can be summarised as a word equation:

$$glucose \rightarrow lactic\ acid\ (+ energy)$$

During the conversion from glucose to energy, a waste product called **lactic acid** is created. Lactic acid makes your muscles tired and painful. It also prevents further energy being created until it is removed.

Oxygen is needed to break down lactic acid into carbon dioxide and water, which is then removed from the body. The extra oxygen needed to do this is called the oxygen debt. Getting this extra oxygen is essential to return the body back its resting state.

Key term

lactic acid: a waste product formed in the muscles during anaerobic respiration, causing muscle fatigue

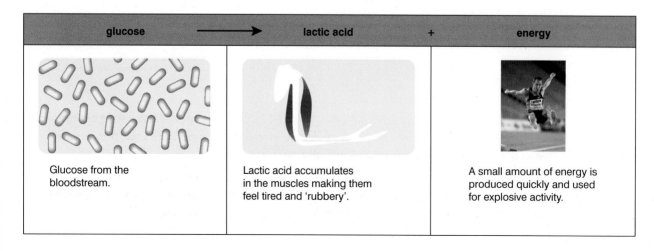

glucose	→	lactic acid	+	energy
Glucose from the bloodstream.		Lactic acid accumulates in the muscles making them feel tired and 'rubbery'.		A small amount of energy is produced quickly and used for explosive activity.

3. Deep breathing is one way of reducing the oxygen debt. How do think this works? (You will look at this in more detail in the next topic.)

4. Write out the word equation for anaerobic respiration. Illustrate or describe on the equation where the glucose comes from and what happens to the lactic acid.

5. In pairs, see how many star jumps you can do in 10 seconds. Discuss what happens to your heart rate and your breathing rate. Why do these things happen? Think about the needs of your muscles for energy and what happens to the glucose stored in the muscles as glycogen.

Applying the skills

Different physical activities make different demands on the body. We use aerobic and anaerobic respiration at different times to meet those demands.

Most of the time your body relies on aerobic respiration: for example, when you are resting or are doing activities with low to medium levels of intensity, such as walking and jogging.

During periods of high levels of intensity, such as sprinting, anaerobic respiration takes over. Muscles require energy quickly and you can't breathe fast enough or deeply enough to meet those demands. Glucose is converted to energy faster, but in smaller amounts, for muscle contractions.

6. Create a table to identify the advantages and disadvantages of aerobic and anaerobic respiration during exercise.

7. Draw up two lists of sports where a) aerobic and b) anaerobic respiration would be the main process of creating energy from glucose.

8. Which sports might use both types of respiration during a game or a race?

REFLECTIVE LOG

a) Which sports, events or activities have you taken part in that require you to work with all-out effort? How long does this last for? What happens to your heart rate and breathing rate at the end of these activities?

b) Which sports, events or activities have you taken part in that require a lower-level, but more sustained, level of activity? How long does this last for? What happens to your heart rate and breathing rate at the end of these activities?

Checklist for success

✔ Memorise and practise writing out the word equations for both types of respiration.

✔ Draw a flowchart to show where glucose comes from, how it is produced and where it is stored.

✔ Make lists of sports and physical activities that depend on different types of respiration.

Sound progress

• I know the names of both types of respiration.

• I know which one requires oxygen and which one does not.

• I can write out the word equation for both types of respiration.

Excellent progress

• I can explain the process of aerobic and anaerobic respiration.

• I can explain what the products of both types of respiration are.

• I can explain which actions, activities and sports require aerobic and anaerobic respiration.

Recovery

How do we recovery after exercise? What is meant by 'oxygen debt', and how do we 'pay back' this debt?

Starting point

In Topic 4.1 you learnt about anaerobic respiration and how lactic acid is created in the cells and the blood. This can happen after as little as 60–90 seconds of maximum effort from muscles. The lactic acid builds up to a point where muscles can no longer operate and the lactic acid must be removed before the muscles can be used again.

1 Think of a time where you have exercised flat out, such as sprinting for 75–100 metres until you are exhausted. What does this feel like? What happens to your heart, lungs and muscles at this point?

Exploring the skills

After intense exercise, the body requires more oxygen than is normally needed to remove the lactic acid in the cells. This is essential to bring the body back to its resting state.

The amount of oxygen needed to bring the body back to normal is called the **oxygen debt**, as the body needs to 'pay back' oxygen into the cells. The process of taking in this additional oxygen is called **excess post-exercise consumption** (or **EPOC**).

The lactic acid equation summarises how this works:

lactic acid + oxygen → water + carbon dioxide (CO_2) + glucose

The oxygen is used to convert the lactic acid into:

- water – which can be used elsewhere in the body or excreted in urine

- carbon dioxide – which is carried to the lungs by the blood and exhaled

- a small amount of glucose – which can be re-used as energy by the muscles.

Key terms

oxygen debt: a temporary oxygen shortage in the body tissues arising from exercise

excess post-exercise oxygen consumption (EPOC): the process of taking in the additional oxygen needed by cells in the body to remove the lactic acid created by anaerobic respiration

A 100 m sprinter barely breathes during the race, but this changes at the end of the race when the oxygen debt has to be paid. Elite athletes will have used anaerobic respiration during the 10 seconds. However, this cannot be maintained for a long period, as the muscles' cells require a huge amount of oxygen to sustain sprinting. The only way they can get enough oxygen to the muscles is to remove the lactic acid through EPOC.

2 When might lactic acid build up in the muscles of a tennis player during a match? Why is it important that they are fit enough to recover quickly and be able to remove the lactic acid from their bodies?

3 Think of a mnemonic to help you remember the definitions of oxygen debt and EPOC, and the difference between them.

Developing the skills

Deep breathing is an essential part of recovering after an intense period of exercise. Large quantities of oxygen are needed to convert lactic acid into carbon dioxide and water. Our breathing rate increases, becoming deeper and faster in order to supply more oxygen to the blood. The heart pumps faster to maintain this increased volume of oxygen through the body. The high breathing rate will continue until the oxygen debt has been paid off.

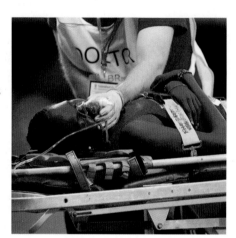

In extreme cases oxygen can be given directly through oxygen tanks. This has happened when athletes have collapsed during or after races.

Sports coaches will spend time training their athletes in techniques of deep breathing to ensure the quickest possible recovery.

When the intense exercise activity has finished and enough oxygen is available again, a fast heart rate helps keep the blood flowing to carry oxygen to the muscles, cells and remove waste products: lactic acid and CO_2.

4 Explain the benefits of deep breathing after exercise in terms of the bodily processes you have studied so far (the respiratory and circulatory systems).

5 Create a poster or leaflet illustrating the lactic acid word equation and explaining the following:

a) how lactic acid is created

b) the role oxygen plays

c) how more oxygen is introduced into the body

d) what happens to the water, carbon dioxide and glucose that are created.

Applying the skills

The ability to recover quickly after exercise is clearly vital for people who want to compete in sports at a high level. There are many factors that influence how quickly someone can recover after exercise, as outlined in the table.

Factor	Explanation
Overall strength and fitness	The stronger your muscles are, the quicker they will be at absorbing the oxygen needed to remove lactic acid.
Genetics	Some people inherit from their parents the ability to recover quickly from exercise; they will recover quickly from a hard bout of exercise, whereas others will feel exhausted.
Age	As you get older, you will generally need a longer recovery time.
Gender	Research has found a gender difference in fatigue and muscle repair, factors that influence recovery. Studies have found that physically fit women have a greater resistance to fatigue than their male counterparts, especially at low to moderate intensities.
Sleep	The amount of sleep you get, and its quality, can affect recovery rate. Good sleep helps your body recover physically and mentally; poor or interrupted sleep has the opposite effect.

In addition, many athletes use various therapies in order to speed their recovery:

- hot and cold contrast therapy – with this technique you alternately apply heat (via heat packs or a hot bath) and cold (via ice packs or a cold bath) to muscles in order improve blood flow and reduce any inflammation

- massage therapy – this is also used to improve blood flow and relax muscles.

You can train your body to be effective at removing lactic acid. An elite athlete is able to recover quickly, removing the lactic acid from their muscles in a short period of time so they can continue intense exercise very soon after. You will look at this in more detail in Topic 4.4.

 6 Draw up a table summarising the factors affecting recovery time. Include a column to say whether the factor is one you can control in any way.

 REFLECTIVE LOG Think about how well you recover from vigorous exercise. Are you quick to recover, or does it take you longer than other people? What steps can you take to improve your recovery time?

Checklist for success

✔ Describe the physical effects on the body when there is an oxygen debt.

✔ Memorise the lactic acid equation and describe how lactic acid is broken down in the presence of oxygen.

✔ Draw a flowchart to outline the processes of lactic acid removal after exercise.

✔ Practise summarising the factors that influence recovery after exercise.

Sound progress

• I know what is meant by the term 'oxygen debt'.

• I can state the word equation for the removal of lactic acid.

• I can give sporting examples of when excess post-exercise oxygen consumption occurs.

Excellent progress

• I can explain what the term 'oxygen debt' means in terms of the circulatory and respiratory systems.

• I can describe how oxygen removes lactic acid from muscles and what happens to the three substances that are then created.

• I can summarise the factors that speed up recovery after exercise and suggest ways of improving recovery time.

Short-term effects of exercise

LEARNING OBJECTIVES
- Identify the immediate effects of exercise on the body.
- Describe what happens to the body during exercise.
- Explain the negative effects that impair performance.

What are the short-term effects of exercise and what are the explanations of these effects?

Starting point

The body reacts to exercise from the moment you start to move. Changes occur inside it that last for a short period after you have finished exercising.

 1 What happens when you start to exercise? How does your body react? Write down as many words, statements or phrases describing how you feel when you start performing a physical activity.

Exploring the skills

Heart rate and breathing

The first effect you probably notice during exercise is that your **heart rate** increases, as the heart pumps faster to send more oxygen through the blood to the muscles to turn glucose into energy (see Topic 4.2). Exercise also causes **adrenalin** to be produced, which is sent to the heart causing it to beat faster.

You probably also notice that your **breathing rate** increases. As you know from your work so far on this chapter, increased breathing means an increase in the amount of oxygen entering the bloodstream via the lungs. This is needed to supply the muscles with energy needed for the exercise (see Topic 4.2).

These two graphs (here and on the next page) show the effect of exercise a) on heart rate in two typical people, one fit and one less fit, and b) on breathing rate.

> **Key terms**
>
> **heart rate:** the number of times the heart beats in a minute
>
> **adrenalin:** a hormone created in the body that causes the body to beat faster
>
> **breathing rate:** the number of breaths taken in a minute

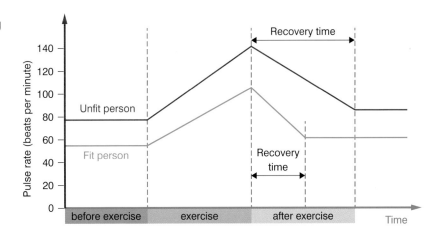

2 Look at the first graph (on page 69) and try to interpret the information to identify what is happening. The following questions will help you:

a) What is the resting heart rate of the two people?

b) What is the maximum heart rate during exercise for each of them?

c) Who recovers more quickly? Why?

d) Why do you think the 'unfit person' has a higher heart rate than the 'fit person'?

3 Look at the second graph (on this page) and explain what is happening. The following questions will help you:

a) What is the resting breathing rate?

b) What is the maximum breathing rate?

c) At what point does the breathing rate increase fastest?

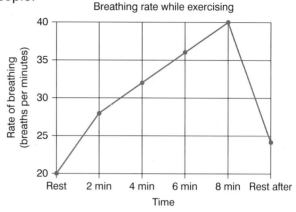

Breathing rate while exercising

— Breathing rate

Heat control and reddening of the skin

Another effect of exercise that you may have noticed is that you start to feel hot. You probably start sweating and your skin may turn red.

In Topic 4.2 you learnt that heat is one of the results of aerobic exercise. Heat occurs when muscles are contracting. The body has to control the temperature. If it didn't, the muscles would stop working to prevent damage to vital organs.

The skin will become red as a result of blood vessels close to the surface of the skin becoming enlarged. The body sends warm blood to the surface of the skin, where it can be cooled by the air.

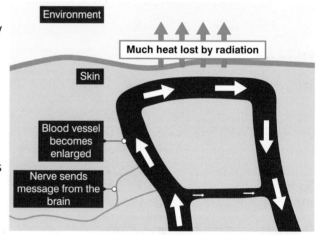

Sweating

Sweating also enables the body to control its temperature by sending water to the surface of the skin released by sweat glands. The sweat evaporates from the skin, removing the body heat and cooling you down.

Water is very effective at cooling the skin, which is why it feels so good to splash water on your face after exercise or in hot weather. This is because water is 25 times better at conducting heat than air. The water absorbs the heat and takes it away from the body.

This quality of water also explains why you quickly begin to feel cold when stepping out of a swimming pool. The water on your skin and your damp swimming costume are both 'stealing' your body heat. As soon as you dry yourself, or change out of the damp clothing, you stop feeling so cold.

Developing the skills

Fatigue

Another noticeable effect of exercise is that you begin to feel tired. **Fatigue** happens when muscle fibres work at their maximum for too long.

In fast twitch fibres (see Topic 1.6), fatigue is caused by lactic acid, which causes pain and stops energy being supplied to the muscle cells. Fatigue may be felt all over the body, or it can be localised to a few muscles, or even to just one muscle. For example, after running a 100 m sprint, your legs suffer from fatigue, although your arms may still be able to lift things.

Slow twitch fibres can work for several hours before they suffer fatigue. If the exercise was quite low intensity, the fatigue will be caused due the body running out of glucose (energy). After a marathon, fatigue would be felt throughout the body, as there is no glucose left to provide energy to the muscles.

 Explain how a trampolinist might struggle to walk after a 30-minute training session but wouldn't struggle so much picking up their kit bag.

> **Key term**
>
> **fatigue:** extreme tiredness resulting from physical exertion

Nausea

Nausea can occur during exercise or shortly after it has stopped, especially if you over-exert during exercise or do high-intensity exercise too quickly. Nausea is a result of blood flow being diverted away during exercise from the stomach to the working muscles, to meet these muscles' need for oxygen and to remove waste products. Digestion in the stomach slows down, and a feeling of sickness can result. If there is anything in the stomach at this time, it may lead to vomiting.

Dehydration (lack of water) can cause the feeling of nausea if the right amount of water has not been drunk. Drinking too much water during exercise (over-hydration) can also lead to feelings of nausea. This is because the excess water dilutes levels of electrolytes (useful minerals) in the body and also stops them from working.

> **Key term**
>
> **nausea:** a feeling of sickness with an inclination to vomit

Light-headedness

After you finish a strenuous exercise session you may feel unsteady, slightly dizzy or light-headed. This is a result of a change in blood pressure, as when you exercise, your heart works harder to pump more blood to your muscles. This causes your blood vessels (see Topic 3.1) to enlarge to allow the stronger flow of blood.

When you stop exercising, your heart rate reduces, but your blood vessels may take longer to get back to their normal size. Hence your blood pressure can drop, causing you to feel light-headed or dizzy. This is normally not something to be worried about.

Deep breathing can help to reduce this as it increases the amount of oxygen into your body. Another approach is to lie down and raise your leg up onto a chair to help the blood flow back to your heart.

Applying the skills

5 Create a poster or wall chart to illustrate the short-term effects of exercise. Using an outline of the body, add labels to show which parts of the body are affected, what the effects are and how to cope or deal with those effects.

6 Working with a partner, test each other's understanding of the effects of short-term exercise. Give your partner one of these key words: pulse, breathing, skin, temperature, sweat, fatigue, nausea, hydration, dizziness. Your partner has to quickly describe the short-term impact of exercise that the key word relates to.

Checklist for success
✔ Practise listing all the effects of short-term exercise on the human body.
✔ For each effect, summarise the causes and the processes going on inside our bodies.
✔ List the negative effects (e.g. nausea) and describe ways of dealing with them.
✔ Sketch an outline of the human body and label the parts affected, and give explanations.

Sound progress
• I understand why heart rate and breathing rate increase during exercise.
• I can explain why we get hot and red, and sweat more during exercise.
• I can explain why we may feel sick and/or light-headed during and after exercise.

Excellent progress
• I can present accurate descriptions of the immediate effects of exercise on the body.
• I can give full explanations of why these effects occur and the physiological processes involved.
• I can suggest ways of countering the negative effects and explain how they work.

Long-term effects of exercise

LEARNING OBJECTIVES
- Identify what happens to the heart after training for a period of time.
- Understand the effects that changes to the heart have on the body.
- Understand how blood is able to tolerate lactic acid.

What are the long-term effects of exercise and what are the explanations of these effects?

Starting point

People exercise and train their bodies to make them fitter. But what does this mean in terms of the changes going on inside your body? And how can we explain this scientifically? This topic looks at the longer-term effects of regular exercise.

1 Discuss what changes take place when you exercise regularly over an extended period. What changes can you see in the body? What about heart rate and breathing? Write down as many words, statements or phrases describing what can happen as a result of long-term exercise.

Exploring the skills

Some of the changes you mentioned in your discussion will relate to obvious changes to the shape of your body: increase in the size of muscles and the loss of body fat, for example.

You may also have mentioned changes not visible on the outside: things such as improved speed (exercising faster) and stamina (being able to exercise for longer). You will explore these in this topic and the reasons for these changes.

Heart size (hypertrophy)

One organ that feels the benefits of regular exercise is the heart. Long-term aerobic training will causes changes in the muscle walls of the heart, making it thicker and stronger. It will increase the size of the heart, making it a more efficient pump. The heart is able to hold more blood and the muscle walls contract more strongly.

This process, called **hypertrophy**, means that the body can work harder, stronger, faster and for longer. In particular, it means an increase in stroke volume, the volume of blood pumped out by each ventricle in one beat (see Topic 3.3). A person of average fitness has a stroke volume of around 70 ml, while for an athlete it is around 90 ml.

Key term

hypertrophy: the process whereby the muscle walls of the heart get thicker and stronger as a result of training

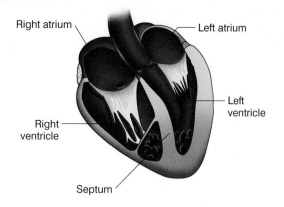

Right atrium
Left atrium
Left ventricle
Right ventricle
Septum

Normal heart

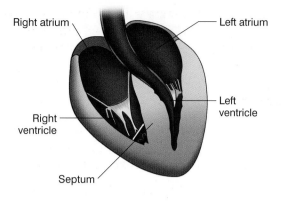

Right atrium
Left atrium
Left ventricle
Right ventricle
Septum

Hypertrophied heart

An elite athlete with a hypertrophied heart will also have a low resting heart rate, pumping larger volumes of blood with fewer beats per minute. A person's heart rate when resting is called their resting pulse. An elite athlete will have a resting pulse of between 40 and 60 beats per minute (bpm), compared with an average person's pulse of 70 bpm. This lower-than-normal heart rate is called **bradycardia**.

2 Can you describe to a partner what happens to the muscle walls of the heart after months of training? Why is this now going to improve your performance?

3 Practise sketching a diagram of the heart, showing the effects of long term-exercise on heart rate and stroke volume.

Key term

bradycardia: a slower than normal heart rate (typically fewer than 60 beats per minute)

Developing the skills

In Topic 4.1 you learnt about anaerobic respiration and how a product of this is lactic acid, which can cause fatigue and impair your ability to exercise further. An elite athlete running at a moderate pace can remove the lactic acid as quickly as it is produced in their muscles. If they increase their speed, more lactic acid will be produced than their muscles are able to remove and this will cause them to slow down or experience pain.

Regular exercise will increase the body's ability to tolerate lactic acid through training programmes that focus on intense activity with periods of rest. This is known as interval training and should match the types of movement the athlete performs in their sport.

During an interval training session the body works at high intensity over a short period time to the point where the lactic acid threshold is reached or exceeded. This is followed by a period of recovery, allowing the lactic acid to be removed. This pattern is repeated several times. Over time, the body will build up a tolerance to the effects of lactic acid.

4 Carry out some research into interval training. What are the benefits of interval training for aerobic and anaerobic fitness? What types of exercise would you perform?

> ## Applying the skills

5 Look at the following discussion points and create a promotional poster aimed at runners, outlining the effects and benefits of exercising in the ways described:

   a) Why would anaerobic training help a 100 m runner be better at the 200 m?

   b) How might a marathon runner benefit from anaerobic training?

   c) How might a 100 m runner benefit from aerobic training?

6 Think of a mnemonic to help you remember the long-term effects of exercise, including the technical terms used to describe these (hypertrophy, bradycardia, stroke volume, lactic acid tolerance).

Checklist for success
✔ Summarise the four main effects of long-term exercise, explaining the physical processes involved.
✔ Sketch a diagram of the heart showing the benefits of long-term exercise.
✔ Outline a training programme to increase the body's tolerance of lactic acid, relevant to a sport you are interested in.

Sound progress
- I can outline the effects of long-term exercise on heart size, stroke volume and pulse rate.
- I can explain how the body's tolerance of lactic acid can be improved.

Excellent progress
- I can define the terms 'hypertrophy', 'stroke volume' and 'bradycardia', and relate these to the benefits of long-term exercise.
- I can describe how the body's tolerance of lactic acid can be increased through exercise and specific training programmes.

Check your progress

Use these statements as a way of evaluating your progress throughout this chapter.

Sound progress

- I know the names of both types of respiration.
- I know which one requires oxygen and which one does not.
- I can write out the word equation for both types of respiration.
- I know what is meant by the term 'oxygen debt'.
- I can state the word equation for the removal of lactic acid.
- I can give sporting examples of when excess post-exercise oxygen consumption occurs.
- I understand why heart rate and breathing rate increase during exercise.
- I can explain why we get hot and red, and sweat more during exercise.
- I can explain why we may feel sick and/or light-headed during and after exercise.
- I can outline the effects of long-term exercise on heart size, stroke volume and pulse rate.
- I can explain how the body's tolerance of lactic acid can be improved.

Excellent progress

- I can explain the process of aerobic and anaerobic respiration.
- I can explain what the products of both types of respiration are.
- I can explain which actions, activities and sports require aerobic and anaerobic respiration.
- I can explain what the term 'oxygen debt' in terms of the circulatory and respiratory systems.
- I can describe how oxygen removes lactic acid from muscles and what happens to the three substances that are then created.
- I can summarise the factors that speed up recovery after exercise and suggest ways of improving recovery time.
- I can present accurate descriptions of the immediate effects of exercise on the body.
- I can give full explanations of why these effects occur and the physiological processes involved.
- I can suggest ways of countering the negative effects and explain how they work.
- I can define the terms 'hypertrophy', 'stroke volume' and 'bradycardia', and relate these to the benefits of long-term exercise.
- I can describe how the body's tolerance of lactic acid can be increased through exercise and specific training programmes.

Chapter 5

Simple biomechanics

Starting points

In this topic, you will understand the key functions of simple biomechanics and its relationship with movement and sports performance. Biomechanics is the study of the mechanics of human movement and its application of forces. In sport this can also be extended to the application of these mechanical forces by the sportsperson onto sports equipment and the environment. This area of study looks at the forces acting on the body (kinetics) and the movement of the body (kinematics).

You will learn how to:

- identify different forces used in physical activities
- apply the equation involving force, mass and acceleration
- identify and explain the forces exerted by gravity, air resistance and muscular force
- define ground resistance force and explain its importance to sprinters
- draw force diagrams to illustrate the forces acting on performers and objects in sport
- identify and sketch the three classes of lever
- state examples of the three classes of lever within the human body
- describe how levers help performance in different sporting situations.

Chapter contents

The activities you complete will primarily relate to theoretical work, but you will also be encouraged to think about the theoretical aspects in a practical setting.

You will:

- memorise Newton's Laws of Motion and the concepts they help to explain.
- practise calculations involving the equation: force = mass × acceleration
- collate examples of sporting situations that describe how forces are used
- memorise the definitions of gravity, air resistance, muscular force and ground reaction force
- draw up tables describing the forces acting upon objects flying through the air
- practise drawing force diagrams to illustrate the forces acting upon moving performers and sprinters in the blocks
- discuss the forces acting upon people taking part in the sports and objects used in them
- practise drawing sketches of the three classes of lever, indicating where the fulcrum, resistance and effort are
- sketch examples of levers found in the human body, indicating FRE on each
- collect examples of how levers help performance in different sporting situations
- build each of the three types of lever
- use mnemonics to help you remember the three types of lever and examples of them.

Biomechanics explores the how movement and structure of living things are connected.

Principles of force

What are the concepts of force, mass and acceleration? How do we use these concepts in sporting situations?

Starting points

Sport employs many different **forces**. To be successful in sport, you need to be able to apply these forces to your advantage in many different ways. Sometimes it will be in very large amounts such as:

- power lifters completing many repetitions of the log lift
- a rugby player making a tackle
- a sprinter running out of the blocks at the start of a race.

These actions all require large, explosive use of forces. Force can be use in a more controlled way, such as:

- a tennis player using spin on the tennis ball to make it dip over the net
- a golfer playing a chip high onto the green.

1 Think of and discuss other examples of forces used in sport. Think in particular of sports you take part in or are especially interested in.

Key terms

force: a push or a pulling action applied upon an object (measured in Newtons, or N for short)

inertia: the resistance of an object to any change in its state of motion

Exploring the skills

Newton's First Law of Motion (also known as the law of **inertia**) states that:

> 'An object in motion stays in motion at the same speed and in the same direction, and an object at rest stays at rest unless acted upon by an external force.'

This First Law suggests that all objects, whether moving or at rest, will stay at the same state unless acted upon by another force. In other words, force is required to cause:

- an object/body at rest to move
- a moving object/body to change direction, accelerate or decelerate
- an object/body to change shape.

English scientist Isaac Newton discovered the laws that govern motion and gravity

For example, a football will stay at rest on the penalty spot until it is acted on by an external force, such as a player kicking it. However, after it has been kicked, the football will continue to travel at the same speed towards the goal until it is acted upon by another external force, which could be:

- the goalkeeper saving it
- the net stopping it
- the bar causing it to change direction
- gravity and air resistance acting as greater forces on the ball, causing it to slow down and eventually come to rest on the ground.

2 Produce a similar table to the one here and provide information for either 'Scoring a penalty kick' or 'A gymnastic vault' to show how forces applied during that action affect the motion of the object or sportsperson.

Effect of force	Example from a serve in squash	
A force can cause an object/body at rest to move.	The racquet will remain at rest until the player applies a force to move it backwards to cause a backswing to prepare to hit the ball.	
A force can cause a moving object or body to change direction.	When the ball comes back from the wall, the squash player's racquet will hit the ball and exert a force to change the direction that the ball will travel. The ball will now travel back towards the wall.	
A force can cause a moving object/body to accelerate.	When squash players need to increase their speed to run across the court, they will apply a greater force against the ground. This causes them to accelerate in the desired direction to reach the ball.	
A force can cause a moving object to decelerate.	As players reach the ball, they need to slow down. They will apply force to the ground in the opposite direction to that in which they are running. This will cause them to decelerate.	
A force can cause an object/body to change its shape.	When the ball hits the wall/racquet, it will deform as it transfers momentum from one direction and transfers it to the new direction in which it is forced to travel.	

All the examples of force described so far have been 'push' forces, e.g. striking a football, hitting a squash ball or air resistance acting against an object. A force can also be a pull.

3 These teams are both exerting forces: which is a push and which is a pull? Can you think of other examples in sport where force is exerted through pulling?

Developing the skills

Force can be calculated using the formula:

Force (N) = **mass** (in kg) × **acceleration** (a)

or $F = ma$

Every object is made up of matter and its **mass** is how heavy the object is without gravity. The more matter an object has, the more it weighs, and the bigger the mass, the harder it is to move.

Newton's Second Law of Motion explains the link between force and **acceleration**:

'An object will accelerate when acted upon by an external force. The acceleration of the object is proportional to this force and is in the direction by which the force acts.'

Acceleration can be either a positive number (meaning an object is getting faster) or a negative number (meaning it's getting slower). For example, a shuttle in badminton will accelerate (go faster) when hit by the racquet. The speed at which it accelerates is proportionate (directly related) to the force the performer has used to hit the shuttle. The shuttle will reach a maximum speed and then begin to decelerate as air resistance and gravity apply forces to slow it down.

Key terms

mass: the quantity of matter in a body regardless of its volume or of any forces acting on it (measured in kilograms or kg)

acceleration: the rate at which an object changes speed (measured in metres per second per second, or m/s^2)

Using curling as an example, imagine a curler pushes a curling stone that weighs 20 kg with a force of 12 N. What is the acceleration of the stone?

This can be worked out using the formula above:

12 = 20 × acceleration

12/20 = acceleration

acceleration = 12/20 = 0.6 m/s²

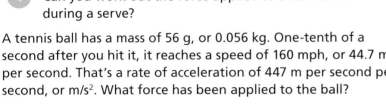

4 Can you work out the force applied to a tennis ball during a serve?

A tennis ball has a mass of 56 g, or 0.056 kg. One-tenth of a second after you hit it, it reaches a speed of 160 mph, or 44.7 m per second. That's a rate of acceleration of 447 m per second per second, or m/s². What force has been applied to the ball?

Applying the skills

Newton's Third Law of Motion states that:

'For every action there exists an equal and opposite reaction.'

Imagine a hockey player collides with an opponent. The hockey player will exert a force on the opponent, and the opponent will exert a force of equal and opposite force back. This will decelerate the opponent and potentially accelerate them in the opposite direction.

5 Using the scenarios below can you explain how Newton's Laws apply to these sport-specific scenarios?

a) There is contact between hockey players fighting over a ball with 500 N of force.

b) A goalkeeper makes a save of a ball that is exerting a force of 200 N and alters the path of the ball.

c) The force applied to the floor at take-off during the long jump is around 300 N.

d) The force used to propel a rowing boat through the water can be around 1300 N.

e) The force applied by the wind to the boat when sailing lessens as the wind drops.

REFLECTIVE LOG

Spend time to produce an information sheet looking at Newton's Laws of Motion and explain how each law applies to a sport or a selection of sports. Why is it important to that sport and how you can use your knowledge to your advantage?

Checklist for success

✔ Memorise Newton's Laws of Motion and the concepts they help to explain.

✔ Practise calculations involving the equation: Force = mass × acceleration (F = ma).

✔ Collate examples of sporting situations that describe how forces are used and the effects they have.

Sound progress

- I can identify the effect of forces that are present in different sporting environments.
- I know what is meant by force, mass and acceleration.
- I understand how forces can affect and improve performance in a physical activity.

Excellent progress

- I can describe, with examples, how different forces are used to help sports performance.
- I can define the terms 'force', 'mass' and 'acceleration' accurately.
- I can apply the equation $F = ma$ to calculate the forces used in different sporting situations.

Applications of force

LEARNING OBJECTIVES
- Identify and explain the forces exerted by gravity, air resistance and muscular force.
- Define ground resistance force and explain its importance to sprinters.
- Draw force diagrams to illustrate the forces acting on performers and objects in sport.

Starting points

When we take part in sport we are exposed to different forces and we use different forces to our advantage. Many of these are invisible and have a continuous effect on us. For example, **gravity** is a force acting on all of us at all times. If we are to run and propel ourselves forwards, we require friction on the ground to apply the force to push ourselves forwards.

In Topic 5.1 you have already explored the effects of other forces, including **muscular force** – the force we consciously apply in activities such as kicking a ball or pulling a rope – and **air resistance**, which affects the speed of objects (such as tennis balls) moving through the air.

The table shows how these forces are applied to the ball during a rugby match.

Key terms

gravity: the force that attracts a body towards the centre of the earth, or towards any other physical body having mass

muscular force: a push or pull applied to an object provided by muscular contraction

air resistance: the frictional force that air applies against a moving object

Forces applied to a rugby ball during a match	
Gravity	• Gravity will always pull the rugby ball towards the pitch, so you have to judge the correct height when passing the ball. • With experience, you automatically make the judgement about height. If you didn't, you would pass the ball short to your teammate. • You use the effects of gravity when you perform a high kick to put a full back under pressure with a ball that falls from a great height.
Air resistance	• When you kick and pass the ball, air resistance will affect the distance and accuracy achieved with a kick. • With a long kick, air resistance slows the ball down the further it goes.
Muscular force	• If you don't apply enough muscular force at the release of the ball, then a pass might not reach your teammates. • When you kick for goal, it might not reach the posts to score. • However, if you release too much muscular force at release, it might be harder to catch or the ball will be kicked too long for your teammates to chase it.

1 Think of another object used in sport and create a table like the one above to explain the effect on the object of

a) gravity

b) muscular force

c) air resistance.

As an object moves, air resistance slows it down. The shape and surface area of the object can increase or decrease the degree of air resistance it encounters.

2 Think about sporting objects of various shapes, such as a tennis ball, shuttle, javelin, shot put or sail. Discuss with your classmates how the forces acting on the object might affect sporting performance.

Exploring the skills

On a forces diagram each force is shown as an arrow. The size of the force is shown by the size of the arrow. The larger the arrow, the bigger the force. The arrows are generally labelled with the name and size of the force being applied. They also show the direction of the force on the object or person.

When two forces acting on an object in opposite directions are equal, then the object is experiencing balanced force.

Look at the picture of the rowing boat. The downward force is the mass of the boat and rowers combined with gravity; the upthrust is the upward force of water buoyancy. In order for the boat to float, the total mass force of the boat and the upthrust force applied by the water must be equal.

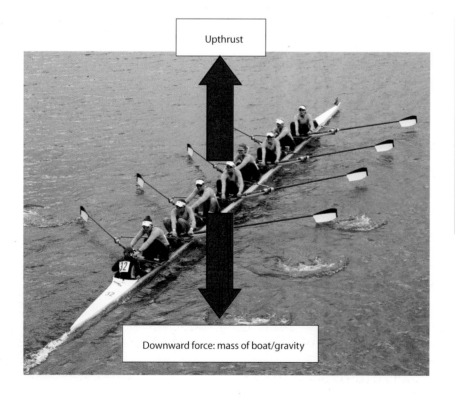

Upthrust

Downward force: mass of boat/gravity

When two forces acting on an object are unbalanced, i.e. not equal, then the object will start to accelerate or move in the direction in which the larger force is pushing or pulling it.

> To move when you are cycling, the muscular force you apply to the pedals will have to be greater than the air resistance and friction placed upon it. To maintain a constant speed, these forces will need to stay the same.
>
> However, if you are cycling on the flat and start to free wheel (stop pedalling and roll), the bike will start to slow down. This is because the forces of the air resistance and friction become larger than the muscular force, which has now become zero.

Let's think about what happens to the forces as the cyclist accelerates:

Muscular force

- To travel at 16 kmph, the cyclist has to apply muscular force of 100 N per metre.

- If he were to produce a muscular force of 1600 N per metre in a sprint finish, you might expect the same equation to apply, i.e. he would reach a speed of 257 kmph – this is clearly impossible!

- In fact, the amount of air resistance increases the faster you travel (as the cyclist is travelling through more air every second).

- As he doubles his speed, then the air resistance could effectively quadruple, so he will only reach around 72 kmph as he closes in on the finish line.

3 Using a similar picture of a cyclist, complete a forces diagram showing the forces acting on the cyclist as he accelerates. Remember: the forces of air resistance and gravity will be lower than the muscular force he is producing as he accelerates to full speed.

4 Choose another sport and produce a forces diagram that shows how the muscular force and air resistance act on them as they change speed and maintain speed.

Developing the skills

In sprinting each runner tries to get the best start possible, with an explosive burst of energy out of the blocks. What are the forces acting in this situation?

As well as gravity, air resistance and muscular force, another force comes into play: the **ground reaction force**. Because of gravity, we are in constant contact with the ground, with forces interacting between them. In a sprint race, the starting blocks are in effect an

> **Key term**
>
> **ground reaction force:** the reaction to the force that the body exerts on the ground

angled extension of the ground. When a sprinter pushes against the blocks, the muscular force applied to them results in an equal reaction force from the blocks (remember Newton's Third Law of Motion in Topic 5.1). This allows the sprinter to make an explosive horizontal burst.

The images below of Jamaican sprinter Usain Bolt summarise the forces in action at different parts of a sprint race.

The athlete has gone from a state of balanced forces to unbalanced forces, meaning acceleration occurs. The muscular force is much greater than that of air resistance.

As speed increases and muscular force reaches its optimum balance against air resistance, acceleration stops and maximum speed is reached.

Acceleration phase

Maximum speed

When pushing against the blocks at the start, the ground reaction force from the blocks results in an explosive start.

Muscular force continues to be applied through to the ground, with friction between the feet of the athlete and the ground essential to aid propulsion.

As the race continues, muscular force reduces as fatigue sets in.

Gravity also plays a part during the race, as gravity forces Usain Bolt's feet to return to the ground after each stride. Applying muscular forces correctly against gravity and air resistance allows him to generate the stride pattern that works best for him.

5   Produce a poster or a leaflet that can be displayed in your classroom, illustrating the forces that act upon a performer and/or object in a particular sport (e.g. triple jump, pole vault, javelin). Include pictures in the form of a forces diagram showing the various forces and their relative sizes during the various phases (e.g. point of release, acceleration, terminal velocity, deceleration).

REFLECTIVE LOG Think about a sport you take part in or are keen on. Identify and explain the forces acting on you and other performers and/or any objects involved. Create a small presentation to show your findings.

Checklist for success

✔ Learn and memorise the definitions of gravity, air resistance, muscular force and ground reaction force.

✔ Draw up tables describing the forces acting upon objects flying through the air.

✔ Practise drawing forces diagrams to illustrate the forces acting upon moving performers and sprinters in the blocks.

✔ Discuss a range of sports and the forces acting upon people taking part in the sports and objects used in them.

Sound progress

• I can describe the various forces that act upon objects in different sporting situations.

• I can explain the size of the forces that generate these actions and can provide examples.

Excellent progress

• I can demonstrate my understanding of the laws of motion by explaining how different forces act upon people and objects in sport.

• I can use my understanding to analyse the effects of forces at different stages of a sporting activity.

Levers

LEARNING OBJECTIVES
- Identify and sketch the three classes of lever.
- State examples of the three classes of lever within the human body.
- Describe how levers help performance in different sporting situations.

What are the three classes of lever? Where in the human body do we see examples of the three types of lever in action?

Starting points

All movements that an athlete performs are produced by **levers** within the body. The muscular system and the skeletal system combine to create lever systems. When a muscle pulls on a bone at a joint to create movement it uses the bone as a lever. These levers work together to apply forces that allow us to run, jump, throw, hit and kick.

The picture of a seesaw illustrates how a lever works.

Key terms

lever: a solid bar (bone/s) that turns around an axis to create movement and contains three main components: fulcrum, resistance and effort

fulcrum: a fixed point about which the lever can turn; sometimes referred to as the axis or pivot

resistance: the load or weight that the lever must move (this could range from the weight of a body part to an external load such as dumb bells)

effort: the amount of force required to move the load

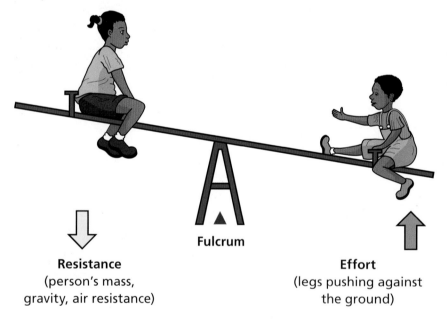

Fulcrum

Resistance
(person's mass,
gravity, air resistance)

Effort
(legs pushing against
the ground)

In our body our bones act as the bars, our joints represent fulcrums, and muscle contractions act as the force.

Exploring the skills

Lever systems have three possible arrangements, described as first-class, second-class and third-class.

First-class levers

The first-class lever is a simple seesaw configuration: the fulcrum is in the middle and the resistance and effort are at either side of the fulcrum. Nodding the head is an example of a first-class lever in the body in action.

First-class levers can produce a wide range of motion and speed of movement.

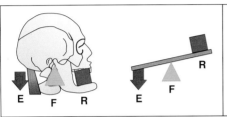

	E Effort = force supplied by muscle contractions in the neck
	F Fulcrum = joint where skull meets the spine
	R Resistance = weight of head + resistance from other muscles in the neck

1. Slowly nod your head backwards. As you do so, think about the forces being applied by muscle contractions at the back of the neck. Now nod your head forwards. Which muscles are applying force now?

2. Can you describe how the first-class lever (the oar) works to enable the sculler to travel along the lake? In this situation, what are the effort, the fulcrum and the resistance? What are the benefits of this type of lever for the rower to apply force and generate speed efficiently?

Second-class levers

The feature of the second-class lever is that the resistance is between the fulcrum and the effort. An example is lifting and moving a wheelbarrow, where the resistance is the load inside the barrow.

The benefit of the second-class lever is that the effort used to move the load can be much less than that of the moving the load itself.

In the body there are few examples of second-class levers, but standing up on your toes is one. Here the foot is the bar at the centre of the lever system.

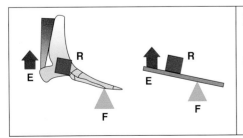

	E Effort = force supplied by muscle contractions in the gastrocnemius (see Topic 1.4)
	F Fulcrum = ball of the foot and joints of the toes
	R Resistance = the weight of the body going through to the foot

3 Think of sporting situations that use second-class levers (hint: look at the photo of the gymnast). Think about some exercises you might perform when completing a circuit training session. Describe how these exercises would fit into this category.

Developing the skills

Third-class levers

Third-class levers are common in the body and in sport. With a third-class lever the effort is placed between the fulcrum and the resistance. Doing a bicep curl is a good example of a third-class lever in action.

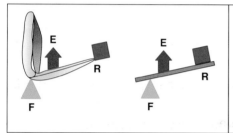

E	Effort = force supplied by muscle contractions in the biceps (see Topic 1.4); the bicep muscle inserts (is attached) about one inch below the elbow joint
F	Fulcrum = elbow joint
R	Resistance = the weight being lifted

Third-class levers require more work to perform a task, but they have the advantage of being able to move with a great range of motion and increased speed. A sporting example where these advantages are important is in cricket or baseball. Here the bat is the bar of the lever system, one hand acts as the fulcrum and the other applies most of the effort. The resistance is supplied by ball.

4 In discussion with classmates, try to think of three more examples of third-class levers being used in sport. Draw a simple diagram and label the components of fulcrum, effort and resistance. For each example, explain why the third-class lever is the best form of lever to perform this action or skill.

Applying the skills

5 The quadriceps (thigh) muscles are attached to the tibia (shinbone) just below the knee joint. The photo shows an athlete performing a leg extension exercise, with her leg forming a lever system. What type of lever is this?

Draw a diagram of this system, indicating where the fulcrum, effort and resistance are located.

(6) Using the diagrams shown in this topic, try to build examples of the three classes of lever using a pivot (e.g. a pencil case), a ruler and string.

REFLECTIVE LOG

Think of mnemonics to help you remember the three types of lever and examples of them within the body.

One way in which you can remember the class of lever and the middle component of the lever is **1-2-3, F-R-E**.

A class **1** lever has the **F**ulcrum in the centre;
a class **2** lever has the **R**esistance in the centre;
and a class **3** lever has the **E**ffort at the centre.

Checklist for success

✔ Practise drawing sketches of the three classes of lever, indicating where the fulcrum, resistance and effort are.

✔ Sketch examples of the three classes of lever as found in the human body, again indicating FRE on each.

✔ Think of examples of how levers help performance in different sporting situations.

✔ Build each of the three types of lever.

✔ Use mnemonics to help you remember the three types of lever and examples of them.

Sound progress

• I can identify and draw diagrams of each class of lever.

• I can give an example of each type of lever in the body.

• I can give examples of levers being used in sporting situations.

Excellent progress

• I can describe the three types of lever and draw diagrams of each, identifying fulcrum, effort and resistance.

• I can give an example of each type of lever in the body and analyse body movements to identify the levers involved.

• I can explain how levers can be used to improve performance in sporting situations.

Check your progress

Use these statements as a way of evaluating your progress throughout this chapter.

Sound progress

- I can identify the effect of forces that are present in different sporting environments.
- I know what is meant by force, mass and acceleration.
- I understand how forces can affect and improve performance in a physical activity.
- I can describe the various forces that act upon objects in different sporting situations.
- I can explain the size of the forces that generate these actions and can provide examples.
- I can identify and draw diagrams of each class of lever.
- I can give an example of each type of lever in the body.
- I can give examples of levers being used in sporting situations.

Excellent progress

- I can describe, with examples, how different forces are used to help sports performance.
- I can define the terms 'force', 'mass' and 'acceleration' accurately.
- I can apply the equation $F = ma$ to calculate the forces used in different sporting situations.
- I can demonstrate my understanding of the laws of motion by explaining how different forces act upon people and objects in sport.
- I can use my understanding to analyse the effects of forces at different stages of a sporting activity.
- I can describe the three types of lever and draw diagrams of each, identifying fulcrum, effort and resistance.
- I can give an example of each type of lever in the body and analyse body movements to identify the levers involved.
- I can explain how levers can be used to improve performance in sporting situations.

Chapter 6

Health and well-being

Starting points

In this topic, you are going to investigate what is meant by health and well-being and what factors affect them. You will explore the links between health and fitness, and examine the different components of fitness that allow you to operate both on a day-to-day basis and to train to become an elite athlete.

You will learn how to:

- provide definitions and examples of health and well-being using the WHO definitions

- identify the relationship between health and fitness

- show understanding of where the body gets its energy from and the importance of diet

- recognise and carry out specific tests to improve both heath-related and skill-related fitness

- describe what your VO_2 max level is and what factors affect it.

Chapter contents

The activities you complete will primarily relate to the aerobic and anaerobic systems, but you will also be able to identify links to other topics to help reinforce your learning as a whole.

You will:

- learn key words relating to health, well-being and fitness

- draw thought clouds to summarise the factors that contribute to your health and well-being

- create a blog or social media page to promote a healthy and active lifestyle

- complete a lifestyle assessment to examine how 'fit' you are to meet the demands of daily life

- discover how your diet can be improved through awareness of different nutrients in food and the way your body uses them to gain energy

- analyse the different components that contribute to fitness both for general health and to improve the skills needed in different sports

- carry out a wide range of fitness tests that measure all aspects of fitness

- create mnemonics to recall key terms and phases relating to health and fitness

- design and create games to explore components of fitness.

Fruit and vegetables are integral to a healthy diet.

Health and well-being

LEARNING OBJECTIVES
- Explain what is meant by 'health' as defined by WHO (World Health Organization).
- Describe, with examples, what is meant by physical, mental and social well-being.
- Explain the benefits of working to improve aspects of physical, mental and social well-being.

What is meant by 'health and well-being'? What physical, mental and social factors contribute towards our health and well-being?

Starting point

In this topic you will look at health and well-being, and what factors affect these important areas of our lives.

1 In pairs or small groups discuss the following questions: What is 'health'? How would you define 'being healthy'?

If you look up 'health' in the dictionary, you may find health defined as 'the state of being free from illness or injury'. Not having an injury, illness or disease is important, of course, but health is about much more than that.

The World Health Organization (WHO) defines health as 'a state of complete **physical**, **mental** and **social well-being**, not simply the absence of disease or infirmity'.

2 How would you define 'well-being'? How does it differ from 'health' in your view?

3 Read through this list of suggestions about what 'well-being' is. How much does each one contribute to feelings of 'well-being'? Rate each one on a scale of 1 to 5, where 1 is not important and 5 is very important.

Aspects of well-being

- having a healthy diet
- taking regular exercise and feeling physically fit
- spending lots of time doing things you enjoy
- feeling good about yourself
- getting on well with your family
- spending lots of time with friends
- having a boyfriend or girlfriend.

Key terms

physical health and well-being: being well in the body and free from injury and illness

mental health and well-being: feeling well in the mind, with a positive outlook and a sense of your own value

social health and well-being: a positive sense of involvement with family, friends and others in the community

All these suggestions can contribute to feelings of well-being. If you eat well and feel fit, that will help you to feel relaxed and happy. So will having lots of interests and a good social life.

4 In pairs or small groups research the six main areas of work that WHO focuses upon by looking at: www.who.int/about/what-we-do/en/
Create a small presentation for your class.

Exploring the skills

Physical health and well-being

What factors contribute to our physical health and well-being? Several factors have already been mentioned in this topic: being free from illness and injury, a healthy diet, regular exercise and feeling fit.

5 On a large piece of paper, copy and complete the diagram below, adapting it to suit you. Focusing first on the physical aspects, what factors contribute to your health and well-being? Add further thought clouds where you think more information is required.

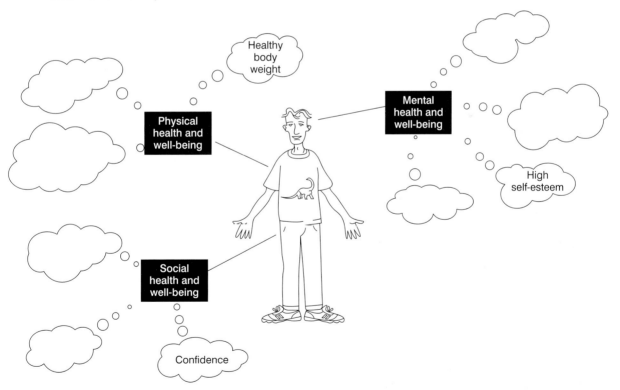

Part of physical health is ensuring that all our body systems (heart, lungs, etc.) and body parts (limbs, overall shape) are working as well as they can, so that we can carry out everyday tasks to the best of our ability.

6 Looking back over the first five chapters of this book, make a list of the body systems described in these chapters and describe how they help us carry out everyday tasks. For example, having strength in our muscles enables us to carry out lifting tasks.

Mental health and well-being

Being healthy should make you feel positive and good in yourself – the idea that a healthy mind and a healthy body are linked. Aspects of mental well-being include:

- feeling good about yourself – having high self-esteem
- being able to cope with stress
- feeling motivated, e.g. to train hard in sport
- being able to control emotions.

7 Returning to the diagram you started in question **5**, now complete the branch focusing on factors that contribute to mental health and well-being. Add further thought clouds where necessary.

Social health and well-being

Many aspects of well-being have to do with the ways in which we relate to other people – the social aspects of health and well-being. We can improve and maintain our well-being through being active and interacting with other people. Aspects of social well-being include:

- our essential need for social contact and interaction
- our friendships with others
- gaining support from and giving support to other people
- confidence to mix with people
- feeling valued within society.

8 Returning to the diagram you started in question **5**, now complete the branch focusing on factors that contribute to social health and well-being. Add further thought clouds where necessary.

Developing the skills

You now should be aware of the many factors that contribute to your health. Each factor brings its own benefits and they combine to improve your overall well-being.

9. Discuss in pairs or as a group the factors shown in the table and the benefits they bring. Identify two more examples for each area – physical, mental and social. Then copy and complete the table below using a computer if possible.

Physical factors	Benefits gained
Improved fitness	Increases your cardiovascular endurance
Healthy diet	Helps you lose weight if you are overweight
Regular exercise	Develops body shape and positive body image

Mental factors	
High self-esteem	Improves your approach to tasks and general confidence
Feeling motivated	Helps you to be active and to feel good about yourself
Coping well with stress	Stops you feeling anxious or depressed

Social factors	
Friendships	Encourages interaction with others, helps you have fun
Being part of a team or club	Helps you make new friends, work to a common goal and gives a sense of belonging
Getting on well with family	Instils a positive attitude towards cooperating with others

Applying the skills

We are all individuals and with unique experiences that affect our health and well-being. Identifying ways of improving your well-being is important for everyone, however. How you do this will depend on your own situation; some of the factors discussed in this topic will be more relevant than others.

10 Create a blog or social media page to promote a healthy and active lifestyle and the benefits of this. You could focus on one of the three aspects: physical, mental and social. Draw on the work you have done in this topic to identify top tips to be included.

REFLECTIVE LOG

For many people, especially in developed countries, life seems to be lived at an extremely fast pace, demanding instant input and high motivation. Technology is a major reason for this and is having a big impact on our lifestyle. Think about your own life and the way technology impacts on your health and well-being:

- Overall, does technology have a good or bad effect on your health and well-being?
- What are the benefits and drawbacks of technology for keeping well and healthy?
- How can you use technology to track and monitor your lifestyle?
- Does it give you access to useful information?
- Are there ways it can make you more motivated to become healthy?

Checklist for success

✔ Remember the World Health Organization's definition of health.

✔ Practise summarising the physical, mental and social factors that contribute to a healthy lifestyle.

✔ Outline the benefits to health and well-being of various factors.

✔ Think of ways of improving your own health and well-being, and promoting that of others.

Sound progress

- I can define what is meant by health and well-being, as supported by the World Health Organization.
- I can list physical, mental and social factors that help keep us well and healthy.

Excellent progress

- I can explain the benefits to health and well-being of a wide range of physical, mental and social factors.
- I can provide clear guidance on how to improve aspects of health and well-being.

Fitness

LEARNING OBJECTIVES
- Provide a definition of fitness.
- Explain the relationship between health and fitness.

How does having a healthy lifestyle tie in with being fit and active?

Starting point

What do we mean by **fitness**?

1 In a group discuss what is meant by the term 'fitness'. What does it mean to be 'unfit'?

Most people think fitness has to do with being physically active and fit, as you would expect top athletes or sportsmen and women to be. But there is more to fitness than that. If you think about what being 'unfit' means, it describes people or things that are unable to cope with something. Fitness, then, is the ability to cope, physically and mentally, with whatever demands are placed upon us.

Having the ability to cope with demands of our environment requires a combination of physical and mental fitness. Being able to carry out everyday tasks without getting too tired whilst balancing home, school, family and friends is enough pressure for anyone.

2 Create a mind map of the demands you have to cope with, using different branches for: home, school, family and friends. Include extensions on each branch to show reasons for each of these demands.

> **Key term**
>
> **fitness:** the ability to cope with (or meet) the demands of the environment

Exploring the skills

From your work in Topic 6.1, you will know that any form of exercise will improve your health. The more you exercise, the more you will improve your overall fitness. You will also develop your performance in physical activities, and as you get better, you will become more confident and gain more enjoyment.

The chart shows the connections (and their definitions) between each of the components in our everyday lives.

3 List some of the activities that you undertake on a typical school day from when you get up to when you go to sleep. Think about the following questions in relation to these activities:

a) What exercise or physical activity is involved? What demands are placed on you?

b) How is this linked to your fitness, i.e. how do you cope with the demands?

c) How do you assess your performance, i.e. how well you have coped with the demands?

How do feel after each one? Are there any you struggle with?

Developing the skills

You know that exercise and fitness can have positive effects on physical, mental and social health. There are times, however, when ill health strikes or we are affected by an injury, such as a sports injury or accident. Illness and injury can lead to decreased fitness – for example, because of an inability to train.

At the same time, people suffering ill health can experience an increased level of fitness. Indeed, exercise may form part of a programme aimed at maximising the fitness of someone who is ill to aid their recovery and improve their overall well-being.

4 Read the following two case studies. Which of these people is experiencing an increase in fitness? And which is experiencing a decrease?

Carl is a keen sprinter, who has been selected to represent his club in national competitions. In a recent event, he suffered an injury to his Achilles tendon and has been instructed to rest for several weeks, with his leg raised whenever possible.

Shirley has been suffering from severe arthritis, especially in her knees. Recently, with the help of a physiotherapist, she has started a programme of seated stretches and movements to increase her heart rate and exercise her muscles and joints. This aim of this exercise is to increase her strength and flexibility, and may also help improve her posture.

HEALTH
'a state of complete physical, mental and social well-being, not simply the absence of disease or infirmity' (WHO)

EXERCISE
a form of physical activity that maintains or improves health and fitness

FITNESS
the ability to cope with (or meet) the demands of the environment

PERFORMANCE
how well a task is completed

5. Thinking about your own experiences, or people you know, think of another example of:

   a) someone who has suffered decreased fitness because of ill health

   b) someone who has benefited from increased fitness despite ill health.

Applying the skills

As you have seen, there are many aspects to maintaining fitness. These include:

- living a healthy, active lifestyle
- eating a balanced diet
- avoiding habits that reduce fitness (such as smoking).

You will look in more detail at aspects of fitness in the next few topics, starting with diet in Topic 6.3.

6. John has been asked to complete a lifestyle assessment to identify ways he can improve his overall health and fitness. He has completed the questionnaire shown here. What is John doing that will help maintain or improve his health and fitness? What areas does John need to change and can he do this?

   How would you present your recommendations to John? Think of different options – report, action plan, presentation, promotional video – and decide which would be the best way to offer your suggestions.

Lifestyle assessment	YES	NO
Eats 5 portions of fruit/veg per day?		✓
Adds salt to food?		✓
Eats fast food at least once per week?	✓	
Drinks alcohol every day?		✓
Has a stressful job?	✓	
Exercises at least three times per week?		✓
Takes the stairs rather than the lift?		✓
Is a smoker?	✓	

6.2

REFLECTIVE LOG

Create your own lifestyle assessment questionnaire or survey that you could use with family members or friends. Ask them if they would be willing to complete the form, making sure that you protect their confidentiality.

Checklist for success

✔ Understand that fitness refers to the ability to cope with the demands of life.

✔ Sketch a flowchart showing how health, exercise, fitness and performance are connected.

✔ Draw up case studies illustrating the relationship between health and fitness.

Sound progress

• I can define fitness.

• I can identify the physical and mental demands of daily life that I have to be fit for.

• I can describe links between health, exercise, fitness and performance.

Excellent progress

• I can write a clear definition of fitness and the link between fitness and the demands of everyday life.

• I can analyse aspects of my daily life and explain how fitness is important for meeting those demands.

• I can encourage others to think about the relationship between fitness and health, and can promote ways to encourage a positive approach to fitness.

Diet and energy sources

LEARNING OBJECTIVES
- Outline the functions of carbohydrates, fats and proteins in providing energy.
- Describe which foods are sources of the different nutrients.
- Explain how food sources contribute to energy produced for different activities.

How does a balanced diet provide the energy our bodies require to work, exercise and recover?

Starting point

As you know from your work on Topics 6.1 and 6.2, a healthy diet is an essential part of staying healthy and well. But what does eating healthily mean?

Different foods contain different **nutrients**, the substances that our bodies need to function and perform. The main nutrients are **carbohydrates**, **fats**, **proteins**, vitamins and minerals. Water is also essential as it transports nutrients to cells and assists in removing waste products from the body.

The table summarises which foods we get different nutrients from and the functions of each type of nutrient.

Key terms

nutrients: the substances in food that our bodies process in order to survive and grow

carbohydrates: the sugars, starches and fibres found in fruits, grains, vegetables and milk products; the body's main source of energy

fats: an essential part of our diet and a rich source of energy: 1 gram of fat contains 9 calories (compared with only 4 calories in a gram of protein or carbohydrate)

proteins: the building blocks of life found in every cell in the human body; proteins are made up of a chain of smaller units called amino acids; they help your body repair cells and make new ones

Nutrient	Source	Function	Energy provision
Carbohydrates	Fruits, breads and grains, starchy vegetables (e.g. potatoes), sugars, pasta, rice	Provide the body's main source of fuel, needed for physical activity, brain *function* and operation of the organs. Also provide fibre helping to regulate digestion.	Up to 55% of our energy intake
Fats	Red meats, butter, cooking oils, cheese, bacon	Supply a very concentrated source of energy that you can store in your body for later use.	Up to 30% of our energy intake
Proteins	Low-fat meat (such as chicken), dairy, beans, eggs, fish	Help body cells grow. Repair cells and muscle tissue.	Up to 15% of our energy intake
Water	Drinks, foods with a high water content such as soup and watermelon	Transports nutrients to cells. Assists in removing waste products from the body. Helps maintain body temperature.	

Because we need more of some nutrients than others, a balanced diet contains all of these nutrients in the right proportions to stay healthy. The final column of the table shows the typical percentage of energy intake the different nutrients provide.

As most foods contain more than one kind of nutrient, trying to work out what a balanced diet looks like can be difficult. Governments sometimes use images of food on a plate such as this one to guide people on what proportions to eat.

Different groups of people may have different needs for nutrients at different times of their lives, so this balance can change. For example, children require more protein than adults because they are still growing rapidly. Also, some groups of people have a greater need for a specific nutrient. For example, pregnant women require more iron than usual to help develop blood cells in their babies.

Other reasons for choosing a particular diet include:

- health conditions (such as diabetes or allergy)
- a desire or need to lose or gain weight
- reasons of religion or culture
- a regime in sport.

1 In small groups, discuss the reasons why some people would require special diets. Think of examples of the different groups of people above.

> **REFLECTIVE LOG**
>
> Look again at the diagram of the food plate and think about the balance of nutrients that you eat in a typical week. Which of the foods do you eat? Does your diet contain a good balance? Or are there foods you might want to add?

Exploring the skills

How much energy you require depends on many different factors, including your age, gender and lifestyle. For example, someone working at a desk all day will require fewer calories than someone whose work involves physical activity, e.g. in the building trade. Energy is measured in kilocalories (kcal), usually referred to as just calories. A teenager (15 years) typically requires 2820 calories (male) and 2390 calories (female), whereas an active adult requires 2500 calories (male) and 2000 calories (female).

The table shows how many calories are burnt up doing various types of activity. As it suggests, watching TV uses about 75 calories of energy in an hour, whereas playing competitive sport can use up over 400 calories in an hour.

Activity	Energy expenditure (calories per minute)	
	58-kilo woman (calories)	70-kilo man (calories)
Sleeping, resting	0.5–1	1–1.5
Sitting, reading, desk work, watching TV	1–1.5	1.5–2
Sitting typing, playing piano, operating controls	1.5–2.5	2–3
Light work, serving in a shop, gardening, slow walking	2–3.5	3–4
Social sports, cycling, tennis, cricket	3–5	4–6
Heavy physical labour, carrying, jogging, competitive sports	4–7	6–8.5
Very hard physical labour, intense physical activity, heavy lifting, very vigorous sporting activity	over 10	over 12

2 How many calories do you burn up during the day? Keep a record of the different activities you carry out in a 24-hour period and estimate how much energy (i.e. how many calories) you are using up. Are there days when you need and use much more energy than others?

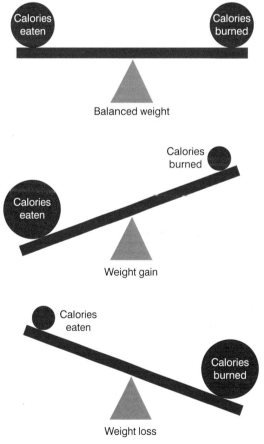

Balanced weight

Weight gain

Weight loss

Developing the skills

Eating healthily also involves matching the amount of energy we need with the amount of energy we use. If we take in a lot more than we need, the unused energy is stored in the body as fat. In the long term, this can lead to cause obesity. Health problems related to obesity can be serious and include high blood pressure, diabetes, liver disease, heart disease, stroke and cancer.

At the other end of the scale, taking in too little nourishment can lead to a person being underweight and not getting enough nutrients to stay healthy. Weighing too little can contribute to a weakened immune system, fragile bones and feeling tired.

In many countries, pre-packaged foods have nutrition labels on the packaging. This is to help people see what the food contains and whether or not it is a healthy choice. These labels include information on energy in kilojoules (kJ) and/or kilocalories (kcal). They may include information on fat, saturates (saturated fat), carbohydrate, sugars, protein and salt. The information is often colour-coded, as in the example shown. This uses a 'traffic light' system where:

- Red means high.
- Amber means medium.
- Green means low.

If you buy a food that has all or mostly green on the label, you know straight away that it's a healthier choice.

3 The example shows the label on a tin of baked beans. How healthy would you say this food item is based on the nutrition information?

4 Look through some of the pre-packed food you have at home and find the nutrition labels. Try to identify foods that are healthy, i.e. contain mostly green. Are there any foods that are less healthy, i.e. have red on the label?

5 As the food label suggests, there are different types of fats: saturates, unsaturates and trans fats. Some types are regarded as healthier than others. Carry out some research into the different types of fat and whether they are healthy or unhealthy.

REFLECTIVE LOG
Over the next week keep a food diary along with the number of calories (check the food labels) you have consumed. Compare this with the estimate you have already made of how much energy you typically use up in a day. You could present your results in the form of a digital presentation to promote a balanced diet.

Applying the skills

You have learnt how our food sources provide nutrients to give us energy. A key element in the process is glucose. Glucose is the carbohydrate transported by the bloodstream to the various tissues and organs, including the muscles and the brain. The muscle cells release energy from glucose in a process called respiration. If the body does not need glucose for energy, it stores it in the liver and the skeletal muscles in a form called glycogen.

You learned all about this process in Topic 4.1. Look back over that topic now and then answer the following questions:

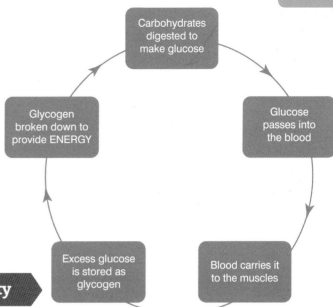

6. What is aerobic respiration? What is the word formula for aerobic respiration?

7. What is anaerobic respiration? What is the word formula for anaerobic respiration? What is the waste product of this process and why is it an important factor for people doing sports?

8. What happens to the glucose that is not used? Where is it stored? When will it be used?

Energy balance for physical activity

Consuming the right amount of nutrients for specific functions can improve performance and fitness. Different athletes will take different approaches depending on the demands of their sport.

Carbohydrate loading is one approach used by endurance athletes, e.g. marathon runners, cyclists, swimmers and rowers. This involves eating excess carbohydrate foods one week before an event to increase glycogen stores in the muscles. This helps delay tiredness by providing a slow release of energy. Athletes on this regime may consume as many as 4000 to 5000 calories a day.

Another approach is a high-protein diet, used by bodybuilders to gain muscle and lose fat. However, eating extra protein does not directly add muscle and can be difficult to digest.

In some sports, participants may even reduce their calories intake to low levels just before a performance, in order to maximise the body's lightness and litheness, e.g. gymnastics, diving.

Water is an essential part of any athlete's diet, as it is important to keep hydrated especially when exercising to replace what the body has lost through sweating. It also helps to maintain the temperature in the body.

9. Identify two essential nutrients that should be included in football players' diets and how they can impact on their performance in the game.

10. Explain why a runner would use a carbohydrate loading diet before a marathon race.

Checklist for success

✔ Describe what makes up a balanced diet and why it is important.

✔ Practise summarising the food sources and functions of these nutrients: carbohydrates, fats, proteins and water.

✔ Think of examples or case studies of athletes from different sports and their energy needs.

✔ Revise the process of aerobic and anaerobic respiration to explain how energy is derived from food sources.

Sound progress

• I can state the main nutrients the body needs and outline their function in providing energy.

• I can identify which food sources provide different nutrients.

• I can describe the importance of a balanced diet for individuals and specific groups.

• I can explain how different physical activities use different amounts of energy.

Excellent progress

• I can identify the main nutrients the body needs and explain their different functions in providing energy.

• I can explain which energy source will benefit a particular activity and the food sources that will be required.

• I can explain in detail how our body gets energy through the processes of aerobic and anaerobic respiration.

• I can describe different dietary regimes needed by athletes for different sports.

Components of fitness

LEARNING OBJECTIVES
- Recognise the components of health-related and skill-related fitness.
- Explain the links of these components to performance of sports and physical activities.

What is meant by health-related and skill-related fitness? What are the different components and how are they used in different physical activities?

Starting point

Our bodies deal with different levels of activity on a daily basis, all of which require a certain amount of fitness. If we find these activities too tiring, then we may regard ourselves as 'being unfit'. An example of this is having enough energy to run for a bus and being able to cope with it afterwards by recovering quickly.

Fitness can be regarded in two ways: as **health-related** or **skill-related**.

Health-related fitness has six components that can help protect your body and keep it free from injury and illness. These are as follows:

- **Cardiovascular endurance** (or **stamina**) allows you to work for long periods of time with the lungs, heart and blood working efficiently to supply oxygen to the muscles. Needed in many sporting activities such as football, netball and swimming.

- **Flexibility** is the range of movement around a joint, demonstrated in activities such as bowling in cricket, gymnastics, karate and taekwondo.

- **Muscular endurance** is the ability of your muscles to work continuously without getting tired. Used in activities such as climbing, long-distance running events and cycling.

- **Power** refers to being able to perform strength movements at speed and includes boxing, shot put and smash shots in tennis and badminton.

- **Speed** is the ability to perform a movement quickly over a distance such as the 100 m sprint or throwing a rounder's ball to a base.

- **Strength** is the ability to exert the maximum amount of force in one go. This can be either explosive, such as a weightlifter lifting a maximum amount in one attempt, or static, such as rugby players in a scrum pushing against the other team.

Key terms

health-related fitness: the components of physical fitness directly related to good health and meeting the demands of everyday life

skill-related fitness: the components of physical fitness that focus on skills and abilities needed to perform successfully in sporting situations

1. Health-related components are abilities you need for everyday life. For each of these six components, think of an example of an everyday activity where you need it. For example, you may need speed to run for the bus!

2. Using the images for each of the six components, create a table with the following headings: Component / Definition / Sporting activity / Everyday activity.

Exploring the skills

The four components of skill-related fitness are described below:

- **Agility** – the ability to change the body position quickly under control.

- **Balance** – being able to maintain a position, either static (still) or dynamic (moving).

- **Coordination** – the ability to use two body parts at the same time.

- **Reaction** – the time it takes to respond to a stimulus (such as a starting pistol).

Note: the distinction between health-related and skill-related fitness components is not always clear-cut. For example, some websites will refer to speed as a skill-related, rather than a health-related, factor.

3. Think of more examples of sports and physical activities that depend on these four skill-related components. Which sports do you practise that require them?

4 Working in pairs, take turns to test each other on your understanding of each component. One person reads out the definition or describes a component without mentioning its name or using words related to it (e.g. 'reacting to …' or 'coordinating your …'). The other has to name the component and state whether it is health-related or skill-related. Vary the task by having one person read out the name of the component, while the other has to describe it and give an example of its use in a sporting activity.

REFLECTIVE LOG

Think of mnemonics to remember the two sets of fitness components. An example for skill-related components is suggested here. Adapt it to something you will remember and create a second one to recall health-related components. Write them on sticky notes to include in your log.

All	**A**	agility
Boys	**B**	alance
Can	**C**	oordination
Run	**R**	eaction

Health-related fitness components

C

M

F

P

S

S

Developing the skills

In any physical activity or sport, if you want to achieve a high level of skill, it is important to identify key areas that need to be developed or improved. The health-related and skill-related components of fitness provide a useful framework for doing this.

Look at this conversation between an athlete (a heptathlon or decathlon specialist) and their coach.

5 Create a similar conversation for another sport or athlete, identifying two skills that they need to improve and the reasons for this.

Applying the skills

Comparing the health-related and skill-related components between people in the same sport is helpful for identifying methods of improving training and performance.

Hi Kim. How are you today?

Yes, I am good thanks. I've just been looking at how I could improve my skill-related fitness – first my reaction time in my sprint start and also coordination when throwing the javelin.

This sounds great. What skills could you improve when hurdling?

6 Shireen is a 200 m sprinter who finds that she is slower out of the blocks than people she races against. She wants to analyse why she is a slower starter than the others and asks her coach for advice. What fitness components do you think the coach would try to help her improve?

Another useful form of analysis is to identify similarities in fitness components between different sports. For example, a badminton player may need similar levels of agility and reaction time to that of a sprinter. Comparing training techniques could benefit both of them.

7 Working in a small group, design a set of fitness 'Top trump' cards using some health-related and skill-related components, as shown in the example. Choose eight sportsmen and women and discuss in your group what rating to give them out of 20, in each component. Doing this will help you to identify physical activities that have similar components and how they could use similar methods for improvement and development.

Rory McIlroy

Speed	15
Strength	14
Flexibility	16
Muscular endurance	14
Cardiovascular endurance	10

Checklist for success

✔ Learn the 10 components that make up a person's fitness and whether each is health-related or skill-related.

✔ With a partner, quiz each other by naming a component and asking the other person to describe it and give an example of its importance to a particular sport.

✔ Use mnemonics to remember whether components are health-related or skill-related.

✔ Make lists of different sports that use the same fitness components and explain why the same skill is essential for both sports.

Sound progress

• I can explain what is meant by health-related and skill-related fitness components.

• I can give examples of both health-related and skill-related fitness components.

• I can describe physical activities that use specific skill-related or health-related fitness components.

Excellent progress

• I can define the 10 recognised components of fitness and categorise them as either health-related or skill-related.

• I can use my knowledge of physical activities to describe which health-related or skill-related components they use.

• I can explain how different activities use similar skill-related or health-related components in their performance.

Fitness testing

LEARNING OBJECTIVES
- Identify the different tests used to assess health-related and skill-related fitness.
- Be able to carry out the different health-related and skill-related fitness tests.
- Outline the main reasons for carrying out fitness tests.
- Explain how fitness tests can improve performance in specific physical activities.

What are the various tests that can be used to identify performance and ability in both health-related and skill-related fitness?

Starting point

Measurement and testing take place at all stages in sport and physical activity. At the simplest level, it happens when counting the score in a game such as squash or cricket. The score shows which individual or team is the most able, or at least the most successful on that occasion. Scores can be recorded for successive matches, giving an overall picture of a person's or team's performance or improvement.

On a more complex level, it is possible to measure many aspects of an individual's fitness: for example, how strong, powerful, supple or fast they are. Further, by comparing measurements before and after training, it is possible to measure the effects that training has had and what improvements are still to be made.

Discuss with your partner some of the physical tests you have undertaken in your PE lessons or with your local sports team. What were they like? Were there precise instructions you had to follow? What results did they give? Do you think the results were generally accurate?

Exploring the skills

For each of the six health-related fitness components discussed in Topic 6.4, there are specific tests that can be used to measure ability in that component.

Cardiovascular endurance or stamina – 12-minute run test (Cooper test)

In the 12-minute run test, or Cooper test, you run and/or walk as far as you can in 12 minutes (a maximal test). The fitness level is judged by comparing the distance run to established norms for the test.

Example Ratings for Cooper test (in metres):

Gender	Excellent	Good	Average	Below average	Poor
Male	>2800m	>2500m	>2300m	>2200m	2200-m
Female	>2200m	>2000m	>1800m	>1600m	1600-m

Cardiovascular endurance or stamina – multi-stage fitness test

In the multi-stage fitness test, you perform continuous shuttle runs between two lines drawn 20 m apart. The pace is established by a recording that sounds a bleep at the end of each leg of the shuttle run. As the test progresses, the time between the bleeps get shorter and a level is indicated. When three bleeps in a row are missed, your fitness level has been established. Again this is a maximal test because you are working as hard as you can.

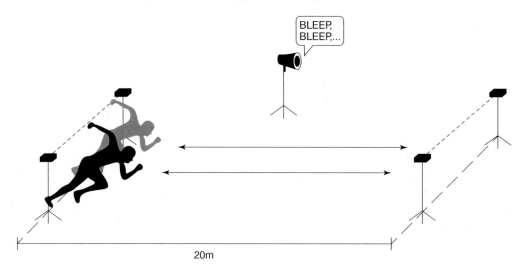

Flexibility – sit-and-reach test

This test measures suppleness in the back and hamstrings. You sit on the floor with your legs fully extended, feet flexed and hands touching the sit-and-reach box. You stretch forward (in an even manner, not jerking) with both hands keeping your legs straight and sliding your palms along the box. The distance your fingertips reach beyond your toes is the measurement. If you cannot reach beyond your toes, the distance from the fingertips and toes is measured – this is a negative score.

Example Ratings sit-and-reach (in cms):

Gender	Excellent	Good	Average	Below average	Poor
M/F	10+	5+	0	−1 to −4	−5

Muscular endurance – multi-stage abdominal conditioning test

Muscular endurance is when a muscle or group of muscles works continuously without tiring for a long period of time. In pairs conduct the following test. You will require:

- a mat
- a stopwatch
- a partner to record the number of sit-ups.

Over a 30-second period perform as many sit-ups as you can. Your partner will time you and keep count. Then use a table like the one below to identify your level of muscular endurance.

Gender	Excellent	Above average	Average	Below average	Poor
Male	>30	26–30	20–25	17–19	<17
Female	>25	21–25	15–20	9–14	<9

Power – vertical jump test

Power is a combination of speed and strength. It can be measured in the legs by using the vertical jump test (see diagram).

Facing the wall, you stretch both arms above your head with your hands side by side so that fingertip level whilst standing can be marked on the wall or a jump board. You then turn sideways to the wall and, with both feet together, jump as high as you can, touching the wall or jump board with the fingertips of one hand. You may swing your arms before jumping if you wish. The distance jumped is the distance between the two marks.

Speed – 30 m sprint

The 30 m sprint measures how fast you can run over a short distance. This is a maximal test, as you need to run as fast as you can.

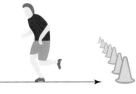

30 m

Strength – one-repetition maximum test

The one-repetition maximum test (1-RM) is a measure of the greatest weight a person can lift with just one repetition. It is only for advanced weight trainers and anyone attempting it needs to have good technique. For reasons of safety the test should be performed with a spotter (someone positioned to observe the performer and minimise the risk of accident or injury).

After a warm-up, the person chooses a weight they know they can lift. Then they rest for several minutes, increase the weight and try again. If successful, they rest for a few more minutes. They keep increasing the weight until they can only repeat one full and correct lift of that weight. It is important to reach the maximum weight without fatiguing the muscles – hence the need for several minutes' rest between lifts.

Strength – hand-grip dynamometer

A hand-grip dynamometer is used to test hand and forearm strength. Before using the dynamometer, check that the scale is set to 0. You then grip and squeeze as hard as you can. Measurement is shown on the display or read off the dial. The test is repeated three times.

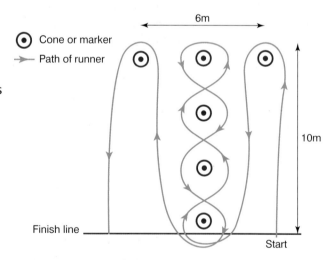

2 Choose three of the health-related fitness components and think of a sport or physical activity where it is an essential skill. For example, speed is used in badminton to move from the back to the front of the court to play a shot. Using the test outline described above, create your own test suitable for that sporting activity. For example, how fast can you move from the back court to the front court? How many times can you do this?

Developing the skills

Skill-related fitness tests focus on the following components:

Agility – Illinois agility run test

Agility is a combination of speed and coordination. In the Illinois agility run, both of these aspects are tested as you run as fast as possible while changing direction around a series of cones on a preset pathway (see diagram).

You start by lying face down behind the starting line with your chin on the floor. On the command 'Go', you stand up and run around cones following the set pathway as fast as possible. The measurement is the time taken to complete the run. This can be compared with established norms.

Ratings for the Illinois agility run (in seconds):

Gender	Excellent	Good	Average	Below average	Poor
Male	<15.2 sec.	<16.1 sec	<18.1 sec	<19.3 sec	<20.0 sec
Female	<17.0 sec	<17.9 sec	<21.7 sec	<23.0 sec	<24.0 sec

Balance – stork stand test

In the stork stand test, you stand on one foot and place the other foot against the inside of the knee. Hands are placed on hips.

Timing starts when both eyes are closed. Timing stops when either you open your eyes, your foot parts from your knee or you lose your balance.

Coordination – Anderson wall toss test

This test measures hand–eye coordination. Standing 2 m from a wall, you toss a tennis ball underarm against the wall with one hand and catch it in the other hand. You immediately throw it back against the wall to and catch it in the initial hand. This action is repeated with the throwing and catching being continuous. Measurement is the total number of catches made in 30 seconds.

Ratings for Anderson wall toss test:

Gender	Excellent	Good	Average	Below average	Poor
Male	>35 catches	30–34	20–29	15–19	10–14
Female	>35 catches	30–34	20–29	15–19	10–14

Reaction – metre-rule drop test

A metre rule is held against a flat wall and you stand with your thumb alongside, but not touching, the 0 cm mark. Without warning, the ruler is dropped and you must catch it by gripping between the thumb and index finger (see diagram). Measurement is the distance between the bottom of the ruler and the index finger.

 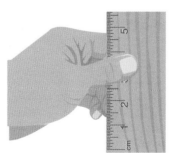

Ratings for the meter-rule drop test (in cm):

Gender	Excellent	Good	Average	Below average	Poor
Male	<8cm	<9–12cm	<13–20cm	<25cm	<30cm

 3   Choose two of the skill-related fitness components and think of a sport or physical activity where it is an essential skill. For example, reaction is used in sprint starts in athletics

to gain advantage in a race. Using the test outline described above, create your own test suitable for that sporting activity. For example, look at which position, such as standing, sitting or lying down, provides the best method of getting into the lead in a race. For example, lie on your back with your head pointing down the track. On the command 'On your marks, get set, and go', see how quickly you can get up into a sprinting position to run the race.

Applying the skills

It is important that the tests are conducted in the correct way using the **test protocol**. This is not only for safety, but to ensure that results are accurate. It is also important that the test gives results that are **valid**.

(4) Set up and complete as many of the health-related and skill-related fitness tests as you can, recording your results.

(5) Identify which tests you scored high scores on. Can you give a reason why? Which tests did you score low on? Do you think further training would improve this component of fitness?

Carrying out these tests yourself will help you appreciate the main reasons for using them. These include:

- Assessing someone's suitability for different physical activities – for example, someone who performs better on strength, power and stamina tests rather than flexibility or balance may decide to concentrate on an activity where those components are particularly important (e.g. rowing).

- Identifying strengths and weaknesses – test results give clear indications of areas where you are strong and others where you need to do more work.

- Monitoring improvement – an individual's tests results can be gathered over the course of a season (or several seasons) and improvements measured.

- Comparison to others – having different people's results from the same test allows individuals to compare their performance with that of other individuals.

- Informing the design of a training programme – athletes and their coaches can identify areas of fitness that need to be focused on, e.g. during pre-season training; the test results can provide a baseline against which goals can be set and progress measured.

- Motivation – the desire to improve your results in a particular test can be a great motivator; seeing improvements in test results should also give confidence and encourage you to perform even better.

Key terms

test protocol: the correct procedure for carrying out a test; if done incorrectly, this might affect the results

valid: the test succeeds in measuring what it sets out to measure: a test for leg strength should not use muscles in the arms

6 In a small group, discuss these reasons for carrying out fitness tests. Which are the most important for you and your classmates? Can you give examples of how fitness tests have proved useful?

7 Create a PowerPoint or promotional video focusing on two health-related and two skill-related fitness components, outlining some of the sports they are essential for. Provide demonstrations of how to perform the tests with examples of the ways they link into a particular sport or physical activity.

REFLECTIVE LOG

Identify a sport or physical activity you are involved in and link this to at least two of the fitness components and their tests. Practise the tests and record your results. Keep a diary for three weeks to see whether this improves the ability and has an impact upon your overall performance.

Checklist for success

✔ Practise carrying out each of the health-related and skill-related fitness tests following test protocols while thinking about safety at all times.

✔ Record your tests accurately and keep a diary of results gathered over a period of time.

✔ Create a mind map or table to summarise the reasons for carrying out fitness tests, with examples.

✔ Think of ways of incorporating fitness tests into your own training programme or as a way of setting goals for yourself.

Sound progress

• I can identify each of the tests for the components of health-related and skill-related fitness.

• I can perform each of the tests and acquire some baseline data to improve my ability.

• I can state the reasons for carrying out fitness tests.

Excellent progress

• I can conduct each of the health-related and skill-related fitness tests with another person following test protocols and ensuring safety.

• I can use the results gathered to help identify strengths and weaknesses, improvements made and areas for further development/training.

• I can explain how each test can improve a sporting or physical activity by implementing them into training sessions.

VO$_2$ max (maximum oxygen uptake)

What is VO$_2$ max and what factors affect VO$_2$ max levels?

Starting point

It is now recognised that regular exercise improves our anatomy in such a way that we can perform at competitive and elite level (with constant training). A major benefit is improved functioning of the blood vessels, especially the capillaries, the minute blood vessels that deliver oxygen into the body's tissues (see Topic 3.1). By increasing the density and functioning of the capillaries, more oxygen can be absorbed by the body and sent to the working muscles.

Measuring the amount of oxygen you can consume while exercising is a good way of assessing your fitness. **VO$_2$ max** does just this by measuring the volume of oxygen you can consume while exercising at your maximum capacity. (VO$_2$ max is sometimes also called maximal oxygen consumption, maximal oxygen uptake, peak oxygen uptake or maximal aerobic capacity.)

VO$_2$ max is measured in millilitres per kilogramme of body weight per minute (ml/kg/min). The typical average VO$_2$ max values for untrained healthy individuals are 35–40 ml/kg/min for males and 27–31 ml/kg/min for females.

> **Key term**
>
> **VO$_2$ max:** the volume of oxygen that can be consumed while exercising at a maximum capacity

1. Using the internet, research the VO$_2$ max values for elite athletes in different sports. Which sports typically have the highest values? How would you explain this in terms of the fitness components required for those sports?

Exploring the skills

A test can be set up to calculate accurately your VO$_2$ max. However, this requires sophisticated equipment in a laboratory on either a treadmill or a cycle ergometer. The multi-stage fitness (bleep) test or 12-minute Cooper run (see Topic 6.5) can be used instead to collect and compare these results.

2. In your next practical session take part in the 12-minute Cooper run around a designated course such as a 400 m athletics track. The aim is to run without stopping for 12 minutes at a fast pace while counting the number of laps and calculating the distance from that.

People who are fit have higher VO_2 max values and can exercise more intensely than those who are not as well conditioned. Studies have shown that you can increase your VO_2 max by working out at an intensity that raises your heart rate to between 65% and 85% of its maximum for at least 20 minutes three to five times a week.

By carrying out either the multi-stage fitness or 12-minute Cooper test, you can establish a baseline identifying your level of cardiovascular endurance (stamina). It allows you to measure improvement by re-testing after a few weeks and aiming for the next level (bleep test) or further distance (Cooper test).

3 Compare your results from the Cooper test (i.e. distance run) to times run by athletes for 1500 m (3.75 laps), 3000 m (7.5 laps) and 10 000 m (25 laps). Look at the world records for each and compare these with your 12 minutes. What did you find out?

4 Present your results using bar charts and graphs to show your results in comparison to others in your class and to elite athletes.

> **REFLECTIVE LOG**
> Research the different ways we can use technology to help monitor our fitness levels. Is it a cheap way of motivating us to stay fit? Record your findings in your reflective log.

Developing the skills

There are different factors that can affect your VO_2 max level. These include:

- Age – oxygen uptake is at its strongest in 18–25 year olds, but reduces with age at the rate of about 1% per year.
- Gender – values of VO_2 max are typically 25–35% higher in men than in women; females have a lower VO_2 max due to the smaller amount of blood pumped (lower stroke volume).
- Genetics – the types of muscle fibres you have and size of your heart are partly dependent on the genes you inherit from your parents.
- Lifestyle – smoking and a sedentary lifestyle are two factors that will prevent your VO_2 max improving.
- Training – focusing on cardiovascular activities such as running, swimming and cycling will increase your VO_2 max and improve your performance.

Applying the skills

5 You are going to set up a circuit of stations that will identify how your breathing copes and adapts to the type of activity it performs.

a) Find out your resting breathing rate by sitting still for 3 minutes. (See Topic 2.3 to recap key terms such as tidal volume, vital capacity, residual volume and minute ventilation.)

b) Record how many breaths you take in 30 seconds, then multiply this by 2 (one breath = one inhalation and one exhalation). Aim for normal breathing and if you wish, place your hand on your chest. Repeat this three times altogether and record the results in a copy of the table. Calculate the average of the three scores by adding them together and dividing by 3.

Measurement	Number of breaths in 30 seconds	Number of breaths in 1 minute
1		
2		
3		
Average resting breathing rate		

c) Conduct a light warm-up including stretches to ensure your body is prepared.

d) Along with your classmates, devise a circuit divided into stations such as skipping, step aerobics, burpees (squat thrust to standing jump) and 5-metre shuttle runs. Write the names of the activities in the first column of a copy of the second table.

e) At each station perform the activity specified for 1 minute and then take your breathing rate for 30 seconds. Then rest for 30 seconds and repeat this four more times, completing your copy of the second table.

Activity	Breathing rate = number of breaths in 30 seconds × 2 30 seconds interval before next record					
	Immediately after activity	Interval 1	Interval 2	Interval 3	Interval 4	Interval 5
1						
2						
3						
4						

f) Analyse the data and compare across your class to answer the following questions:

- Which activity required the greatest number of breaths to recover?
- Which activity did people feel was the hardest to perform regardless of the results?
- Which activities did boys find hardest? Which did girls find hardest?

g) Present your results.

Checklist for success

✔ Summarise the definition of VO_2 max, the units it is measured in, the typical levels for trained and untrained people and the role of VO_2 max in measuring cardiovascular endurance (stamina).

✔ Draw up a list of the different factors that affect the level of VO_2 max.

Sound progress

- I can show an understanding of what VO_2 max is and provide examples of how to test it.
- I can identify what factors will affect VO_2 max in different people.

Excellent progress

- I can explain how to set up a test to measure VO_2 max showing the levels of endurance.
- I can show what factors affect VO_2 max and how it can be improved using evidence from fitness tests.

Check your progress

Use these statements as a way of evaluating your progress throughout this chapter.

Sound progress

- I can define what is meant by health and well-being, as supported by the World Health Organization.
- I can list physical, mental and social factors that help keep us well and healthy.
- I can define fitness.
- I can identify the physical and mental demands of daily life that I have to be fit for.
- I can describe links between health, exercise, fitness and performance.
- I can state the main nutrients the body needs and outline their function in providing energy.
- I can identify which food sources provide different nutrients.
- I can describe the importance of a balanced diet for individuals and specific groups.
- I can explain how different physical activities use different amounts of energy.
- I can explain what is meant by health-related and skill-related fitness components.
- I can give examples of both health-related and skill-related fitness components.
- I can describe physical activities that use specific skill-related or health-related fitness components.
- I can identify each of the tests for the components of health-related and skill-related fitness.
- I can perform each of the tests and acquire some baseline data to improve my ability.
- I can state the reasons for carrying out fitness tests.
- I can show an understanding of what VO_2 max is and provide examples of how to test it.
- I can identify what factors will affect VO_2 max in different people.

Excellent progress

- I can explain the benefits to health and well-being of a wide range of physical, mental and social factors.
- I can provide clear guidance on how to improve aspects of health and well-being.
- I can write a clear definition of fitness and the link between fitness and the demands of everyday life.
- I can analyse aspects of my daily life and explain how fitness is important for meeting those demands.
- I can encourage others to think about the relationship between fitness and health, and can promote ways to encourage a positive approach to fitness.

- I can identify the main nutrients the body needs and explain their different functions in providing energy.
- I can explain which energy source will benefit a particular activity and the food sources that will be required.
- I can explain in detail how our body gets energy through the processes of aerobic and anaerobic respiration.
- I can describe different dietary regimes needed by athletes for different sports.
- I can define the 10 recognised components of fitness and categorise them as either health-related or skill-related.
- I can use my knowledge of physical activities to describe which health-related or skill-related components they use.
- I can explain how different activities use similar skill-related or health-related components in their performance.
- I can conduct each of the health-related and skill-related fitness tests with another person following test protocols and ensuring safety.
- I can use the results gathered to help identify strengths and weaknesses, improvements made and areas for further development/training.
- I can explain how each test can improve a sporting or physical activity by implementing them into training sessions.
- I can explain how to set up a test to measure VO_2 max showing the levels of endurance.
- I can show what factors affect VO_2 max and how it can be improved using evidence from fitness tests.

Chapter 7

Training

In this topic, you will examine the principles of successful training in sport and identify what makes a good training programme. You will look in detail at six commonly used methods of training, as well as more specialised approaches. You will also explore the reasons, both physical and mental, for warming up thoroughly before exercise as well as cooling down afterwards.

You will learn how to:

- apply the principles of effective training (SPORT and FITT) to design high-quality training programmes

- identify and avoid the dangers of overtraining

- use different training methods to target specific aspects of fitness

- explain the reasons for warming up thoroughly before physical activity, as well as cooling down afterwards

- design effective warm-up and cool-down schedules.

Chapter contents

The activities you complete will primarily relate to theoretical work, but you will also be encouraged to think about the theoretical aspects in a practical setting.

You will:

- memorise the five principles of training known as SPORT

- memorise the four principles of overload known as FITT

- outline examples of how you can apply these principles to your own training programme

- summarise the dangers of overtraining in a personal exercise plan, with examples relevant to your own sport or activity

- memorise the six main types of training methods

- practise describing each method, making links to fitness components targeted and outlining the advantages and disadvantages of each method

- remember the safety issues with each training method

- summarise the advantages and disadvantages of specialised high-altitude training

- use blank body templates to summarise both the physiological (bodily) and psychological (mental) reasons for a warm-up and cool-down

- draw a three-phase diagram to outline the stages of a warm-up and cool-down

- perform a targeted warm-up and cool-down you have designed for a specific physical activity.

Training is essential to improve performance in any kind of sport.

Principles of training and overload

LEARNING OBJECTIVES
- Understand the principles of training known as SPORT.
- Apply these principles to a training programme.
- Provide examples of the principles of overload known as FITT.
- Explain the dangers of overtraining.

What is required to create a high-quality training programme that includes positive principles and avoids the risk of overtraining?

Starting point

To improve your performance in any sport, a well-designed and carefully planned training programme is essential. This should be based on a clear set of training principles, as you will explore in this topic.

Training programmes also need to be personalised, based on the person's individual circumstances, needs and ambitions. It is important to gather background information to support the analysis of their needs as a performer. Look at the training programme template – this includes key questions that will provide the structure to an individual's training.

Using the headings in this example programme as a structure, make notes summarising what you would include in the various sections. Record all of this information and try to identify whether your own training programme should focus upon health-related or skill-related fitness components (see Topics 6.4 and 6.5).

An introduction to a training programme.

1 Personal details -

Name					
Gender		Date of birth		Age	

2 Physical activity goals -

Identify your short term goals for the next three months	✓ ✓ ✓
Identify your medium term goals for the next six months	✓ ✓ ✓
Identify your long term goals for this year.	✓ ✓ ✓

3 Current training status -

What are your main training requirements? (tick)		
Muscular strength	Coordination	
Speed	Reaction	
Cardiovascular endurance	Balance	
Muscular endurance	Agility	
Flexibility		
Power		

Identify your current fitness status (tick)	Sedentary (unfit)	Active (participating)	Fit (involved)
How many times a week will you train?			

4 Your nutritional needs -

Using the scale of 1–10 (1 being low quality and 10 being high quality) score the quality of your diet.			
Do you follow any particular diet?	Yes No		

Describe a typical day's intake	Breakfast	Lunch	Dinner

5 Your lifestyle -

Do you experience stress?	If yes, what causes you stress (if you know)?
What do you do to cope with it?	

6 Physical health -

Do you experience any of the following? (tick)		
Back pain or injury	Ankle pain / injury	Knee pain / injury
Swollen joints	Shoulder pain / injury	Head injuries
Nerve damage	Hip or pelvic pain or injury	

If yes please give details	
Are any of these injuries made worse by exercise?	
If yes, what movements in particular will cause pain?	
Are you currently receiving any treatment?	

7 Medical history -

Do you have, or have you had, any of the following medical conditions?		
Asthma	Heart problems	Bronchitis
Diabetes	High blood pressure	Chest pains
Epilepsy	Other	
Are you taking any medication? If yes, state what, how much and why		

Exploring the skills

Once you have identified the individual's background, needs and goals, a personal exercise plan (PEP) can be drawn up using the five principles of **SPORT**.

Key term

SPORT: the five principles of training, relating to **S**pecificity, **P**rogression, **O**verload, **R**eversibility, **T**edium

S	**Specificity** Training must focus on specific types of activity to improve: • the type of fitness needed • particular muscle groups. Training may need to be adapted for the individual. **For example:** • Marathon runners focus on endurance. • Swimmers exercise muscles specific to swimming.
P	**Progression** Happens when the body adapts to the training and moves to a new level of fitness. Progress is achieved through an increase in intensity leading to overload. **Note that:** • Most progress is made early on. • At higher fitness levels, there is less progress. • A plateau may occur when higher levels of fitness are hard to reach.
O	**Overload** Occurs when level of training is raised to a level higher than normal. Your body adapts to these extra demands. Can be achieved by an increase in: • intensity • frequency • duration.
R	**Reversibility** Training effects are reversible. If training intensity is reduced or stopped, there can be deterioration of speed, strength or agility. Muscle 'atrophy' (loss of muscle tone) may occur.
T	**Tedium** Tedium = boredom! Signs of boredom are an important indicator that training needs to be more interesting and useful.

2 Create a mind map to summarise the principles of training of SPORT.

3 Think of one sport or activity you are keen on or excel in. For that activity, outline how you could (or already do) implement each of the five principles of SPORT.

Developing the skills

As well as having the structure of the SPORT principles, training programmes should also include the concept of overload. This works on the basis that in order to improve, athletes must continually work harder as their bodies adjust to existing workouts. The four overload principles are summarised as **FITT**.

Key term

FITT: the four principles of overload – Frequency, Intensity, Time, Type

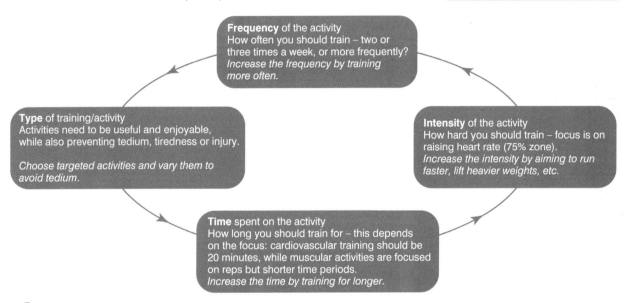

Frequency of the activity
How often you should train – two or three times a week, or more frequently?
Increase the frequency by training more often.

Type of training/activity
Activities need to be useful and enjoyable, while also preventing tedium, tiredness or injury.
Choose targeted activities and vary them to avoid tedium.

Intensity of the activity
How hard you should train – focus is on raising heart rate (75% zone).
Increase the intensity by aiming to run faster, lift heavier weights, etc.

Time spent on the activity
How long you should train for – this depends on the focus: cardiovascular training should be 20 minutes, while muscular activities are focused on reps but shorter time periods.
Increase the time by training for longer.

4 Thinking again of your chosen sport or activity, outline ways that you could implement the four principles of FITT. Give specific examples of goals you could set yourself to increase frequency, time and intensity of activities, and to choose and vary types of activity.

Applying the skills

Copy the example here of a PEP that has been created for a hockey central midfield player. Identify how the principles of SPORT and FITT have been covered in this plan. Use one colour for SPORT and another colour for FITT. Which principles have *not* been included?

Week 1:	Cardiovascular focus to improve stamina
Monday	Jogging for 20 minutes at a steady pace
Tuesday	Rest – no intense activity
Wednesday	Thought swimming would be good, tried 10 lengths but got bored
Thursday	Rest day as muscles ached
Friday	Went jogging again – used some hills but limited to 10 minutes
Saturday	Did not want to run so tried cycling, but had a puncture so did not train.
Sunday	Rest day

6 Frank is training for a badminton tournament. He has identified two areas that he needs to improve: speed around the court area and his backhand smash. Using both the SPORT and FITT principles, design a suitable training programme for Frank. Write a short summary of the reasons why these will benefit him.

Key term

overtraining: excessive exercise that gives the body more work or stress than it can handle

Continuous training will allow your body to adapt, improving your fitness and overall performance. However, training must be monitored to make sure the activities are overloaded but do not cause **overtraining**.

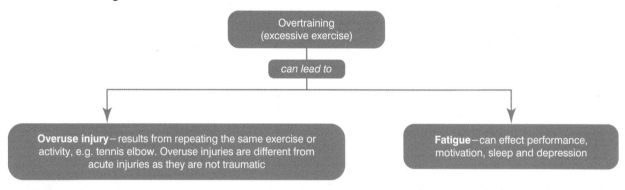

Overtraining (excessive exercise)

can lead to

Overuse injury—results from repeating the same exercise or activity, e.g. tennis elbow. Overuse injuries are different from acute injuries as they are not traumatic

Fatigue—can effect performance, motivation, sleep and depression

REFLECTIVE LOG Identify your sport or physical activity. You have just been selected to represent your country in the World Championships of that sport/activity. You need to create a training programme that would allow you to compete. Use the principles of SMART and FITT to design your programme. Include a section identifying situations where possible overtraining may occur. How can you avoid the dangers of overtraining?

Checklist for success

✔ Memorise the five principles of training known as SPORT.

✔ Memorise the four principles of overload known as FITT.

✔ Outline examples of how you can apply these principles to your own training programme.

✔ Summarise the dangers of overtraining in a personal exercise plan, with examples relevant to your own sport or activity.

Sound progress

• I can identify the training principles of SPORT and FITT, and use examples to describe them.

• I can use these principles when creating a training programme to improve my fitness.

Excellent progress

• I can apply all the principles of SPORT and FITT successfully into a training programme, and can describe what the outcomes should be for the performer.

• I can explain what overtraining is and provide examples of how to avoid it.

Methods of training

What training methods can be used to improve targeted areas of fitness? What are the strengths, drawbacks and safety implications of these methods?

Starting point

The reason for training is to improve your ability and achieve success in whichever physical activity you want to focus on. For this to happen, it is important to match the type of training to your training aims. There are many different **methods of training** to choose from.

In this topic, you will explore six commonly used types of training, listed below, as well as a more specialist method – high-altitude training:

- Continuous training
- Weight training
- 'Fartlek' training
- Plyometric training
- Circuit training
- High-intensity interval training (HIIT).

Key term

method of training: a systemic to improving ability in specific areas of health-related or skill-related fitness

Exploring the skills

There are six different types of method of training that will improve the chosen activity you wish to target. The table below provides a description of each method and what aspects of fitness it is good for, along with the benefits and challenges it offers. The final column suggests aspects of safety that need to be considered when using each method.

1. Read through the table on page 132 carefully and make sure you understand everything in it. If there are terms or phrases that you are not familiar with, make a list of them and find out what they mean by researching on the internet (e.g. Borg scale for intensity, squat jumps). You will be able to revise some things by looking at earlier chapters in this book – for example, eccentric muscle movements are covered in Topic 1.5.

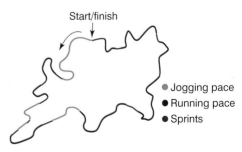

Start/finish

● Jogging pace
● Running pace
● Sprints

Description	Training aim	Advantages	Disadvantages	Safety
Continuous training				
• Consists of continuous activities • Max heart rate between 60 and 80% • Examples: running, swimming, cycling, rowing	• Cardiovascular endurance	• Does not require much equipment • Good for aerobic fitness • Burns fat	• No anaerobic fitness • Requires motivation	• Correct footwear • Safe environment
Weight training				
• Involves using free weights, kettle bells, resistance weights • Repetitions are the number of times the weights are lifted • Sets are the number of times a weight activity is carried out	• Muscular endurance • Speed • Power • Strength	• Improves muscular strength • Easy to show progression • Muscle size and power increased	• Can be expensive (gym fees, equipment) • Prone to injuries • Specialist equipment may be needed	• Correct use of equipment • Use of spotter to prevent injury • Risk of overtraining
Fartlek training				
• Also known as 'speed play' • Involves fast and slow activity over a variety of terrain or hills (running, cycling, etc.) • Uses the Borg scale for intensity	• Aerobic endurance • Anaerobic fitness	• Easily adapted for different sports and fitness levels • Good for sports that have a change of pace	• Difficult to monitor effort • Easy to avoid challenging parts	• Correct footwear and equipment • Safe environment
Plyometric training				
• Eccentric muscle movement (see Topic 1.5) • Methods: squat jumps, box jumps	• Power • Explosive strength	• Over time a greater force is created when muscle contracts • Provides more energy • Provides fast powerful movement	• High amount of stress on muscles • No benefit to aerobic fitness	• Correct use of equipment • Need to prevent injury

Description	Training aim	Advantages	Disadvantages	Safety
Circuit training				
• Complete exercises for different muscle groups at stations • Exercise over time or repetition • The muscle groups should be on alternate stations • Useful for team sports	• Anaerobic fitness • Strength • Muscular endurance • Cardiovascular • Speed	• Varied, so doesn't get boring • Easily adapted • Can include skill stations	• Requires a lot of equipment and time to set up	• Correct use of equipment • Risk of overtraining • Time limitation
High-intensity interval training (HIIT)				
• Involves periods of intense work followed by rest periods • Can be short or long intervals • Allows rest time to remove waste products – lactic acid, CO_2	• Speed • Muscular endurance • Anaerobic fitness	• Benefits game players • Combines aerobic and anaerobic exercise • Can be adapted for activities or fitness levels • Specialist equipment not required	• Can become boring • Needs to include rest	• Correct use of equipment • Risk of overtraining • Time limitation

2 Design your own images of the six methods of training above to help you remember what each one involves. Draw your images onto separate cards. Test your knowledge with a partner by playing the 'say what you see' game. You show the card and your partner has to describe what the method of training involves (without using the name of training method itself).

Developing the skills

Training should improve your ability and motivate you to want to succeed at whatever level. Whether for fitness in a physical activity or for success in a sporting competition, a personal exercise plan (PEP) allows this to be achieved. It is important that your training matches your goals (see Topic 9.1) that can be identified through the test protocols.

3 You are going to create a basic PEP for a friend or teammate. You need to work through the following stages:

- Identify their sport and identify baseline levels using the specific tests that are most appropriate (see Topics 6.5 and 6.6). For example, football requires sprinting and agility, so suitable tests will include the Illinois agility test and the 30 m sprint.
- Then identify suitable methods of training to improve these areas over a 3–6 week block.
- Remember to use the principles of SPORT and FITT (see Topic 7.1) to take account of the needs of the individual.

Applying the skills

As well as these commonly used training methods, there are other, more specialised forms of training. When we hear the term **high-altitude training**, we tend to think in terms of athletes who are just about to compete in the Olympics or World Championships. What are the reasons for doing this kind of specialised training? Is it to improve their VO_2 max? Or develop their technique in running?

However, there are several disadvantages to training at high altitude:

- Training at high altitude places more stress on the body.
- It is not possible to train as intensively as at lower altitudes. This can lead to overtraining.
- It can also have a negative effect on the immune system.
- There can be a loss of muscle mass because the body is using up energy reserves in the muscles.
- Some people experience dizziness or nausea and can't complete their training.
- Many people don't have easy access to high altitude locations.

> **Key term**
>
> **high-altitude training:** specialised training at over 5000 ft (1524 m) above sea level to help the body improve the production of red blood cells

High-altitude training increases your VO_2 max, which in turn improves your endurance and athletic performance.

To compensate, the body produces more red blood cells to help carry oxygen to the muscles. This leads to an increase in the body's oxygen-carrying capacity.

Aerobic exercise is carried out at higher altitudes (usually above 5000 ft).

The air is less dense and oxygen levels are lower, so each breath delivers less of what working muscles require.

The adaptation of increased red blood cells will last about 2–3 months when athletes return to sea level.

A less extreme form of specialist training is warm weather training, where an individual or team moves to a training centre in a location with a consistently good climate. This has several benefits:

- Athletes can train consistently in good conditions.
- There are psychological benefits, as mood is lifted with the sun.
- Other pressures they have at home may be removed, such as media intrusion.
- The risk of injury risk is reduced as muscles are warmer.

4 Using the information in this topic and additional research, create a blog entry that describes (in no more than 120 words) what specialist training is and how people could access it.

REFLECTIVE LOG Using the 'Training year' example below, choose from one of the following physical activities: athletics, cricket, mountain biking. Create a mindmap to include the same headings as the example, and identify the different methods of training and components of fitness to be covered.

Training Year

Pre-Season:
- The time leading up to competition
- Initial preparation
- Time to develop technique and fitness.

Peak Season:
- Main competition period
- Participation in competitions
- Concentration on skills and on-going fitness.

Post-Season:
- Period of rest and recovery
- Maintain general fitness.

Example sessions for a footballer

- Jogging
- Shuttle sprints
- Ball-skills work
- Small sided games

- Warm up
- Speed shuttles
- Team shape and set plays

- Cool down
- Cycling
- Running
- Swimming

Checklist for success

✔ Memorise the six different types of training method.

✔ Practise describing each method, making links to fitness components targeted and outlining the advantages and disadvantages.

✔ Remember the safety issues with each training method.

✔ Summarise the advantages and disadvantages of specialised high-altitude training.

Sound progress

• I can identify the six main types of training method used within a programme.

• I can describe the activities involved and provide examples of physical activities to support this.

• I know what is meant by 'high-altitude training' and why athletes might use this method of training.

Excellent progress

• I can describe the six main training methods and explain how they can be used to meet specific fitness improvement goals.

• I can clearly explain the benefits and drawbacks of different methods.

• I can explain the advantages and disadvantages of using specialised training techniques, such as high-altitude training.

Warming up and cooling down

LEARNING OBJECTIVES
- Understand the physiological reasons for a warm-up and cool-down.
- Identify the psychological reasons for a warm-up and cool-down.
- Explain the phases required in a warm-up and cool-down.
- Create a warm-up and cool-down for a specific physical activity.

What is involved in a warm-up and a cool-down, and what mental and physical benefits do they have?

Starting point

In the previous two topics, you have looked in detail at methods of training and the types of exercise involved. What you do at the start and end of any training – the warm-up and the cool-down – are crucial parts of a good training session. There are many studies that have examined the benefits of warming up and cooling down, and have found them to have both **physiological** and **psychological** benefits.

The physiological and psychological of warming up and cooling down can be summarised in a table.

Key terms

physiological: to do with the body; physical activities that get the body ready for exercise or wind-down afterwards

psychological: to do with the mind; activities that stimulate the mind and help the performer prepare mentally for exercise/competition or to relax afterwards

	Physiological benefits	Psychological benefits
WARM-UP	• Raises the body temperature and heart rate • Increases blood flow (oxygen supply) to the muscles • Stretches the muscles and gets them ready for action • Gets joints moving and increases the range of motion • Help avoid sprains and strains • Gives practice in skills and techniques to be used in the session/game	• Focuses the mind on the exercise • Helps prepare mentally for competition • Part of the build-up to 'match readiness'
COOL-DOWN	• Helps reduce the oxygen debt and clear any lactic acid in the muscles (see Topic 4.1) • Allows heart rate and blood flow to reduce gradually to normal levels • Gentle stretching reduces muscle soreness and stiffness later • Reduces risk of injury	• Gives time for performer to calm down • Helps transition to less physical daily activities • Offers chance to reflect on performance

1 Using a blank outline of the human body, summarise the physical and mental benefits of warming up by adding arrows and labels to show which parts of the body benefit from the warm-up. Then take a second blank outline and summarise the benefits of a cool-down.

Exploring the skills

Preparing the body and mind to ensure the best possible performance is an important role for both athlete and the coach. While a warm-up and cool-down cannot be clinically proven to prevent injuries, they certainly help keep the athlete's body in top condition. In particular the psychological benefits, such as rehearsal or motivation, can be focused on through clear, simple instructions or visualisations. Positive words – such as 'commitment', 'motivation', 'drive' – can be used to provide encouragement. In the words of the philosopher Aristotle:

> *'We are what we repeatedly do.*
> *Excellence, then, is not an act, but a habit.'*

2 Create a 'word cloud' that identifies key words that could be used during a warm-up to engage and motivate the performers.

3 Choose one these words and create your own motivational quote, which you could use as a mantra in when exercising or in competition.

Developing the skills

Encouraging a three-phase warm-up before the physical activity ensures that the performer can thoroughly prepare physically and mentally. The overview below provides a guide to the stages that could be included. The focus is on preparing to perform/compete by raising the pulse, dynamic stretching and skill familiarisation in ways that are appropriate for the physical activity being done.

Pulse raiser	Increases your heart rate	e.g. running, jumping, skipping
Dynamic stretches	Engages the muscles to increase flexibility	e.g. lunges, hurdle steps, heel flicks
Skill familarisation	Imitates actions / performance of sport	e.g. dribbling in basketball, demonstrating speed, agility and coordination

As well as **dynamic stretches**, **static stretches** and mobilisation of the joints could be a focus – for example, ball-and-socket joints (shoulder and hip) in preparation for bowling in cricket.

A phased cool-down will mirror the first two warm-up phases with less intensity and focusing on the removal of lactic acid. Typically a cool-down will involve:

- 5 to 10 minutes of light jogging/walking – to decrease body temperature and remove waste products from the working muscles

- 5 to 10 minutes of static stretches (e.g. hamstring, gastrocnemius and quadriceps as well as upper body) – to help muscles relax and reestablish their normal range of movement

- breathing exercises – to aid relaxation and transition back to daily life.

4 Carry out more research into warm-ups and cool-downs by looking at websites such as: www.nhs.uk/Livewell/fitness. What other suggestions can you find for phases to include in a warm-up or cool-down?

Applying the skills

As research into sports science has become more sophisticated, so too has preparation before and after a physical activity. As well as engaging the body physically, concentrating the mind during the warm-up may give a competitive advantage over the opposition. An example of such a warm-up is shown below and on page 140, with an exercise known as 'protecting the ball' played in basketball.

> **Key terms**
>
> **dynamic stretches:** controlled leg and arm movements that take the limbs to the limits of their range of motion; used to engage muscles and mobilise joints simulating the action used in the activity (for example, lunging simulates a tackle in rugby)
>
> **static stretches:** involve gradually easing into the stretch position and holding the position for 15–20 seconds; a focus for activities such as dance, gymnastics and diving that require the muscles to engage beyond their normal range

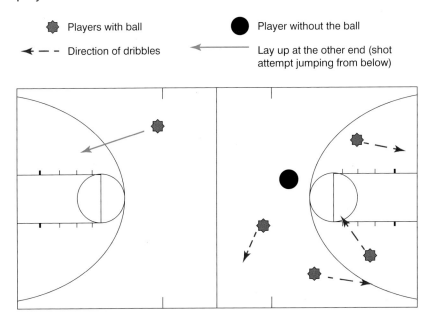

Players with ball

Player without the ball

◄ – – Direction of dribbles

Lay up at the other end (shot attempt jumping from below)

AIM:

- Students to dribble around an area **(pulse raiser)**.
- One student must try to touch the ball each person has **(dynamic stretches)**.
- If your ball is touched, a lay up shot must be scored at the other end **(skill/familiarisation)**.
- To make it harder: reduce the area/use weak hand only/more defenders **(psychological challenges)**.

5 Using the example above and information in this topic, create your own warm-up with illustrations designed for a specific sport. It should include movements that match or simulate movements in the sport. Also include a cool-down with specific focus on muscle groups and mobilisation of joints to get rid of lactic acid.

 REFLECTIVE LOG Think about the way you usually warm up before physical activities and cool down afterwards. From what you have learnt in this topic, what changes will you make to your regime?

Checklist for success

✔ Practise summarising both the physiological (bodily) and psychological (mental) reasons for a warm-up and cool-down.

✔ Draw a three-phase diagram to outline the stages of a warm-up and cool-down.

✔ Perform a targeted warm-up and cool-down you have designed for a specific physical activity.

Sound progress

- I can outline both the physiological (bodily) and psychological (mental) reasons for warming up and cooling down.
- I can identify the different phases of a warm-up and cool-down.
- I can link types of warm-up and cool-down to particular activities or sports.

Excellent progress

- I can explain the phases of a three-phase warm-up and a corresponding cool-down, explaining the physiological benefits to be gained.
- I can analyse the psychological reasons for choosing particular forms of warm-up and cool-down, and explain how these can give a competitive edge.
- I can create and perform a three-phase warm-up using a specific sport as the focus.

Check your progress

Use these statements as a way of evaluating your progress throughout this chapter.

Sound progress

- I can identify the training principles of SPORT and FITT, and use examples to describe them.
- I can use these principles when creating a training programme to improve my fitness.
- I can identify the six main types of training method used within a programme.
- I can describe the activities involved and give examples of physical activities to support this.
- I know what is meant by 'high-altitude training' and why athletes might use this method of training.
- I can outline both the physiological (bodily) and psychological (mental) reasons for warming up and cooling down.
- I can identify the different phases of a warm-up and cool-down.
- I can link types of warm-up and cool-down to particular activities or sports.

Excellent progress

- I can apply all the principles of SPORT and FITT successfully into a training programme, and can describe what the outcomes should be for the performer.
- I can explain what overtraining is and provide examples of how to avoid it.
- I can describe the six main training methods and explain how they can be used to meet specific fitness improvement goals.
- I can clearly explain the benefits and drawbacks of different methods.
- I can explain the advantages and disadvantages of using specialised training techniques, such as high-altitude training.
- I can explain the phases of a three-phase warm-up and a corresponding cool-down, explaining the physiological benefits to be gained.
- I can analyse the psychological reasons for choosing particular forms of warm-up and cool-down, and explain how these can give a competitive edge.
- I can create and perform a three-phase warm-up using a specific sport as the focus.

Chapter 8

Skills and skill acquisition

Starting points

In this topic, you are going to explore what is meant by skill (as opposed to ability) and how people go about acquiring skills. You will investigate different aspects of learning, including how we process information and the benefits of good feedback and guidance.

You will learn how to:

- explain what is meant by skill and ability
- identify the elements that make up a skilled performance
- classify skills in different ways
- describe how people process information
- identify the different stages that learners go through to become skilled
- explain the function and importance of feedback and guidance in helping people learn.

Chapter contents

The activities you complete will primarily relate to theoretical work, but you will also be exploring practical situations and your own experiences to understand the theories of skill acquisition.

You will:

- learn the definitions of the terms 'skill' and 'ability', and summarise the difference between them
- find examples of the eight factors that affect level of sporting performance
- research events from the Paralympic Games to show an appreciation of the skills perfected by athletes with disabilities
- learn the six characteristics of a skilled performance, with examples from different sports
- suggest ways of using these characteristics as a focus for coaching/training and overall improvement in skills
- describe examples of different types of skills: basic/complex, fine/gross, open/closed
- place sporting skills on a scale or continuum to describe the level of skill involved
- analyse a sport you regularly play in terms of the skills involved

- draw a flowchart of the four-stage information-processing model
- apply the information-processing model to a sport you are interested in
- memorise the three stages of learning and the characteristics of each stage
- think of examples of how you can apply the three stages of learning to become proficient in specific sporting activities
- give examples of different types of feedback (extrinsic/intrinsic, knowledge-based/results-based)
- use case studies to explore the importance of giving and receiving feedback
- memorise the four types of guidance and give sporting examples of each one.
- draw a mind map to summarise how guidance can be given to learners at different stages of development.

All sport requires a range of skills which need to be developed alongside natural ability.

Skill and ability

LEARNING OBJECTIVES
- Define the terms 'skill' and 'ability'.
- Describe the differences between skill and ability.
- Show an awareness of the idea of mastering of an ability against adversity (e.g. Paralympics).

Sports performers need to develop a perfect range of skills to be able to perform at the highest level.

Starting point

Some people are born with natural **ability**, but they still need to develop and perfect their **skills** over time with frequent practice.

The psychologist Anders Ericsson identified that it takes 10 000 hours of practice to become an expert. If we break this down and think of a committed athlete who trains an average of 5 hours a day for 7 days a week over 365 days, how long would it take them to become an expert? The answer is about five and a half years. An average performer might train, say, 2 hours a day over 2 days a week. On that basis, it would take them 48 years to reach the 10 000-hour threshold!

 Identify a group of different sports performers whom you think are experts. Find out their ages and calculate how many years it might have taken them to achieve 10 000 hours.

Key terms

ability: the qualities and characteristics a person is born with, such as speed, agility, coordination, flexibility, balance, reaction time, that allow a person to learn or acquire skills

skill: a learned and practised ability that brings about the result that you want to achieve with maximum certainty and efficiency

Exploring the skills

So what is the difference between skill and ability?

Muhammad Ali had the natural ability to punch with speed. He developed his speed punching skills by practising again and again on the speed bag.

A person's ability will help them to learn a skill. Someone with good hand–eye coordination and fast reaction times will possibly be good at racquet sports. Their innate ability will help them to become good at the skills they practise. Table tennis, tennis and badminton need similar abilities, but the specific skills needed to play each sport are very different. Being good at tennis does not automatically make you good at table tennis, although your general ability may help you play decently and help you learn the skills quickly.

2 How are the skills in each sport different? Why might tennis-style strokes not be the best to use in table tennis or badminton? Think of the different types of strokes each player would need to perform (smash, spin, slice, half-volley, etc.)

Developing the skills

There are eight key factors that can affect the variation of skill level within a performer.

Age and maturity:
How young a person is can affect how good they become. Starting younger provides more time to become expert.

Arousal conditions:
Someone who is calm and enjoys low arousal may perform well in shooting or archery, which require fine motor skills. People with high arousal levels may prefer football or boxing, which require more gross motor skills.

Culture:
Background can impact upon the skills you learn. A person with the ability to play striking sports is likely to play baseball in USA, but cricket in India.

Facilities:
The kinds of facilities that available and accessible will impact on the sports that are offered.

Motivation:
This will influence the skills you choose and how well you master them. A desire to succeed will encourage you to practise and seek new challenges.

Environment:
Where you live will affect your choices. If you live where there is snow, you are likely to ski than if you live in a tropical climate.

Anxiety:
If you see the skill as difficult, for example, it may stop you improving. The coach must break the skill down to help motivate you.

Teaching and coaching:
The quality and provision of coaching available will affect the skill level. For example, Andy Murray left the UK for Spain to develop his tennis skills.

You will look in more detail at these factors in the following topics, but for now answer the following questions.

3 Think about your culture and background. Which sports were you always most likely to play due to your culture? What motivates you to play the sports you do? What motivates you to persevere and master the skills of that sport? Write a tweet or a blog to identify key points from above and use the # to identify key words or phrases.

4 Which sports do you play regularly? How good are the facilities and coaching available to you locally? What impact has this had on the sports you play? Are there any sports you are unable to play because of a lack of facilities or teaching/coaching?

Applying the skills

There are many factors that can influence the participation and competitive performances a person might follow. Sports such as hockey and rugby are not played in many schools, reducing the likelihood of students taking them up. Furthermore, there are two types of rugby played in the UK: Rugby League (popular in the north of England) and Rugby Union (more southern in comparison). The two sports have strongholds in different parts of the UK.

Investment in sports facilities can create opportunities for local people to become skilled in a sport. There was massive investment in facilities for the London Olympics in 2012; the Aquatics Centre and the Copper Box Arena are still accessible to the general public. The same applies to the Commonwealth Arena and Sir Chris Hoy Velodrome built for the 2014 Commonwealth Games in Glasgow.

5 How can investment in the facilities available in an area help develop the skills the people in that community use?

In London 2012 the GB Paralympic squad won 120 medals, a huge number that helped raise the profile of disabled athletes in the UK. It was their *ability* that enabled them to develop their skills in the face of adversity, overshadowing their disability. These were people who had shown determination and courage to use their other abilities to master a new set of skills.

REFLECTIVE LOG

Research one of the events from the Paralympic Games, what the event involves and who some of the most skilled and talented athletes are in that field. Present your findings to the class in a PowerPoint presentation. Alternatively, re-create the activity they performed in and attempt to test your skills at it. Write up a summary of your research and experiences in your reflective log.

Checklist for success

✔ Learn the definitions of the terms 'skill' and 'ability', and summarise the difference between them.

✔ Practise listing the eight factors that affect level of sporting performance, with examples of each.

✔ Research events from the Paralympic Games to show an appreciation of the skills perfected by athletes with disabilities.

Sound progress

• I can define skill and ability.

• I can describe the difference between skill and ability with sporting examples.

• I can list the factors that affect how well skills are performed.

Excellent progress

• I can define skill and ability, and explain the difference between the two.

• I can summarise the factors that affect skill level, using examples from sport.

• I can provide a description of a Paralympic sport and describe the impact it has had.

Skilled performance

LEARNING OBJECTIVES
- Identify the six main characteristics of a skilled performance.
- Explain the role and importance of these characteristics in different sports.
- Use these characteristics as a focus for coaching/training and improvement.

What are the qualities that characterise a skilled performance?

Starting point

To learn the skills needed for a sport or physical activity requires practice, perseverance and experience over a long period of time. Having a clear direction and determination will motivate you towards your overall goal of performing with accuracy and fluency. But what is skilled performance?

1 Discuss with classmates what you would look for in a skilled performance. What would be the characteristics of that performance? To focus your discussion, think of two or three sports that everyone is familiar with.

Exploring the skills

In Topic 6.4, you learned about the 10 components of health-related and skill-related fitness – such as stamina, flexibility, balance and coordination. These are clearly vital for anyone aiming to produce a skilled performance. These are also combined with other skills, which you will explore later in this chapter:

- gross skills – how we move
- cognitive skills – how we think and make decisions
- perceptual skills – how we visualise and anticipate things.

Putting all these skills together should result in a performance that demonstrates all the following six characteristics: accurate, consistent, fluent, coordinated, aesthetically pleasing, goal directed.

2 Look at the pictures and discuss how the performer in each one would display the skills listed above. Are some of the skills more important in particular sports than others?

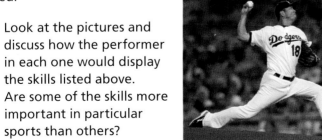

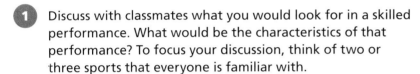

Developing the skills

When we observe a performance or watch a player perform a movement, we are able to identify whether they are skilful by one or all of the characteristics. For example, a centre in netball playing skilfully will control and distribute the ball to each teammate with **accuracy** and **consistency**. A gymnast performing a floor exercise will also need accuracy and **fluency** of movement, not only showing **coordination**, but being **aesthetically pleasing** to watch. Both need to be goal-directed.

3   The image shows the stages of a handspring vault in gymnastics. Using the six characteristics of a skilled performer, shown in the 'Key terms' box, choose one of the skills as the main focus for each stage. Write this down and give a reason for your choice.

4   Research an image or video of an unskilled performer or someone who is a beginner in a sport. Using the six characteristics of a skilled performance as a guide, identify what they need to improve and how.

Applying the skills

Skilled performers are those who strive to demonstrate the six characteristics discussed in this topic. To achieve success, they will need to use different components of fitness, as discussed in Topic 6.4.

5   Look back at Topic 6.4, which explores the 10 components of health-related and skill-related fitness. With classmates discuss how these link to the characteristics of skilled performance outlined in this topic. For example, a fluent performer will certainly need agility and coordination. What else?

6   Set up a game of handball in your class to explore the six characteristics of skilled performance. Divide yourselves into teams of 10, with seven players and three coaches who will observe and identify how the players demonstrate each characteristic. Swap players in and out so that everyone has a chance to be both player and coach.

Key terms

accurate: achieving precise, reliable movements

consistent: performing to a high level every time with control and quality

fluent: using movements that are quick, smooth and flowing, without hesitation or stumbling

coordinated: moving different parts of the body together with efficiency and control

aesthetically pleasing: a display that looks good to the eye of the spectator, judge or coach

goal directed: focusing performing on a specific target and being determined to achieve that target

At the end of the game, think of positive feedback you could give to another player, e.g. 'As goalkeeper, you showed good coordination when saving the ball using both hands and legs'.

Think about your own performance and note down areas where you showed particular skills. Think, too, of characteristics that you think you could improve. How do these relate to areas of health-related and skill-related fitness?

REFLECTIVE LOG Write up your own definitions of the six characteristics of a skilled performance in your reflective log. Describe how they would apply to you when performing a sport you regularly play or are keen on. Draw or find pictures to illustrate each skill as demonstrated in your sport.

Checklist for success

✔ Learn the six characteristics of a skilled performance, with examples of their importance in different sports.

✔ Create your own definitions of the six characteristics, illustrated with examples from your own sport.

✔ Suggest ways of using these characteristics as a focus for coaching/training and overall improvement in skills.

Sound progress

• I can identify the six characteristics that a skilful performer would demonstrate.

• I can provide examples of sports or physical activities that show each of the characteristics.

Excellent progress

• I can explain the role and importance of the six characteristics of a skilful performer.

• I can use these characteristics to analyse performance and suggest goals for improvement.

Skill classification

LEARNING OBJECTIVES
- Identify the different types of skills: basic/complex, fine/gross, open/closed.
- Understand that these can be placed on a continuum.
- Justify the choice of these skills with sporting examples.

How can skills be classified and how is this useful in analysing performance and training?

Starting point

Skills have different characteristics that allow them to be classified. Classifying skills is useful as it helps us to understand how the skill can be taught most effectively. Giving targeted guidance and training enables a performer to be successful at the skill.

Basic and complex skills

On the most straightforward level, skills can be either **basic** or **complex**.

Basic skills tend to need less concentration and coordination to perform compared with complex skills.

A performer's coordination will develop and improve as they master basic skills. Typically, they would need to master basic skills before being able to learn and perform complex ones, which tend to need more time to learn and perfect.

> **Key terms**
>
> **basic skills:** simple skills such as throwing, catching, hitting a ball and running
>
> **complex skills:** more difficult skills that require a higher level of coordination and concentration

1 Consider someone learning the pole vault. What basic skills would need to be learned first? What complex skills then need to be learned to perform well at the event?

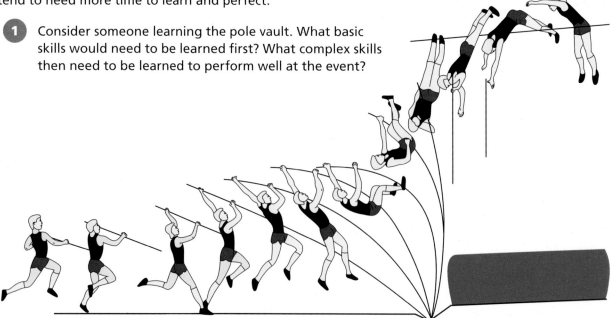

Exploring the skills

Open and closed skills

Another way of classifying skills is between **closed skills** and **open skills**.

2 Look at the skills illustrated in the two photos. Which skills are virtually the same every time you perform it and which one is different?

3 For the skill that is the same, why is this? For the one that is different, what factors make it different each time?

Open skills are most commonly seen in team games such as football, rugby and hockey. The environment may change from game to game, or even during the game. A player may face different weather conditions such as wind or rain. The quality and state of the pitch can vary between games, or may change as the game progresses: for example, if rain makes the pitch muddy or the ball slippery.

4 What other conditions or factors will a player encounter that could affect what happens in the game?

A closed skill is often seen in individual and indoor events. Most swimming events require closed skills, as the swimming pool is a stable and constant environment: that is, most pools have the same characteristics. Also, swimmers compete in individual lanes, so there is no interaction during the race. Many athletics events also require closed skills, such as running the 100 metres.

5 Performing a vault in gymnastics is a similar closed skill. Identify the factors that go towards making the performance similar each time the gymnast performs.

Fine and gross skills

Some sports require a high level of accuracy and precision; other sports depend more on brute strength or explosive power. This leads to another classification of skills as either **fine** or **gross**.

Running, jumping and throwing are examples of gross skills. Firing an arrow in archery needs very precise control and is another example of a fine skill, as is a backhand topspin in table tennis.

6 Use a storyboard structure to explain how a spin bowler in cricket needs fine skills. Draw a set of sketches using stick people or simple images with a written explanation underneath.

Key terms

fine skills: precise movements that require high levels of accuracy and technique; they are often small movements that require small groups of muscles such as in the fingers

gross skills: movements that use large muscle groups to produce big, powerful movements; gross skills are usually performed by the arms and legs

Developing the skills

No individual skill is completely basic or complex, open or closed, fine or gross. Each pair of skills can be charted on a continuum (plural 'continua'), which is a scale that changes gradually from one end to the other, as shown below.

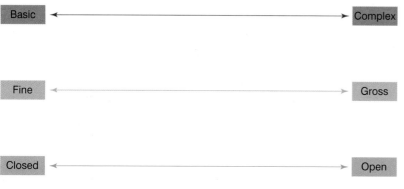

For example, performing the long jump involves the relatively basic skills of running and jumping, although there are of course more technical aspects to the event. In comparison, synchronised diving involves more complex movements of the body, such as twisting and somersaulting, as well as skills of coordination and timing.

7 Where on the basic/complex continuum would you place the following?

a) the triple jump   b) a tennis serve

c) the pommel horse in gymnastics

In terms of other sports, a golf swing is a relatively closed skill, and so would appear near to the closed end of the continuum. In cricket, a wicket keeper catching is a more open skill, and so appears closer to the opposite end of the scale. Here, the player has to adjust to weather conditions and visibility, as well as the height, speed and direction of the ball.

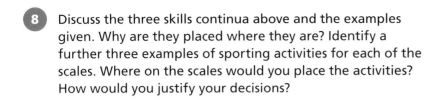

8 Discuss the three skills continua above and the examples given. Why are they placed where they are? Identify a further three examples of sporting activities for each of the scales. Where on the scales would you place the activities? How would you justify your decisions?

Applying the skills

During sport and competitive physical activity, you are constantly making decisions that can be affected by the crowd, the environment, other players or personal choices and feelings. Each of these will affect your skill type and over time you will adapt and learn how to cope with these in order to justify what you have applied.

REFLECTIVE LOG
Think of a sport you regularly play or are keen on. How would you classify the skills involved in that sport? Draw three more skills continua (basic/ complex, fine/gross and open/closed) and place aspects of your sport on what you think is the appropriate point on each one.

Checklist for success
✔ Learn and describe examples of the different types of skills: basic/complex, fine/gross, open/ closed.

✔ Place sporting skills on a scale or continuum to describe the level of skill involved.

✔ Analyse a sport you regularly play in terms of the skills involved.

Sound progress
• I can identify the three pairs of skill types: basic/complex, fine/gross, open/closed.

• I can give sporting examples of the different types of skills.

• I understand that skills can be placed on a scale or continuum.

Excellent progress
• I can classify skills according to whether they are basic/complex, fine/gross, open/closed.

• I can analyse sporting activities in terms of skills classification and place them onto continua using examples.

Simple information-processing model

How do we process information to allow us to make good decisions? What factors might interfere with us making good decisions?

Starting point

Your brain controls everything you do and every action you take, from washing your face to throwing a javelin. The brain is constantly processing information from all kinds of sources:

- your eyes (visual information)
- your ears (hearing or auditory information)
- your skin (sensory information): for example, through your fingers and the sense of touch
- your muscles, that provide the action through movement.

1 Look at the photo. What information is the goalkeeper thinking about at this moment?

Exploring the skills

A performer will go through four steps, known as the **information-processing** model, summarised in the diagram. Good performers will learn to process information very quickly, making the right decisions about the action that should be taken.

Input
- This is information that is received.
- The performer receives it via their senses: sight, hearing, touch.
- It could also come via feedback from previous experiences, or 'intuition' as some call it.
- A great deal of information is received, so the performer has to select which is best to focus on.

Decision-making
- The information is analysed by the performer so they can choose the most appropriate response.
- It is stored in the performer's **short-term memory (STM)** at first.
- If the information is **rehearsed** (repeated), it can be stored in **long-term memory (LTM)**; otherwise it is lost.
- Experienced performers will have more relevant information stored in their LTM because they have had more chances to **rehearse**.

Feedback
- Information is also received about the output or outcome of the decision: that is, whether your decision and action was good or bad.
- This knowledge can be stored and used for future decisions.
- The performer can receive this information in two ways: through **intrinsic** or **extrinsic feedback**.

Output
- The decision is made and then acted upon.
- The brain sends information to the muscles.
- These muscles then move and perform the skill or action.

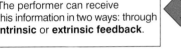
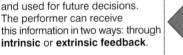
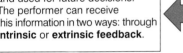
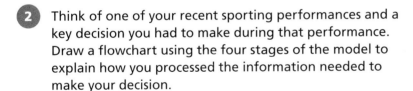

2 Think of one of your recent sporting performances and a key decision you had to make during that performance. Draw a flowchart using the four stages of the model to explain how you processed the information needed to make your decision.

Developing the skills

At any one time we can channel information from various sources (auditory, visual, sensory), but our ability to interpret it is limited. If we try to do more than one thing at once, our overall performance suffers as the brain struggles to process all the information coming at it. Too much information will cause an overload and confusion, so we cannot process and apply it all in time. In the information-processing model, this is known as **limited-channel capacity**.

Key terms

information-processing model: the four-stage process that a performer goes through to make a decision and act upon it

short-term memory (STM): system for storing a small amount of information for a brief period; STM can hold up to seven pieces of information for 60 seconds

long-term memory (LTM): memory store that can hold vast amounts of information for a long period

rehearse: repeat information over and over in order to get the information processed and stored as a memory

intrinsic feedback: information that comes from within, concerning the feel of a movement, such as what it feels like to balance

extrinsic feedback: information that comes from an external source, for example, a teacher or coach or the response of the crowd/teammates

Key term

limited-channel capacity: the idea that our brains can only process a certain amount of information at once; too much information results in overload

3 This situation of a boxing match demonstrates the limited-channel capacity in action. Explain why this is and how the factors shown are contributing it. What is the final outcome?

A theory as to why this happens is the **single-channel hypothesis**. This suggests that the performer's brain can process only one piece of information at a time. Until one stimulus has been dealt with and a decision made about it, another stimulus cannot be acted upon. This might affect performance.

An alternative approach is the **multi-channel hypothesis**. This suggests that the brain has several channels each dedicated to a different task. For example, visual information may be processed in one channel, while verbal information (instructions) may be processed through another channel. Performance suffers only if two similar tasks are attempted.

4 In experiments it has been shown that people can listen to and repeat back speech at the same time as sight-reading piano music. Which of the two theories hypotheses would this support?

5 Can you think of sporting situations where the performer seems able to process and act on different types of information at the same time?

Applying the skills

6 Look at and analyse the photograph of the shooter and goalkeeper in action in a match at the Netball World Championships.

Describe the four steps of the information-processing model as they apply to the player making the shot at goal in this photo.

Key terms

single-channel hypothesis: the theory that when receiving many stimuli from the environment, the brain can only deal with one stimulus at a time

multi-channel hypothesis: the theory that the brain can process different types of information at the same time by using different channels for different stimuli

7 What information is the player making the shot taking in? What are the different decisions that she could make? Are there any pieces of information that are irrelevant and not used to make a decision?

REFLECTIVE LOG

Think of a sport you play regularly or are keen on. Makes note about how an understanding of the information-processing model might help you make better decisions and so become more successful.

- What are the inputs and outputs in the sport?
- What kind of feedback do you receive?
- What are the roles of STM and LTM in the performance of your sport?
- How do the ideas of limited-channel capacity and the single-channel hypothesis apply to your sport?

Checklist for success

✔ Practise drawing flowcharts of the four-stage information-processing model.

✔ Apply the model to a sport you are interested in, think of examples of the types of information processed (input), decisions made, actions taken (output) and feedback received.

✔ Learn the definitions of short-term memory and long-term memory, with examples of information stored in each.

✔ Summarise what is meant by limited-channel capacity and how it is explained by both the single-channel hypothesis and the multi-channel hypothesis.

Sound progress

- I can outline the four parts of the information-processing model.
- I know the difference between STM and LTM and their role in processing information.
- I know what is meant by limited-channel capacity and the single-channel hypothesis.

Excellent progress

- I can describe in detail what happens at each stage of the information-processing model.
- I can explain how the four stages enable us make sporting decisions.
- I can explain the effects of limited-channel capacity in a sporting situation, and explain these in terms of the single-channel/multi-channel hypothesis.

The stages of learning

How does a performer learn a skill and develop from a beginner to a skilled performer?

Starting point

Look at this photo of curling.

Consider curling, or any sport you have never played or participated in before.

1 What is it like learning a completely new sport, skill or technique?

   a) Think about the successes you have and mistakes you make when learning.

   b) How do you know when you have learnt the skill?

Exploring the skills

We can track the learning of skills by watching a baby in its early months. The baby's skills of movement (gross skills) gradually develop, allowing it first to crawl and then learn to walk, run and jump. These are gross gross skills involving larger movements of the legs and arms (see Topic 8.3). We know when a new gross gross skill has been learned, as performances become consistent and fluent.

As we become more proficient, we learn the techniques involved – that is, the way the various skills should be performed. For example, in swimming a high elbow is needed for front crawl instead of it being below the water.

When learning any skill, there are three stages to learning, as outlined in the table below. Here we use the example of a lay-up shot in basketball, a complex gross gross skill, to illustrate the various stages.

Stage	Mistakes	Example
Stage 1: Cognitive stage The **Preparation** stage: you start to learn the new skill or technique. You consciously think about what is involved and the actions you need to perform the skill.	A large number of mistakes will be made. Shooting too far away	
Stage 2: Associative stage Also called the **Practice** stage: you continue repeating and practising skills and techniques so that they improve.	The number of mistakes decreases as your skills improve. Number of misses gradually decreases	
Stage 3: Autonomous stage, Also called the **Automatic** stage: you can perform the skill naturally and without conscious thought. You show control and accuracy, and even flair.	Mistakes are rare. When you do make mistakes, you can analyse what went wrong. Scoring every time, unless impeded in some way	

The three stages of learning form a continuum, with each stage merging into the next. As your skill level develops, you will gradually progress from the cognitive stage to the associative stage to the autonomous stage. There may be times when you have to move back a stage, for example, if you find you are using an incorrect technique and need to 'relearn' the correct technique.

2 Consider skills that you think you are very good at, reasonable at and not very good at. Think of them in relation to each of the three stages named above. What are your experiences of learning and performing skills at each of the three stages?

Developing the skills

The three stages of learning skills – cognitive, associative and autonomous – can be broken down further and analysed in more detail. Consider learning the serve in tennis or badminton. How would you breakdown the skill into different parts to enable someone who has never served before learn to serve?

3 Complete the final column of this table, applying each stage to learning the skills of serving. Use this as guidance to create a coaching storyboard. If possible, make a video of the serve being coached and performed.

Stage	Description / coaching points	Outcome
Stage 1: Cognitive stage The stage of understanding, preparation and planning	• You begin to find out exactly what is involved in the skill. • You breakdown the skill into subroutines (the different parts of an action) and try to master each subroutine. • You make lots of mistakes and need lots of coaching. • You may follow an expert and shadow their movements.	Learning how to stand, racket grip and position, ball toss
Stage 2: Associative stage The stage of repeating and practising skills and techniques	• You combine the subroutines of the skill. • You repeat and practise, so that you become more consistent in performing the skill or technique. • You may practise in a controlled environment, e.g. a reduced-sized court. • You may use specialised equipment to help practise a specific subroutine. • You try out more advanced skills and techniques.	
Stage 3: Autonomous stage The automatic stage	• You can perform the skill naturally and without conscious thought. • You can play full games/matches putting the skills/techniques you have learned into practice. • When you make a mistake, you can identify what went wrong. • The skill is performed with flair, control and accuracy.	

Applying the skills

To learn how to execute a skill with accuracy, fluency and control requires constant practice and rehearsal of the correct skills and technique. There are many ways of approaching the task of practice, for example:

- whole practice
- part practice
- whole–part–whole
- fixed–variable practice.

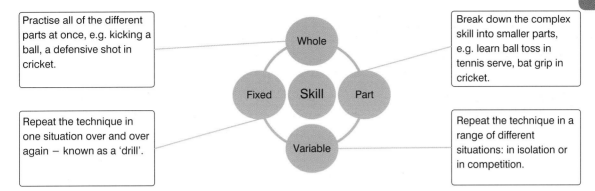

Practise all of the different parts at once, e.g. kicking a ball, a defensive shot in cricket.

Break down the complex skill into smaller parts, e.g. learn ball toss in tennis serve, bat grip in cricket.

Repeat the technique in one situation over and over again – known as a 'drill'.

Repeat the technique in a range of different situations: in isolation or in competition.

Here is an example of the whole–part–whole system as used in swimming:

- Whole – the swimmer does a length of full front crawl; the coach identifies that he is breathing with every stroke turning his head from side to side. Action – to improve breathing and reduce number of breaths.

- Part – the swimmer practises breathing every second breath while standing stationary in the pool.

- Whole – the swimmer does a length of full front crawl using the improved breathing technique.

REFLECTIVE LOG Think of a similar example of how you could use the whole–part–whole technique to improve a technique in a sport you regularly play.

Checklist for success

✔ Memorise the three stages of learning and the characteristics of each stage.

✔ Think of a mnemonic to help you remember the meaning of cognitive, associative and autonomous.

✔ Think of examples of how you can apply the three stages of learning to become proficient in specific sporting activities.

Sound progress

- I can identify the three stages of learning and describe what is meant by the terms cognitive, associative and autonomous.

- I can explain roughly what happens during each stage of learning, with examples.

Excellent progress

- I can outline the three stages of learning and describe the characteristics of each stage in detail.

- I can apply the stages of learning the skills of a specific sporting activity using clear commentary and physical demonstrations.

Feedback

LEARNING OBJECTIVES
- Identify and outline four different types of feedback: intrinsic, extrinsic, knowledge of performance and knowledge of results.
- Explain how each type of feedback links to the stages of learning and can be given to performers at different levels.
- Explain the importance of receiving good feedback and the impact it can have on performance.

What kinds of feedback are there? How does feedback help to improve performance?

Starting point

In your work on Topic 8.4, you looked at the information-processing model and the various stages we go through whenever we make a decision and perform an action, whether in daily life or in sporting situations. One of the key stages in the process is the **feedback** stage.

Feedback is essential for helping us to assess how well we have performed. It can help us to improve by showing us which skills and techniques we need to develop. It can be given during or after a performance.

1 Think about times when you have received feedback about a performance. What form did the feedback take? How did the feedback help you to improve?

Exploring the skills

Feedback allows the performer or participant to identify what they have done well and what needs to be improved. Without feedback you are isolated and have nothing to compare your performance against. You may even regress – that is, get worse at a skill.

'The feedback loop' (see diagram) illustrates the importance of feedback and where it fits into the cycle of creating improved performances.

Feedback can take different forms. One major distinction is between **extrinsic** and **intrinsic feedback**.

Key terms

feedback: the information that a performer receives about their performance

extrinsic feedback: information that comes from an external source: for example, a teacher or coach

intrinsic feedback: information that comes from within, to do with emotions, thoughts and muscles (the feel of a movement, such as what it feels like to balance)

Correct, adjust, practise

Next Performance

Assess performance

Feedback

2 Think of times when you have received each of these types of feedback. Who were the external sources of feedback? (Try to think of as many as possible.) How was the feedback given? How effective was it at improving you as a performer?

Teachers and coaches are key figures in giving extrinsic feedback. This type of feedback can also come from friends or relatives, or from the response of the crowd/teammates. Extrinsic feedback is important for beginners (i.e. those at the cognitive stage of learning – see Topic 8.5), who have yet to develop a 'feel' for movements or techniques.

Autonomous learners are more likely to use intrinsic feedback. This is because they will be at a level where they can judge how well their body has performed and can work out what needs to be corrected purely by the feeling of the skill.

Feedback can come in other forms too:

- **Knowledge of results** – knowing your score, time, distance or place in the race; this allows you to measure or judge how well you have done.
- **Knowledge of performance** – analysing your quality of movement or use of techniques (e.g. how good your timing felt when batting at cricket or whether a landing after a vault was 'clean').

Knowledge of results is an extrinsic form of feedback. Knowledge of performance can be either extrinsic or intrinsic.

3 Explain how a coach giving you feedback on your last performance is both extrinsic feedback and knowledge of performance.

4 Now think of instances when you have received and used feedback from knowledge or results and performance. Give examples of the feedback. How did you use it? How effective was it at helping you to improve you as a performer?

Developing the skills

Different forms of feedback work well depending on the performer's level of ability or the type of competition they are performing in. The table summarises the strengths and drawbacks of the different types of feedback, as well as suggesting some of the situations in which the feedback could be used.

	Advantages	Disadvantages
Intrinsic feedback	• Performers can make immediate adjustments.	• Requires high level of knowledge about the skill or activity being performed (autonomous stage). • Beginners do not have this knowledge. • Better for more experienced and skilled performers.
Extrinsic feedback	• Good for beginners (cognitive stage) as they need constant feedback in order to learn. • Coaches can make beginners aware of basic skills and techniques. • Experienced performers combine extrinsic and intrinsic feedback to get a better picture of their performance.	• Needs a qualified coach to give the feedback. • Incorrect feedback from a poor-quality coach will cause performances to decline.
Knowledge of results	• Results give a quick measure of success. • They should be accurate if recorded properly. • Knowledge of results can give a target for improvement. • Helps show improvement over time if recorded regularly.	• Poor results can be demotivating. • Improvement might slow down and this can be demotivating. • Results may not reflect skill or performance. Coming third in a race with strong performers may be a better result than coming first in a race with weaker performers.
Knowledge of performance	• Feedback can be tailored to suit the performer's ability level. • Can be simple feedback on one or two areas for beginners. • Can be specific, complex and detailed for the experienced performers.	• It can be difficult and time-consuming to analyse the performances of experienced sports people. • There may be many skills and techniques that require feedback. This can take time. • The coach may need to see videos of the performance first in order to get their feedback accurate.

5) Create a mind map using the performer as the central point to include:

a) the different sources of feedback – intrinsic and extrinsic

b) other types of feedback – knowledge of results and performance

c) link to stages of learning (cognitive, associative, autonomous)

d) the role feedback plays in your development, both mentally and physically.

Applying the skills

Feedback can be either positive (focusing on what you did well) or negative (focusing on what you did less well). Positive feedback provides motivation and direction, ensuring that the performer is building towards future success.

The three Fs summarise the qualities of good feedback:

Fast – given as soon after the event as possible

Focused – upon the key areas of concern or development

Factual – based on evidence showing what you did well and not just what you did wrong

6 Consider the following performers. Which types of feedback would benefit each of these performers? Give reasons for your choice.

a) a beginner at hockey

b) a beginner at trampolining

c) a club-level rugby player

d) a club-level basketball player

e) an advanced-level trampolinist

f) an advanced triple-jumper.

Checklist for success

✔ Learn the definitions of extrinsic and intrinsic feedback, and list the various sources of external feedback available to performers.

✔ Make a list of examples of feedback that comes in the form of knowledge of performance and knowledge of results.

✔ Draw up a table to show how each type of feedback links into the three stages of learning.

✔ Use case studies to explain the importance of receiving feedback and the impact it can have on an athlete's development and performances.

Sound progress

• I can define the four main types of feedback and provide examples of when they might occur.

• I can give practical examples of how the feedback links to stages of learning.

Excellent progress

• I can explain the advantages and disadvantages of the four types of feedback.

• I can explain the importance of receiving feedback and the impact that it has on the performer.

Guidance

LEARNING OBJECTIVES
- Identify and outline the different types of guidance: visual, verbal, manual and mechanical.
- Summarise the advantages and disadvantages of different types of guidance.
- Explain how different types of guidance can be used during different stages of learning.

What kind of guidance do we need at different stages of learning? And in what form can that guidance be given?

Starting point

In Topic 8.6, you investigated external sources of feedback, such as teachers and coaches. Whenever we learn a new sport or activity, we rely on **guidance** from sources such as these to help us acquire and perfect the skills needed. The outcome and success of our efforts will rely on the quality of the guidance given.

> **Key term**
>
> **guidance:** help and instruction given to guide learners through movement patterns, skills and techniques, and so help them acquire skills

Exploring the skills

Guidance can be given in many forms. It may be:

- verbal – in the form of words
- visual – in the form of images
- manual – 'hands on' guidance, showing you how to hold a racket or swing a golf club
- mechanical – guidance on how to use physical supports such as harnesses or flotation aids.

Manual and mechanical guidance are often grouped together as they are both concerned with support given physically to the person learning the skill.

 Look at the four photos. What kind of guidance is being given in each one?

a)

b)

c)

d)

2 Study the diagram carefully and then think of examples from sport of different types of guidance given to help people learn skills. How might a coach provide that guidance? Copy and complete the guidance table.

Guidance	Sport example	How a coach would provide it
Visual		
Verbal		
Manual		
Mechanical		

The diagram below gives more details about these four types of guidance.

What you see

The first way you learn a skill is watching images, videos or through a demonstration (other people showing you how to do something).

What you are told

A coach can use words to highlight important images or explain movements or techniques.

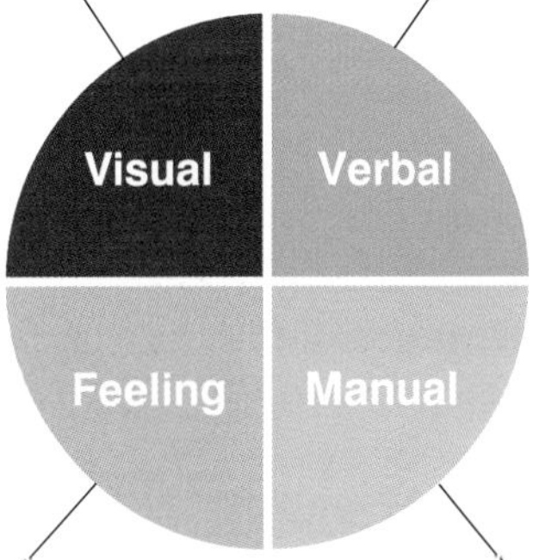

Visual | Verbal

Feeling | Manual

What you feel

A coach can physically guide you through a movement, e.g. a golf swing or shot in cricket (manual guidance), so you begin to acquire the muscle memory. Muscle memory is created through the physical sensation experienced in your muscles being repeated time and again.

What supports you

You may need the support of equipment as you start to learn a skill, e.g. a harness when learning to trampoline. Mechanical guidance involves showing you how to use this equipment.

Developing the skills

There are advantages and disadvantages to the different types of guidance. These are summarised in the table below.

3 In a small group, discuss the advantages and disadvantages of the different types of guidance outlined in the table. Try to think of examples from your own experience of being given guidance in learning a skill.

	Advantages	Disadvantages
Visual guidance	• Learners can see accurate performance and form a mental picture of correct performance. • Demonstrations can be repeated if necessary. • The 'slow motion' option on video allows you to focus in on subroutines or specific aspects of a skill. • Useful in all stages of learning.	• Demonstrations need to be accurate and expertly performed. • Poor-quality videos are not helpful.
Verbal guidance	• It is immediate. Instructions (especially if short) can be acted on straight away. • Coaches/teachers can use questions to assess and check learning and understanding. • Verbal and visual guidance can be combined to paint a more accurate picture for the learner.	• Long or complicated instructions are hard to take in (see limited-channel capacity in Topic 8.4). This can be a particular problem for beginners taking in a lot of new information at once. • Some movements cannot be accurately explained using words.
Manual/ mechanical guidance	• Useful in the early stages of learning when the coach can position or adjust the learner's limbs or body parts: for example, correct racket grip in tennis. • Helps individual to get a feel for the movement and develop muscle memory. • Can provide a safe environment to try out more hazardous activities (e.g. in gymnastics). • Gives performers a sense of security and helps deal with feelings of anxiety or fear.	• Learners can come to depend on support from coach/equipment. • Can give learners an unrealistic 'feeling' of the motion: for example, they do not take their full body weight in a gymnastics movement. • Learners may resist having the manual/mechanical guidance taken away.

4 Write a short leaflet for coaches/trainers with tips on how to give guidance to students learning sports activities. Pick out the key points from the table above and add any other ideas your group came up with. Design your leaflet using a computer, bringing in suitable images.

Applying the skills

Good coaches will modify the types of guidance according to the needs of their learners. As you know from Topic 8.5, people go through various stages as they learn a skill, and the guidance given needs to match the learning stage.

- Visual guidance – this is useful at all stages, but is most effective at the cognitive stage to provide an overall picture of the skill. To analyse performance further, video recordings can used for specific details.

- Verbal guidance – cognitive learners have limited understanding of terms used in the activity and may tire quickly if too much verbal guidance is given. More detailed explanations can be used with more advanced learners.

- Manual/mechanical guidance – this is important during the cognitive stage of learning. It helps the learner to get a 'feel' of a movement (e.g. in gymnastics), and becomes vital when exploring more complex movements. It can also be used by more experienced performers because of safety issues: for example, in rock climbing.

5 Draw a mind map, based on the outline here, to summarise which kinds of guidance you think will be useful to learners at different stages of development.

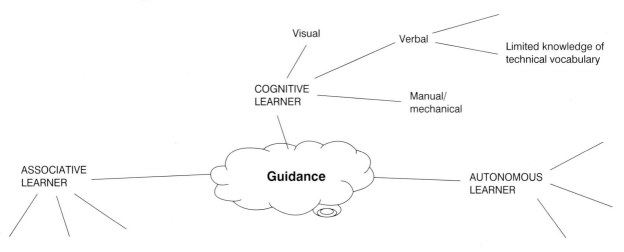

6 Imagine you are a coach for a performer or team. Outline a programme showing how you would offer guidance to learners at different stages of development. Note down the types of guidance you would give, the resources you would use and how you would use them. Explain the reasoning for your choices.

Checklist for success

✔ Memorise the four types of guidance and give sporting examples of each one.

✔ Write bullet point summaries of the advantages and disadvantages of different types of guidance.

✔ Draw a mind map to summarise how guidance can be given to learners at different stages of development.

Sound progress

- I can describe, with examples, four different types of guidance.

- I can give examples of the types of guidance that are suitable for learners at different stages of learning.

Excellent progress

- I can explain the advantages and disadvantages of the different types of guidance.

- I can outline a programme showing how guidance can be given to learners at different stages of development.

Check your progress

Use these statements as a way of evaluating your progress throughout this chapter.

Sound progress

- I can define skill and ability.
- I can describe the difference between skill and ability with sporting examples.
- I can list the factors that affect how well skills are performed.
- I can identify the six characteristics that a skilful performer would demonstrate.
- I can provide examples of sports or physical activities that show each of the characteristics.
- I can identify the three pairs of skill types: basic/complex, fine/gross, open/closed.
- I can give sporting examples of the different types of skills.
- I understand that skills can be placed on a scale or continuum.
- I can outline the four parts of the information-processing model.
- I know the difference between STM and LTM and their role in processing information.
- I know what is meant by limited-channel capacity and the single channel hypothesis.
- I can identify the three stages of learning and describe what is meant by the terms cognitive, associative and autonomous.
- I can explain roughly what happens during each stage of learning, with examples.
- I can define the four main types of feedback and provide examples of when they might occur.
- I can give practical examples of how the feedback links to stages of learning.
- I can describe, with examples, four different types of guidance.
- I can give examples of the types of guidance that are suitable for learners at different stages of learning.

Excellent progress

- I can define skill and ability, and explain the difference between the two.
- I can summarise the factors that affect skill level, using examples from sport.
- I can provide a description of a Paralympic sport and describe the impact it has had.
- I can explain the role and importance of the six characteristics of a skilful performer.
- I can use these characteristics to analyse performance and suggest goals for improvement.
- I can classify skills according to whether they are basic/complex, fine/gross, open/closed.
- I can analyse sporting activities in terms of skills classification and place them onto continua using examples.
- I can describe in detail what happens at each stage of the information-processing model.

- I can explain how the four stages enable us make sporting decisions.
- I can explain the effects of limited-channel capacity in a sporting situation, and explain these in terms of the single-channel/multi-channel hypothesis.
- I can outline the three stages of learning and describe the characteristics of each stage in detail.
- I can apply the stages of learning the skills of a specific sporting activity using clear commentary and physical demonstrations.
- I can explain the advantages and disadvantages of the four types of feedback.
- I can explain the importance of receiving feedback and the impact that it has on the performer.
- I can explain the advantages and disadvantages of the different types of guidance.
- I can outline a programme showing how guidance can be given to learners at different stages of development.

Chapter 9

Psychology

Starting points

In this topic, you are going to develop an understanding and appreciation of the psychological aspects of sport and physical activity. This includes looking at with how individuals approach activities, such as setting goals and motivation, as well as how they deal with the pressures of competing, such as the effects of arousal and anxiety. You will explore the use of relaxation techniques to reduce the negative effects of these.

You will learn how to:

- set goals that are focused and follow sound principles

- appreciate how performers motivate themselves to perform under pressure

- explain how a performer's level of arousal can affect their performance

- identify two types of anxiety (cognitive and somatic) and describe the symptoms of each

- describe and use relaxation techniques to help reduce arousal and anxiety

- identify different personality types and their characteristics, and their links to particular sports.

Chapter contents

The activities you complete will primarily relate to theoretical work, but you will also be exploring practical situations and your own experiences to understand the psychological aspects of sport.

You will:

- write goals for yourself in a sporting activity using the seven principles of SMARTER goal-setting

- note down in your reflective log how you can use goal-setting to control anxiety and other negative factors

- make a list of examples of intrinsic and extrinsic motivation, explaining how they can provide incentives and rewards

- use the example of a sporting hero to illustrate the importance of motivation and to inspire you

- annotate a sketch of the human body with the physical signs of arousal

- draw and explain the inverted U theory of optimal arousal (Yerkes–Dodson law)

- make a list of the negative thought processes (cognitive anxiety) and physical symptoms (somatic anxiety) involved in anxiety

- draw a flowchart to outline the role of adrenaline in the body's physiological response to arousal

- practise using mental rehearsal and visualisation techniques to help reduce anxiety in sporting situations

- regularly practise using deep breathing techniques to reduce arousal and anxiety

- list the characteristics of the two personality types: introvert and extrovert

- draw up suggestions for activities that introverts and extroverts are best suited to, along with reasons for this.

Synapses fire messages around our brains.

Goal-setting

LEARNING OBJECTIVES
- Understand the principles of SMARTER goal-setting.
- Suggest how to set SMARTER targets appropriate to the physical activity.
- Explain how goal-setting can control anxiety.

How can you set targets to able reach your goals.

Starting point

Sports performers who wish to be successful set themselves **goals.**

- Athletes at every level may want to reach a personal best time or distance.
- A school cricket player may want to get into the First Team.
- A professional footballer may want to win the league, the cup or gain a call-up to their national team.

Whatever level you are performing at, it is important to set goals to work towards.

> **Key term**
>
> **goal:** a desired aim or outcome; something that you are trying to achieve

1 Choose a sport you are involved in. Copy and complete the table, identifying the reasons for taking part or performing in that sport equate either goals you have achieved already or future goals you have. Note down the reason for selecting those goals.

Sport	Reason for taking part in this sport
Goals	**Reason for choosing these goals**
1	
2	
3	

Exploring the skills

Having a goal to aim for is a good motivator and can help you prepare mentally for a performance. It can act as a signpost giving you direction with your training and as a marker against which to check your progress.

Goals work best if they follow the SMARTER principles:

S	Specific	Make your goal or target specific: 'I will run faster' is too vague. 'I must run 30 metres in under 4 seconds' is specific.
M	Measureable	You can measure whether you have achieved it or not. For example, 'running 30 metres in under 4 seconds' can be timed.
A	Agreed	You and your coach must discuss and agree your goals. They need to be a challenge and achievable in order for you to make progress.
R	Realistic	A goal that is too difficult will demotivate you and put you off. For example, 'To run 100 metres in 9 seconds' is not a realistic target. Set a realistic target: for example, 'to run under 16 seconds by next June.
T	Time-phased	Goals should be planned out ahead to give you direction over the short, medium and long term. For example: goals for the next week (short-term), month (medium-term) and year (long-term). As you achieve these goals, you know you are making progress.
E	Exciting	Goals that are exciting and challenging will prevent you from getting bored and disillusioned. As you make progress, your goals should get more difficult and more exciting.
R	Recorded	Your goals should be written down, then you will know what you are aiming for, where you are going and can check when you have met your targets.

2 Identify three goals – one short-term, one medium-term and one long-term – that would help you in your development of your chosen sport. Make sure that each of these goals is based on the SMARTER principles. Draw up a table similar to the one above showing how each goal follows each of the principles.

Developing the skills

Goal-setting can be a way of controlling anxiety. If a performer is over-aroused, they can become anxious and nervous, which will affect their performance. (The topics of anxiety and arousal are explored further in Topics 9.3 and 9.4.)

By setting realistic goals, agreed between the performer and coach, the performer will be more confident going into a competitive situation. The goals should still be challenging, but knowing they have trained properly and are well prepared, the performer should believe they can achieve them. They will also feel more in control of the situation – having control has been shown to be an important factor in reducing stress and anxiety.

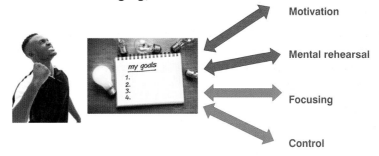

Motivation

Mental rehearsal

Focusing

Control

3 Look back at the goals you set yourself in the previous section. How would achieving those goals give you confidence and stop you from being anxious when it comes to performing in a competitive situation? Look at the key words that make up the picture equation.

Applying the skills

Throughout this chapter the focus has been on setting goals using the SMARTER principles. However, it is the partnership with the coach/mentor that creates the stability to ensure that goal-setting is both challenging and achievable.

4 Look back at Topic 7.2. Identify the different methods of training you might be able to use within your goal-setting. You will need to discuss these and agree on suitable methods with your coach.

5 Goals are just as important for teams as for individual performers. Put yourself in the shoes of a coach of a netball, rugby or football team (or any team sport). Come up with three short-term, medium-term and long-term goals to motivate a team towards success. Try to link in the factors that reduce anxiety as well. What additional factors can help reduce anxiety and other negative factors in teams?

 REFLECTIVE LOG Use your reflective log to record the goals you have worked on during this topic. Note down the key points you will take from this topic in terms of how your goals will help you to succeed and to reduce negative factors such as anxiety.

Checklist for success

✔ Remember the acronym SMARTER and what each letter stands for.

✔ Use the seven principles of SMARTER goal-setting to write goals for yourself.

✔ Note down in your reflective log how you can use goal-setting to control anxiety and other negative factors.

Sound progress

• I can identify the SMARTER principles of goal-setting with physical activities.

• I can describe how anxiety can be reduced by setting SMARTER goals.

Excellent progress

• I can apply the SMARTER principles and set targets for myself, for an individual and for a team of players.

• I can explain how to structure goal-setting strategies within the SMARTER targets to reduce anxiety.

Motivation and mental preparation

LEARNING OBJECTIVES
- Define the term 'motivation'.
- Explain the terms 'intrinsic' and 'extrinsic motivation'.
- Understand what rewards and incentives are.

What is motivation and why is it so important in achieving success in sporting performance?

Starting point

To be a successful sports performer a high level of **motivation** is required.

Exploring the skills

Motivation can be seen by:

- the amount of effort we put into a task
- how well we direct and focus our effort
- how long we stick at a task, especially one that is difficult
- what we are willing to give up and sacrifice for success.

Read the following quotations from some famous sportspeople:

> **Key term**
>
> **motivation:** the desire required to be successful; a driving force that makes you do something and decide how much effort to put in

'Obstacles don't have to stop you. If you run into a wall, don't turn around and give up. Figure out how to climb it, go through it, or work around it.'

Michael Jordan (basketball superstar)

'Fail to prepare, prepare to fail.'

Roy Keane (footballer, paraphrasing Benjamin Franklin)

'To all my doubters, thank you very much because you guys have also pushed me.'

Usain Bolt (sprinter, nine-time Olympic gold medallist)

1   Look at the famous sporting quotes above. Read the quotes with classmates and discuss what aspect of motivation each sportsperson is describing.

2   Consider a sport you play a lot or are very keen to become better at. What motivates you to play that sport? What are the various parts that motivate you to play that sport? Create a quote that could inspire a younger generation to take up the sport.

Developing the skills

Motivation is what drives us on to succeed. It can come in two forms: **intrinsic** or **extrinsic**. The table below summarises these factors.

Intrinsic motivation	Extrinsic motivation
• The desire to do the sport or activity for its own sake	• Praise from a parent, a coach or the crowd
• Feelings of satisfaction or well-being from doing the activity	• Rewards in terms of money, prizes, medals or trophies
• Improved physical fitness	• The desire for attention, publicity or fame
• Social rewards from playing in a team	• At professional level, the search for sponsorship or a better contract

For example, an Olympic gold medal is given as a **reward** for finishing first in an Olympic event. For someone striving to reach the top of their sport, it can be one of their main **incentives**. Similar rewards exist at all levels of sport and can be strong motivating factors.

3   Look back on what motivates you to play a sport. Which of these things are intrinsic factors and which are extrinsic? Work through the list of factors in the table and decide how important each of these factors is for you.

4   Playing in a team can involve different motivating factors compared with performing as an individual. In a small group, discuss what some of the factors are (such as the social enjoyment and pleasure of working with others towards a common goal). Think of examples to illustrate this, either from your own experience or from following a team you support.

Key terms

intrinsic motivation: motivation that comes from simply doing the activity itself, rather than to gain external rewards or prizes

extrinsic motivation: motivating forces that come from outside the person and the activity, such as prizes, trophies, praise from others or fame

reward: something given to someone to recognise their achievements

incentive: something that motivates or encourages someone to do something

Applying the skills

Understanding the factors that motivate an individual or team is important not just for the performer, but also for trainers and coaches:

- If you are intrinsically motivated by a sport or activity, your desire and willingness to continue is a factor that the coach must harness. The coach must ensure that sessions remain enjoyable, so you will continue, whether or not there are any extrinsic rewards.

- If you are motivated more by extrinsic factors, the coach can use that appetite for success to set goals focused on achieving rewards, such as an individual medal or winning a team competition.

If a reward is too difficult to achieve, it can demotivate the performer. For example, someone entered into a competition above their level may feel themselves under too much pressure, which stops them performing at their best. If they are motivated by rewards, then they may become demoralised and lose interest if they do not win the prize.

Good coaches make sure that their performers enjoy the sport and their training through a mixture of intrinsic and extrinsic methods of motivation.

5 Imagine you are a coach of a team that is underperforming and lying at the bottom of their division. Using your knowledge of motivating factors, along with goal-setting (Topic 9.1), think about ways of remotivating the players. What strategies could you develop to strengthen both extrinsic and intrinsic factors? Create a motivational display that you can refer to and use with your players.

6 Think of someone you regard as a sporting hero. What has motivated them to achieve the success they have earned? Do some research on the internet (type in the person's name + 'motivation', and look for interviews they have given or quotations from books. Create a poster outlining the most important factors. Base your poster on a photo of the person, annotated with the various factors. Find a way to indicate whether the factors are intrinsic or extrinsic.

REFLECTIVE LOG Reflect on how you have been rewarded by your parents, teachers or coaches to motivate you to succeed? Which rewards and incentives were effective? Why was this?

Checklist for success

✔ Write a definition of the term 'motivation'.

✔ Make a list of examples of intrinsic and extrinsic motivation, explaining how they can provide incentives and rewards.

✔ Use the example of a sporting hero to illustrate the importance of motivation and to inspire you.

Sound progress

• I can describe what motivates me as a performer in a physical activity.

• I can explain how I am intrinsically and extrinsically motivated in this situation.

Excellent progress

• I can explain what motivates an elite athlete.

• I can explain how elite athletes are intrinsically and extrinsically motivated.

Arousal

LEARNING OBJECTIVES
- Give the definition of arousal.
- Know the signs of optimal arousal for different skills.
- Draw and explain the inverted U-theory (Yerkes–Dodson Law).
- Explain the effects of under-arousal and over-arousal.

What is arousal in a sporting context? In what ways can our level of arousal affect our performance?

Starting point

Delivering a successful performance in any kind of sports activity needs the right level of **arousal**.

Arousal describes an energised state of readiness that motivates you to perform a task. Your level of arousal is determined by how prepared, enthusiastic and mentally ready you are for the activity or event. There needs to be a balance of your arousal levels: not too high (which can result in anxiety and stress) and not too low (which may cause you to under-perform).

Key term

arousal: an increased level of mental excitement and alertness; the state of being excited, keen and mentally and physically ready to perform a task

A

B

C

1. Above are a three of images showing: nervousness, over-excitement, determination – factors that contribute to arousal levels. Identify which picture illustrates which state, and describe to your partner the reasons for your choice.

Developing the skills

> - Dry mouth
> - Increased breathing
> - Increased heart rate
> - Nausea
> - Sweaty palms
> - Tremor (shakiness).

Arousal is a general mixture of both the physiological and psychological levels of activity that a performer experiences. Arousal causes changes in the body, depending on the levels of stimulation being felt. The list on the right shows the symptoms of physical arousal and can lead to us under- or over-performing in a physical or sporting situation.

2 Think of a time where you were too excited or too anxious before a sporting activity and consequently performed badly. Which of these physical symptoms did you experience? What were the factors that made you feel like this? How did it negatively affect your performance?

3 Now consider a time where you have been 'in the zone' and have performed extremely well in a sporting activity. What were the factors that enabled you to perform at this level? How would you describe your level of arousal at that point?

Exploring the skills

Two psychologists, Yerkes and Dobson (1908), identified that there is a optimum point of arousal that will enable us to perform at our best. This level is different for each individual and depends upon:

- the nature of the task – what it involves and how much pressure is applied
- the skill of the performer – their ability to use their physical skill and expertise to execute a good performance
- the personality of the performer – their own mental preparation and motivation.

Yerkes and Dobson illustrated their theory in the form of an 'inverted U', which identified three areas of low, optimal and high arousal.

Arousal is at the optimal level
- Known as being 'in the zone', a state that allows you to perform well.

Arousal level too low
- You will not be excited or focused enough to perform at the required level.
- However, fine motor skills such as darts require low levels of arousal to perform well.

Arousal level too high
- You feel anxious, nervous or stressed.
- You could be 'psyched out' by the opposition.
- You may make mistakes or not give your best performance.

Applying the skills

The 'inverted U' graph provides an indicator as to the level of arousal a performer needs to be at in order to succeed in their sport. If they are under-aroused, the drive and determination will not be at a high enough level. However, if they are at a stage of over-arousal, this will lead to stress and anxiety, which may decrease their performance.

Finding the right level of arousal can be a difficult balancing act. This is because the optimal level of arousal varies for different sporting skills. For example, fine skills (that involve precision and accuracy) often require lower levels of arousal than gross skills (that involve strength, speed or power).

4 Look back at Topic 8.3, which discusses various fine skills, such as those needed for darts, spin bowling in cricket or archery. Why do you think a lower level of arousal is important to execute these skills? What might happen if the player using these skills got too 'pumped up' before a competition? On the other hand, why is getting 'pumped up' a feature of sports such as sprinting or weightlifting?

5 Draw a nine-diamond shape on A4 paper, using the pattern shown here. In discussion with classmates, rank the following sports in order according to which you think needs the highest level of arousal. The one with the highest arousal goes in the top box:

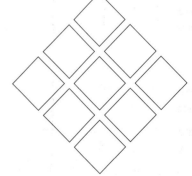

- putting the shot
- high jump
- hockey penalty
- boxing
- archery
- 100 m sprint
- rugby match
- weightlifting competition
- gymnastic vault

Watch a clip on YouTube of the New Zealand rugby team (the 'All Blacks') performing their famous 'haka' before an international rugby match (use search terms 'All Blacks haka'). Why do you think they perform this display? How does it help the players get 'in the zone'? Explain the haka in terms of arousal levels and motivation.

REFLECTIVE LOG — Reflect on the levels of arousal you experience when taking part in sports competitions or physical activity. Where do you typically fall on the inverted U chart? Are there aspects of your preparation that you could improve?

Checklist for success

✔ Learn the definition of arousal and list the factors (mental and physical) that contribute to it.

✔ Annotate a sketch of the human body with the physical signs of arousal.

✔ Draw and explain the Inverted U theory (Yerkes–Dodson Law).

✔ Think of sporting examples illustrating the effects of under- and over-arousal.

Sound progress

• I can state what is meant by arousal in a sporting context.

• I can identify the physical signs of arousal.

• I can draw the Yerkes–Dodson Inverted U theory and identify the key areas of arousal.

Excellent progress

• I can describe the physiological and psychological aspects of arousal.

• I can apply the Yerkes Dodson Inverted U theory to situations I have been in.

• I can explain under- and over-arousal with reference to sporting examples and the impact on performance.

Anxiety

LEARNING OBJECTIVES
- Identify the two types of anxiety (cognitive and somatic) and describe their symptoms.
- Describe four physiological responses to arousal.
- Explain the causes of anxiety in physical activities.

What causes anxiety in sporting contexts and how does it affect performance?

Starting point

The excitement that a competitor feels before a match or competition causes a number of responses in the body, as you learned in the previous topic. Successful athletes are able to manage and control these responses, and so prevent **anxiety** from interfering with a good performance,

Exploring the skills

Anxiety is a negative emotional state associated with arousal; it involves fear, worry and doubt. Anxiety is caused by situations that we perceive as threatening. These fears and worries can be to do with:

- uncertainty – 'I don't know whether I can succeed or not.'
- pressure – 'I have to take that penalty. What if I miss?'
- effect on self-esteem – 'Other people will have a lower opinion of me if I don't perform well.'
- fear of harm – 'I might get hurt or injured.'
- frustration – 'I won't win the trophy I have set my heart on. I might not make the first team.'

The anxieties listed above are all examples of **cognitive anxiety** – the thought processes that lead to worry and stress. Anxiety can also take a more physical form, called **somatic anxiety.**

Some sports performers have such strong somatic symptoms that they actually vomit before an event or match. (Many actors and musicians also experience the same thing.)

Key term

anxiety: negative reaction from a performer to stress, causing the performer to feel worried, nervous or apprehensive

Key terms

cognitive anxiety: the mental symptoms that a performer feels, such as fear, worry and doubt, that can occur if the performer is in a state of under-arousal or over-arousal

somatic anxiety: the physical signs of anxiety that can be termed as 'butterflies in the stomach' (see the physical signs of arousal in Topic 9.3)

1   Look at the following two images of people in sporting situations. Suggest the possible causes of anxiety in each case. What somatic symptoms might affect the players' performance?

a) A golfer who needs to sink a difficult putt in order to progress to the next round

b) A cricketer who is next in line to bat in a championship-deciding game

Developing the skills

Some of the somatic symptoms of anxiety are a result of the body's response to the arousal caused by the excitement of a match, competition or event. The hormone adrenaline plays an important part in this response, as illustrated in the diagram.

Production of adrenaline
Your adrenal glands, found just above your kidneys, release a hormone called adrenaline into the bloodstream.

Increased heart rate
Adrenaline makes the heart beat faster. More oxygen and glucose are then pumped on to the muscles.

Increased respiration
Adrenaline causes you to breathe faster and more deeply to allow oxygen to quickly reach the muscles.

Muscles tense
Adrenaline causes your muscles to tense in readiness for action.

2   Think of a time you were about to perform in a competitive match. Explain how the following can help you to give a good performance:

a) increased heart rate

b) increased respiration

c) muscles tensing.

Applying the skills

Synchronised diving partners Tom Daley and Daniel Goodfellow have performed together in various competitions. Although they will have techniques to cope with anxiety, it can still occur, especially within a team or paired event.

3 Thinking of the example of Tom Daley and Daniel Goodfellow, describe the following:

    a) the signs of somatic (physical) anxiety they might experience

    b) the cognitive (mental) anxiety they might have to deal with

    c) any other factors that might contribute to anxieties in their particular sport.

4 Research the phrase 'eustress'. Explain how some amount of anxiety or stress can help someone to perform.

> **REFLECTIVE LOG**
>
> Keep a log of your physical and mental feelings in the period leading up to a competitive sporting event. What symptoms did you show? How did you control and manage these feelings? Can you identify ways of managing your feelings more effectively?

Checklist for success

✔ Learn the definitions of anxiety and the two forms it can take (cognitive and somatic).

✔ Make a list of the negative thought processes (cognitive anxiety) and physical symptoms (somatic anxiety) involved in anxiety.

✔ Draw a flowchart to outline the role of adrenaline in the body's physiological response to arousal.

Sound progress

• I can define anxiety and describe the two types of anxiety: somatic and cognitive.

• I can describe the physiological responses to arousal.

Excellent progress

• I can explain what is meant by anxiety and link it to arousal.

• I can describe the causes of anxiety in terms of negative thought processes (cognitive anxiety) and physical symptoms (somatic anxiety).

• I can describe the role of adrenaline in the body's response to arousal and anxiety.

Relaxation techniques

LEARNING OBJECTIVES
- Explain the benefits of relaxation techniques in reducing anxiety and arousal.
- Describe and use the techniques of mental rehearsal, visualisation and deep breathing.
- Explain how these techniques control and support the performer.

What are relaxation techniques and how can they help to reduce arousal and anxiety?

Starting point

Everyone suffers from nerves before an important performance, even top-level sports performers. Elite athletes learn how to control these nerves, using relaxation techniques to control their levels of anxiety and arousal before a competitive event.

> I need to reduce my levels of stress and anxious thoughts.

> I need to concentrate on the event and not waste energy.

An over-aroused performer may suffer raised blood pressure and a faster breathing rate, as well as a deterioration in their motor activity:

- They may begin to sweat and shake, which will impair fine motor control.
- They may suffer from lack of sleep leading up to their event, leaving them tired.

A combination of relaxation techniques can be applied to reduce their anxiety or arousal levels, both in the immediate situation and over the longer term.

 Consider a situation where you have suffered from anxiety or over-arousal before an important event and felt nervous. Describe how you felt and what you did to help keep yourself calm.

Exploring the skills

There are various relaxation techniques that athletes will use to control their levels of anxiety and arousal. The most common are **mental rehearsal**, combined with **visualisation**, and **deep breathing**.

Using the technique of mental rehearsal, an athlete mentally practises a skill, running through a whole sequence or event in their mind in advance and in detail. They use all their senses to recreate the event mentally. They try to simulate all the sights, sounds and experiences that may occur such as:

- crowd noise
- what the crowd looks like
- how to react positively to bad situations
- performing skills perfectly under pressure.

When using mental rehearsal, an athlete will also try to visualise themselves performing well, while staying calm and confident.

Key terms

mental rehearsal: running through a skill, sequence or event in your mind, in detail, using all your senses

visualisation: 'seeing' the best positive outcome for the skill/technique you are about to perform

deep breathing: a learned way of breathing in a deep, calm and focused way to promote relaxation as well as physical well-being

Rehearsing mentally

Visualising success

If certain situations create anxiety or arousal, then these can be discussed with a coach, who will help the performer consider how to deal with it. This solution can then be acted in their future mental rehearsals.

2 Think of a skill you perform in your chosen sport. It could taking a penalty, putting in golf or clearing a hurdle.

- Close your eyes and relax your body, getting rid of any tension. Breathe calmly.
- Imagine yourself in that situation. Think about the sights, sounds and smells that you would experience.
- Now visualise yourself completing that skill perfectly.
- Create a story board of mental rehearsal.

9.5

Developing the skills

Deep breathing is the action of breathing deeply as a means of relaxation. With this technique, athletes will spend time breathing deeply and slowly.

Focus on breathing instead of the event, reducing stress.

Use breathing to remove tension from muscles, allowing relaxation.

Fill the lungs with air and let the body take in oxygen efficiently.

Focus on maintaining attention by staying calm, by standing, sitting or lying down.

Using a combination of these and other relaxation techniques can help a performer control their pre-competition arousal. Athletes train themselves to be highly effective at these techniques, enabling their bodies and minds to respond quickly and relax more easily.

A coach encourages a performer to:
- think about their distractions
- use the experience of mental rehearsal to overcome those situations
- visualise successful occasions when performing under pressure.

Relaxation techniques help a performer to:
- increase their concentration by focusing on how to execute the skills successfully
- understand that a reduced resting heart rate will lower the risk of heart disease
- realise that the heart does not need to pump as fast due to the higher levels of oxygen being carried in the blood.

Deep breathing allows a performer to:
- improve their stamina by increasing the efficiency of their oxygen intake
- encourage the correct breathing technique during exercise
- lower the amount of adrenaline released and so prevent the heart rate from rising
- lower their heart rate by getting oxygen absorbed into the blood more efficiently.

Applying the skills

3 Try the deep-breathing relaxation technique. You will need to set aside 10–15 minutes for this activity.

- Find a quiet space where there is little noise and you will not be disturbed.
- You can stand, sit or lie down.
- Close your eyes and breathe evenly and deeply from your abdomen.

- As you breathe in, feel the breath fill your abdomen. Keep your shoulders relaxed.

- When you breathe out, focus on the heaviness occurring in your stomach.

- As you exhale, think of a word that captures the feeling such as 'calm' or 'relax'.

- Repeat that word with each breath and let it become a mantra for you.

 4 Create a self-help blog or leaflet entitled 'Why should athletes train themselves to relax?'

Explain how deep breathing can help an athlete perform successfully. Research an elite performer that you admire and find out what relaxation techniques they used.

> **REFLECTIVE LOG**
>
> Reflect on your experience of trying out mental rehearsal and deep breathing. How did you find it? In what ways did it help? These techniques require practice, so keep trying them. Makes notes in your log of the benefits you find, as well as any difficulties you encounter.
>
> Research other forms of relaxation such as yoga, internal mental imagery, progressive muscular relaxation, massage, meditation, thought redirection and self-hypnosis.

Checklist for success

✔ Summarise the steps involved in various relaxation techniques.

✔ Practise using mental rehearsal and visualisation techniques to help reduce anxiety in sporting situations.

✔ Regularly practise using deep breathing techniques to reduce arousal and anxiety.

Sound progress

- I can describe the techniques of mental rehearsal, visualisation and deep breathing.
- I can identify how these techniques are used to reduce anxiety and arousal in a performer.

Excellent progress

- I can explain how relaxation techniques increase concentration, control breathing and reduce heart rate.
- I can explain how relaxation techniques can help an athlete perform successfully.

Personality types

LEARNING OBJECTIVES
- Define the two personality types: introvert and extrovert.
- Describe the typical characteristics of introverts and extroverts.
- Suggest physical activities that might be taken up by introvert and extrovert personality types.

How might a person's personality type influence the type of physical activity they take up?

Starting point

The type of personality a performer has can have an effect on the types of sport they decide to take up and become successful at. Generally speaking, a marathon runner is likely to be a very different kind of person from a boxer, even though both take part in sports and have to be able to endure a certain amount of pain.

Team sports such as football and netball require performers who are willing to cooperate with others and work to a team plan, which requires a quite different set of skills.

1 Write down 10 sentences about your personality, each starting with 'I am …'. Try to be as honest as possible!

Share these with a partner and ask them to say whether they agree with your assessment.

Exploring the skills

According to psychologists, there are two main personality types: **introvert** and **extrovert**.

The table lists some of the characteristics of the two personality types, and how they might be linked to different sports and physical activities.

A note of caution

These are generalisations: there are plenty of introverts who play hockey or football, and extrovert sportspeople can also enjoy shooting!

Also, many people don't fall neatly into these categories. They may be a mixture of both introvert and extrovert.

Key terms

introvert: a quiet, shy, reserved personality type; associated with individual sports

extrovert: a sociable, lively, optimistic, outgoing personality type; more associated with team sports

Introverts	Extroverts
Are quiet, shy and reserved types of people	Are sociable, talkative, outgoing and active
Prefer taking part in activities and sports by themselves	Prefer team sports
Enjoy their own company and like being on their own	Enjoy interacting with others and get bored easily if on their own
Are often involved in activities that demand high concentration and accuracy	Prefer activities with lower levels of concentration
Excel at sports that require fine movement skills	Can be frustrated by precise, intricate movements and prefer sports that require gross motor skills
Perform better with lower levels of arousal	Prefer sports that require higher levels of arousal and are played at a fast pace
Practise by themselves or in the company of a few others	Enjoy team practice sessions
Tend to dislike contact sports and have a lower tolerance of pain	Enjoy contact sports with lots of action and tend to have a higher tolerance of pain

2 Based on these two descriptions, which personality type do you now consider yourself to be? Do you fit into the patterns above in terms of the kind of sports you prefer to play?

3 Think of examples of top-class performers in a range of sports. How well do they fit into these categories? Can you think of individuals who go against type?

Developing the skills

The table above is a very general assessment of the types of sport each personality type would be suited to. All performers are individuals, with their own characteristics and personality traits that will influence the choices they make about what activities to devote time to.

4 Look at this table, which has divided a number of sports into two columns, according to whether they are more suited to introverts or to extroverts. Do you agree with the sports and the columns they have been put in? If you agree, discuss with classmates the reasons for having them in that column. If you disagree, discuss reasons for having that sport in a different column.

Introverts	Agree	Disagree	Extroverts	Agree	Disagree
Long-distance running			Football		
Archery			Rugby		
Swimming			Boxing		
Diving			Basketball		
Gymnastics			Hockey		
Table tennis			Netball		

5 Which column would you put cricket and martial arts into? Give reasons for your decision.

Applying the skills

Assessing personality types can be used as a way of identifying talented individuals and nurturing their particular skills. There are many different theories of personality, which you will come across if studying sociology or psychology. These include:

- trait theory – the idea that people are born with certain inherited characteristics

- social learning theory – the theory that behaviour is learnt in the social context, through observation or direct instruction

- interactionist theory – the idea that behaviour, beliefs and values are developed through individual and small group interactions.

What these theories also suggest is that many different factors may influence the type of personality we have and hence also our choice of sport.

REFLECTIVE LOG

Note down your own assessment of your personality type and the extent to which it has influenced your choice of physical activities. How important do you think personality type has been in your choice? What other factors have played a role?

Checklist for success

✔ List the characteristics of the two personality types: introvert and extrovert.

✔ Draw up suggestions for activities that introverts and extroverts are best suited to, along with reasons why.

Sound progress

- I can explain the difference between introverts and extroverts.
- I can identify activities to suit both an introvert and extrovert.

Excellent progress

- I can describe the personality traits of introverts and extroverts.
- I can describe how personality traits may influence a person's choice of physical activity, with examples and explanations.

Check your progress

Use these statements as a way of evaluating your progress throughout this chapter.

Sound progress

- I can identify the SMARTER principles of goal-setting with physical activities.
- I can describe how anxiety can be reduced by setting SMARTER goals.
- I can describe what motivates me as a performer in a physical activity.
- I can explain how I am intrinsically and extrinsically motivated in this situation.
- I can state what is meant by arousal in a sporting context.
- I can identify the physical signs of arousal.
- I can draw the Yerkes–Dodson Inverted U theory and identify the key areas of arousal.
- I can define anxiety and describe the two types of anxiety: somatic and cognitive.
- I can describe the physiological responses to arousal.
- I can describe the techniques of mental rehearsal, visualisation and deep breathing.
- I can identify how these techniques are used to reduce anxiety and arousal in a performer.
- I can explain the difference between introverts and extroverts.
- I can identify activities to suit both an introvert and extrovert.

Excellent progress

- I can apply the SMARTER principles and set targets for myself, for an individual and for a team of players.
- I can explain how to structure goal-setting strategies within the SMARTER targets to reduce anxiety.
- I can explain what motivates an elite athlete.
- I can explain how elite athletes are intrinsically and extrinsically motivated.
- I can describe the physiological and psychological aspects of arousal.
- I can apply the Yerkes–Dodson Inverted U theory to situations I have been in.
- I can explain under- and over-arousal with reference to sporting examples and the impact on performance.
- I can explain what is meant by anxiety and link it to arousal.
- I can describe the causes of anxiety in terms of negative thought processes (cognitive anxiety) and physical symptoms (somatic anxiety).
- I can describe the role of adrenaline in the body's response to arousal and anxiety.
- I can explain how relaxation techniques increase concentration, control breathing and reduce heart rate.

- I can explain how relaxation techniques can help an athlete perform successfully.
- I can describe the personality traits of introverts and extroverts.
- I can describe how personality traits may influence a person's choice of physical activity, with examples and explanations.

Chapter 10

Social and cultural influences

Starting point

Sport is a huge industry that involves much more than just participating and competing. It involves jobs, lifestyles and livelihoods, and can play a key role in the life of individuals, communities and the nation as a whole. In this topic, you will develop an understanding of the social and cultural influences on sport and sporting performance.

You will:

- investigate the role of leisure and recreation in modern society, and the growth of the leisure industry
- explore the factors that affect people's access to and participation in physical activities
- describe the role of the media, sponsorship and technology in sport
- explore the role of professional and amateur performers in sport, and the place of sportsmanship and gamesmanship.

Chapter contents

The activities you complete will primarily relate to theoretical work, but you will also be exploring practical situations and your own experiences to understand the social and cultural influences on sport.

You will:

- create a table of factors that influence people's choice of recreational activities
- draw a mind map of the factors influencing the growth in leisure activities
- draw sketches of the sports development pyramid, annotated with descriptions
- chart your own possible pathway up the sports development pyramid
- design a leaflet promoting the role of sports development officer as a career
- find examples of each of the factors that affect access to physical activities
- consider factors that affect participation, identifying who is affected
- suggest strategies for increasing access and participation in a sport you take part in
- draw up case studies of sponsorship deals
- create mind maps to summarise the advantages and disadvantages of sponsorship
- list the different forms of media and the kind of coverage they provide
- complete a diary record of the sports coverage you are exposed to
- draw a mind map of the advantages and disadvantages of media coverage of sport
- investigate the benefits of hosting a global event such as the Olympic Games
- explore the history of sport in terms of amateur and professional participation
- research examples to illustrate acts of sportsmanship and gamesmanship
- investigate the use of different forms of technology in sport
- assess the positive and negative arguments for introducing new technology into sport.

We are influenced by our surroundings – social, cultural and geographical.

Leisure, recreation and the growth of leisure activities

LEARNING OBJECTIVES
- Explain the terms 'leisure', '(physical) recreation', 'play' and 'sport'.
- Outline the factors that influence the recreational activities people take part in.
- Describe the factors that have influenced the growth of leisure activities.

What are leisure and recreation? What has caused the huge growth in leisure activities?

Starting point

People take part in exercise and **physical recreation** for a variety of reasons. For many people this has to happen during their **leisure time**. Your choice of activities can be affected by a wide range of factors, including where you live, what weather your area has, what facilities are available and what your friends also do. You will explore these factors in this topic.

 What leisure activities do you and members of your family take part in? Jot down a few ideas quickly.

Exploring the skills

In recent years, leisure and recreation have become vast industry, with sport being only a section of it. For example, in the United Kingdom it provides around 900 000 jobs with an income of £23.8 billion for the economy. As an indicator of its importance, some 60% of men and women in the UK aged 16–60 participate in sport or leisure activities.

So, what is the difference between leisure, **sport**, recreation and **play**?

 Look at the pictures overleaf. Which category (or categories) does each picture illustrate?

a) leisure

b) physical recreation

c) play

d) sport.

Key terms

physical recreation: a physical activity or pastime that promotes health, relaxation and enjoyment

leisure time: time spent away from work and free from obligations

sport: an activity that involves physical exertion and skill, either as an individual or as part of a team competing against another person or team

play: to take part in a sport or activity for enjoyment

A

B

C

D

E

F

G

H

I

3 Think about your typical day/week. Note down the amount of time you spend performing different activities throughout the day/week. Present the results in a table or a chart (pie chart). Use these categories:

a) school

b) sleeping

c) homework

d) eating

e) travelling

f) chores

g) leisure (computer games, sport, reading, walking, drama).

Developing the skills

There are all kinds of reasons why people choose to take part in certain types of activities rather than others. Consider the recreational activities that you and your family do in your leisure time. There will be many reasons why you have chosen these particular ones. It could be that your friends or other members or your family do them. Or there might be an activity that you would like to do but cannot because it is too expensive or too inconvenient. Each of these factors influences why we take part and what level we want to achieve, whether it is purely for pleasure or to be competitive.

The chart below lists the factors that influence the recreational activities that people choose to do in their leisure time.

Age and health
Your age (and health) are likely to affect the recreational activities you choose, when it comes to activities that require physical activity. Older people may choose less demanding activities, such as walking, football or bowling.

Interests
You are more likely to take part in activities that spark your interest than things you care less about. If you like being outdoors, you are more likely to take up an outdoor activity, such as hiking or road cycling.

Facilities
The facilities and standard of those facilities available to you can affect the activities you take part in. For example: if you don't have easy access to squash facilities, then you are unlikely to take up squash in your leisure time.

Family influences
Your family plays a massive role in the activities you do. Do they show interest and encourage you? Are they part of your family's culture or tradition? Can they transport you to and from these activities? If the answers to these are yes, then you are more likely to participate in these recreational activities.

Factors that influence what recreational activities people do in their leisure time

Peer influences
People in a peer group will often have similar interests and backgrounds to each other and can often influence each other to behave in particular ways. If your peer group approves of or encourages you to take part in something, you are more likely to do so.

Social circumstances
Some activities are expensive, such as skiing, golf, sailing and horse riding. If your social circumstance mean that you cannot afford to do these activities, then the chances are you will find other activities to do.

Where you live
Where you live can affect the activities available to you and influence which activities you can take part in. Factors include the geography and climate of your location, and traditions or cultural activities you are exposed to. For example, ski jumping facilities tend to be found only in certain places in certain countries. If you have very little snow or no indoor facilities, then it is very difficult for you to try ski jumping.

4 Using yourself and members of your family/friends, investigate how all these factors have influenced the recreational activities you have taken part in. Summarise your findings in the form of a table like this one.

Factor	Myself	Grandparent
Age	As a teenager, I can take part in any activity that is high or low intensity and is either contact or non-contact. I prefer to take part in rugby with my friends. I can recover quickly to play and train each week.	I now play golf. It is very sociable and I am able to play at a slower pace. I used to play rugby but now I am older, I cannot get around the pitch anymore or recover to train and play on a regular basis.
Interest		
Where you live		
Family influence		
Peer influence		
Social circumstances		
Facilities		

5 Share your information with a partner. What similarities and differences did you find?

Applying the skills

In recent years, the amount of leisure time people enjoy has increased. There are many reasons for this:

- People generally spend less time working and have more holidays.

- More people are retiring at a younger age and in better health than previous generations – they can look forward to many years of active leisure time.

- Work patterns have changed, with a general increase in part-time and temporary work.

- Advances in technology mean that we spend less time on household tasks: microwave ovens, washing machines and dishwashers mean less time spent on cooking, cleaning and washing.

At the same time, people are now more aware of the health benefits of leading an active lifestyle. Being active can benefit your health as you get older, and there has been a rise in the number of people over 65 years taking part in physical activities (42% of men and 33% of women take part, compared with

53% of the total population). Governments have promoted these benefits over many years through health promotion campaigns.

If you compare your family's leisure activities, you can see there are opportunities for people at all stages of life. For example, younger people may play football, but older people can take part in less physically demanding activities such as walking football, bowls or golf. People are aware that they do not have to do the same activities as when they were younger and can look for new opportunities.

The factors influencing the growth of leisure activities are summarised in the chart.

6 Look at the factors listed above and using a piece of paper, write down the headings, leaving space to write information underneath them.

a) Discuss the reasons why each factor will help to increase the number of leisure activities people take part in.

b) Record your findings under each heading.

c) Discuss your findings with someone else. What similarities did you find in your responses? Did you find any differences?

You may find it useful to summarise the information in the form of a mind map, with separate branches for each of the factors identified.

REFLECTIVE LOG

Take some time to reflect or test yourself on the differences between leisure, recreation, sport and play. Write notes about your own experiences and interests, and the factors that have influenced your own choice of leisure activities and sports.

Choose three factors that have led to an increase in leisure activities and explore the effect of each factor in more detail. Why are these factors so important? What kinds of recreational activities do they affect most?

Checklist for success

✔ Learn the meaning of the terms 'leisure', '(physical) recreation', 'play' and 'sport'.

✔ Draw up a table of factors that influence people's choice of recreational activities, using your own experience to provide examples.

✔ Create a mind map summarising the many factors that have influenced the growth in leisure activities.

Sound progress

• I can identify factors that influence which recreational activities people do in their leisure time.

• I can list the factors that influence the growth in leisure activities.

Excellent progress

• I can explain with examples what factors influence people's choices of recreational activities.

• I can explain the effects of different factors on the growth of leisure activities.

The sports development pyramid

LEARNING OBJECTIVES
- Define sports development and identify the different levels of the sports development pyramid.
- Describe the pathways performers take through the pyramid in different sports.
- Investigate the role of sports development officers.

What is sports development? How does using the sports development pyramid help both individuals and organisations?

Starting point

This topic focuses on the topic of **sports development**, the process of finding ways to enable individuals to start, stay and succeed in sport.

Sports development is about generating as much interest and participation in sport as possible. It is often viewed as a pyramid, as shown in the diagram, with a large mass of people at the base taking part at a foundation level or for recreation, moving through to the peak, where a small number of elite athletes perform at the highest level. The diagram shows the kinds of sports activities and events that take place at the various levels.

Key term

sports development: the promotion of sports activities for the community

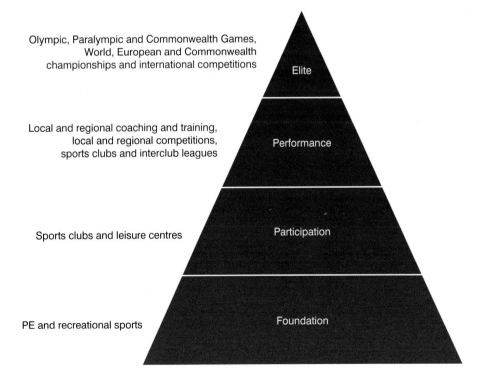

Olympic, Paralympic and Commonwealth Games, World, European and Commonwealth championships and international competitions — **Elite**

Local and regional coaching and training, local and regional competitions, sports clubs and interclub leagues — **Performance**

Sports clubs and leisure centres — **Participation**

PE and recreational sports — **Foundation**

1. On which level of the sports development pyramid would you place:

   a) a badminton player who meets up every week with friends for a game

   b) a medal winner at the Paralympic Games

   c) a pupil at primary school learning rounders

   d) a footballer who plays for their local team in the county league?

Exploring the skills

The sports development pyramid is a widely accepted model that is used in two ways:

- for participants – to identify the level at which individuals are performing, to provide them with a suitable level of support, competition and opportunity to aid their development
- for policy makers and providers – to plan how to use and develop resources that will promote take-up of the sport.

All people involved in sport follow this journey through the sports development pyramid. However, the level you are at on the pyramid may depend on many factors: your abilities, age, experience, determination and luck. This is explored in more detail in Topic 10.3.

Stage 1: Foundation

The Foundation stage is the base of the pyramid, the first stage at which people come into contact with sports. In any sport, the largest number of people taking part will be at this level.

The Foundation stage:

- consists of beginners and younger people
- involves mass participation activities
- is about recreation and having fun
- involves learning and developing basic skills such as running, jumping and throwing
- is found at school age in PE lessons or in 'mini sports' activities.

Having a strong base or foundation in any sport is vital. The more people that take part in sports, then the greater the number that will progress from the bottom of the pyramid to the top – in other words, that will develop from being basic or good participants to becoming top-class, elite performers.

Stage 2: Participation

The Participation stage is all about the enjoyment factor of playing sports. This level is about:

- taking part in organised sporting activities at clubs and leisure centres
- being with friends and like-minded individuals who are there to enjoy playing sport
- having a more structured environment than in the Foundation stage.

Individuals at this stage are making choices about which sports and activities they enjoy and want to pursue. Sports development involves making links between schools, clubs and sports festivals to create a pathway for people from the Foundation stage to the Participation stage.

Sports clubs become more important at this stage because they help link to the next stage: Performance.

Stage 3: Performance

The key characteristic of the Performance stage is competition. There may be lower-level performers taking part in competitive sports, but by now the performers tend to have a higher level of ability to perform the key skills needed for the sport.

At the Performance stage:

- the focus is on developing the level of performance towards the elite level
- participants will concentrate on one or two sports, developing specific skills
- training and competition become more regular and more important
- the emphasis is more on being professional and less about just having fun.

Individuals will have opportunities to develop their performance by representing their county and region. Additional coaching will be available to improve physical, tactical and psychological skills as they progress towards the Elite stage.

Stage 4: Elite

The Elite stage is the pinnacle of the pyramid and involves performers at the highest level. The pyramid is at its narrowest at this point as very few people reach this level.

At the Elite stage:

- performers now move from county/regional to national squads
- governing bodies are responsible for performer's development
- high levels of support are given to prepare the performers both physically and mentally through: coaching, medical care, equipment, diet and mentoring
- performers lead a lifestyle designed to maintain high levels of fitness – sacrifices are required as their lifestyle will centre around performing and competition
- performers will most likely be professional.

In minority sports the choice to become professional may not be possible because of a lack of funding for the sport and/or a reluctance on the part of sponsors to offer support.

 a) What stage do you think you are currently at in the sports development pyramid?

b) Why are you at this stage of the pyramid?

c) What do you need to do to get to the next level of the pyramid?

Developing the skills

Each sport has its own development programme based on the sports development pyramid, with initiatives focusing on the different levels, aimed at:

- raising awareness of the sport
- promoting its values
- raising participation by creating more opportunities
- improving access and removing barriers to taking part.

For example, in the UK, the Rugby Football Union (RFU) invested considerable sums of money in its 'All Schools' programme, established in 2012 as a legacy from the London Olympic Games. The idea was to increase access and participation, delivering the values of the sport to around a million school-aged children in conjunction with 750 partnership schools.

This chart helps us to see how the RFU is active at each stage of the sports development pyramid for its sport.

Stage 4: Elite stage
- Provides national-level coaching, competition and support for those who show high levels of ability and the character to perform at the highest level.

Stage 3: Performance stage
- Provides competitions through schools to develop representative rugby for county and regional levels.
- Generates knowledge of links to club-level rugby for improved coaching, level of competition and support/experience to those who wish to or are able to progress into the Performance stage.

Stage 2: Participation stage
- Provides rugby coaching and opportunities to play in extra-curricular sessions through schools, including festivals and fun games.

Stage 1: Foundation stage
- Provides rugby coaching and access through PE lessons.
- Runs introductory classes and fun sessions through community groups/sports centres.

3 For two sports of your choice, research how each sport provides a pathway through the sports development pyramid. Draw a pyramid similar to the one above.

4 Now focus on one of your sports. Imagine you are a member of a sports development team that has been given an unlimited budget to look at the services provided at each stage of the pyramid.

a) Consider what is already offered by your sport at each stage of the pyramid. What else might performers need to progress to the next stage of the pyramid or, if already at the Elite stage, to improve their performance?

b) What could you improve, in terms of resources, opportunities or organisation?

c) How might you do improve the services? What difficulties might you come across along the way in implementing these changes?

d) Produce a poster/mind map/plan about how you might improve the services offered at each stage of the pyramid to develop your sport further and present it to the group.

Applying the skills

Successful sports development depends largely on effective partnership and networking between a wide range of people and groups. Many professionals and volunteers are involved in providing the skills and support needed for people to progress up the pyramid. These include:

- coaches and trainers
- facilities operators and service providers (e.g. owners of sports centres)
- volunteers and voluntary groups
- community groups
- local councils
- sports governing bodies
- policy makers (e.g. politicians).

In recent years in the UK there has been a steady expansion of sports development programmes, leading to an increase in the number of sports development professionals. One of the key roles is that of the **sports development officer**.

The aim of the sports development officer's work is to increase participation in sport of all kinds and at all levels of the pyramid, from recreational level to those interested in competing at the highest level. This means:

- ensuring that all sections of the community are aware of available activities and where they can go to get involved
- distributing information and promoting sport
- organising classes, programmes, coaching, club development and training
- liaising with schools, governing bodies, councils and everyone involved in sports development.

Sports development officers are employed by a variety of organisations, including local authorities, universities and colleges, sports councils and national governing bodies.

> **Key term**
>
> **sports development officer:** a professional whose job is to identify and support a planned route for participants and performers through the four stages of the pyramid

5. Using the internet carry out further research into the role of sports development officer:

   a) Investigate what opportunities exist to work as a sports development officer in your area. What organisations employ sports development officers?

   b) What abilities and skills do you need? What personal qualities are useful or desirable?

c) What would the pathway be towards becoming a sports development officer? What qualifications are important?

Summarise your findings in the form of a leaflet for fellow students, encouraging them to take up a career as a sports development officer.

 REFLECTIVE LOG Reflect upon your on development and identify a sport or activity you would like to excel in. Using the pyramid, construct your path and what support you would need to progress through the different levels.

Checklist for success

✔ Practise drawing sketches of the sports development pyramid and annotate them with descriptions of what happens at each stage.

✔ Create a case study for a sport you are interested in, illustrating pathways through the pyramid.

✔ Summarise the role and tasks of different people involved in sports development.

Sound progress

• I can identify the different stages of the sports development pyramid.

• I can outline the pathways performers must follow to progress up the pyramid.

• I know what is involved in the work of sports development officers.

Excellent progress

• I can describe the four stages of the sports development pyramid and the characteristics of each stage.

• I can describe in detail what support performers need to progress through the pyramid.

• I can summarise the roles of different people and organisations involved in sports development and the support they offer.

Access and participation in sport

LEARNING OBJECTIVES
- Identify the factors that affect access to physical activity.
- Describe the factors that affect participation in sports and physical activities.
- Explain strategies for increasing access and participation in sports.

What are the factors that can affect access to and participation in physical activities? What strategies can be developed to improve access and participation?

Starting point

In 10.2, you looked at progression through the sports development pyramid and some of the ways in which people can be helped to progress from the lower levels towards the peak.

Unfortunately, many people come across obstacles that hinder their progress up the pyramid – or even prevent them becoming part of the pyramid and participating in physical activities at all. The obstacles fall into two main groups: factors that affect *access* and those that affect *participation*. Some of these are illustrated in the diagram. As you can see, many of the factors are linked, affecting both access and participation, as you will explore further in this topic.

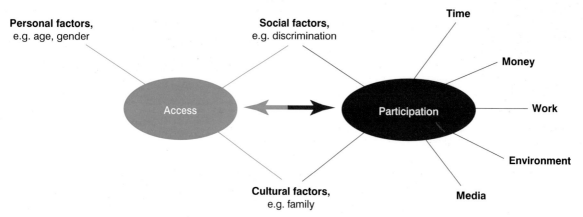

Exploring the skills

Accessing sport and physical activity should be an easy decision to make: you simply decide which sport or activity you have an interest in and want to take part in. However, for many people the decision is not that simple. There are several factors that can affect how easily they access activities certain activities, if at all.

The table lists some of the factors that affect access to sport and the kinds of people affected. The main factors considered are: age, gender, disability, and social and cultural influences.

Factor	Group	How it affects access to sport
Age	Young children	Joints are not fully developed, so some activities should be avoided, such as heavy weight training and extreme distances.
	Older people	May not be able to do some sports because of less strength, disease such as arthritis, poorer eyesight and hearing.
Gender	Females	Some organisations still restrict access to men only (e.g. some golf clubs). Women may be made to feel unwelcome even when access is allowed. Women's sports are not treated equally in terms of finance, sponsorship and development.
Disability	Physical	Lack of provision for people who can't use facilities without additional equipment or support. Lack of parking or disabled-friendly transport means people can't get to facilities.
Social influences	Family	Family may not be able to afford to pay for equipment, fees or tuition.
	School	School may not provide the facilities for particular sports or offer it on the timetable.
Cultural influences	Religion	Local facilities may be segregated on the basis of what faith you belong to. Some faiths treat certain days as holy, so participants cannot compete on those days. Faith may impose restrictions on sports women can play or the clothing women can wear.

1. In a group, discuss these factors and try to think of further examples. Copy this table and add in extra rows to record your ideas.

2. In your group discuss what, if anything, could or should be done to improve access for people affected. Make a record of your ideas: for example, as a table or mind map.

3. You have been asked to write a short article (500 words maximum) for a magazine about factors that affect access to physical activity.

   a) Look at the factors highlighted above and discuss why they can affect people's access to physical activity.

   b) Write your article, focusing on one the factors limiting access to sport and suggesting ideas for improving access.

10.3

Developing the skills

Access is just one of the factors that affect whether or not people take part in physical activity and sport. There are many other factors that influence people's levels of participation. These are summarised in the diagram.

4 Copy and complete this table by doing some research to find out how the various factors listed on the left might affect participation in physical activities. Which groups of people are affected and in what ways?

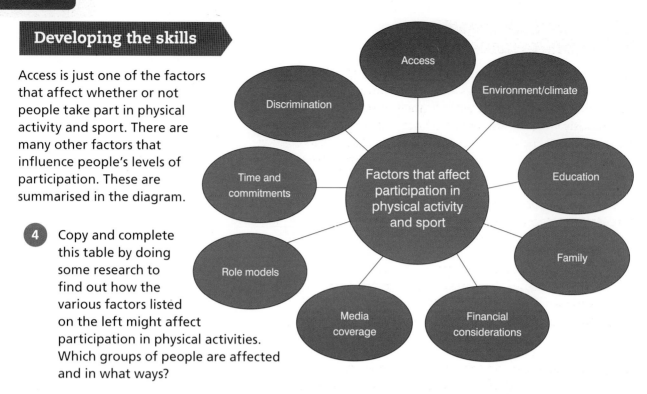

Factor	Whom does it affect and why?
Access	People with disabilities, older people, women – see 'Exploring the skills'
Discrimination	People of minority ethnic groups
	People with disabilities
Education	
Environment/climate	In mountainous areas, activities such as fell walking or hiking might be popular and well-supported.
Family	Traditionally in some countries women are encouraged to look after the family.
	The family's habits can affect the level of exercise and activities they will take part in.
Financial considerations	
Media coverage	Very dominated by male sports, great for male sport.
	Very little female sport covered in any form of media.
Role models	Boys are influenced by poor behaviour of their idols.
	Girls receive very little coverage of female role models.
Time and work commitment	People in full-time work may have less time for activities or may feel too tired to take part.

Applying the skills

In recent years there has been a real attempt to address some of the issues affecting access and participation. For example, opportunities for athletes with disabilities have increased enormously with the success of events such as the Paralympics. The high media profile given to the Olympic Games in London in 2012 and Rio 2016 has undoubtedly helped to increase participation.

The BBC launched a web-based programme called 'Get Inspired' after the London 2012 Olympic Games to raise awareness, increase participation and motivate people to try new sports.

5 Do some research into organisations such as English Disability Sport and strategies such as Sport England's 'This Girl Can' campaign and BBC Sport's 'Get Inspired' pages. Discuss what they are doing to improve access for these groups.

6 Look again at the table you completed for task **4**. For each factor listed, think about strategies that could be used to increase participation in physical activities. Write your ideas in a table like the one here. Some suggestions have been included to get you started.

Factor	Strategies to increase participation
Access	
Discrimination	
Education	
Environment / Climate	
Family	Cheaper memberships when enrolling as a family
Financial considerations	Reducing the cost of participation or memberships for through concessions (e.g. under 16 and pensioners) Local group activities using public spaces to keep costs down and offer easy access, e.g. park runs
Media coverage	Need more coverage of female sports such as netball Programmes aimed at women, e.g. Sky TV's 'Sports Women' programme and web pages More high-profile female presenters on TV
Role models	
Time and work commitment	

> **REFLECTIVE LOG**
>
> Have you been affected by any of the factors you have investigated in this unit? Have you experienced any barriers to access or obstacles to taking part? What strategies have you used to try to overcome these obstacles? What other strategies would help you further – either things you could do yourself or changes that could be made on a wider level?

Checklist for success

✔ List examples of each of the factors that affect access to physical activities.

✔ Learn the list of factors that affect participation, identifying which groups of people are affected and how.

✔ For every example you list, suggest a strategy that could be used to increase access/participation.

Sound progress

• I can list the factors that affect people's access to physical activities.

• I can identify the factors that affect participation, with examples.

• I can suggest strategies for improving access and participation.

Excellent progress

• I can describe how factors such as age and disability can affect people's access to physical activities in a wide range of ways.

• I can explain how various factors affect participation with a wide range of examples.

• I can describe a range of strategies for increasing access and participation, including more promotion, better provision and greater access.

Sponsorship

LEARNING OBJECTIVES
- Identify the different forms sponsorship can take.
- Describe the role that sponsorship plays in sport.
- Explain the advantages and disadvantages of sponsorship in sport.

What impact does sponsorship have both on sports and on individual performers?

Starting point

Professional sport relies on income to:

- pay the wages of their players and employees
- develop and maintain facilities, such as stadia and training grounds
- provide their shareholders with a financial reward for their investment.

Sport generates income in various ways, from people paying to watch at the venue, the media paying to broadcast sport and the sale of merchandise. However, sponsorship has now become one of the major sources of the investment required by sport.

Exploring the skills

Sponsorship is a commercial deal where a business provides support for a team, athlete or event. It is generally financial, although it could come in the form of goods or services. The businesses involved hope to enhance their advertising and **brand** through positive association with a sport or athlete. This can be very expensive, but it can lead to the businesses making larger profits if the performer or team are successful.

Examples of high-profile sponsorship deals are shown in the table.

Key terms

sponsorship: the support given to a sport, sports event or organisation by an outside body or person for the mutual benefit for both parties

brand: The creation of a recognisable image that widely identifies a product and differentiates it from its competitors

Individual	Sportswear company Nike pays Cristiano Ronaldo in the region of £14 million a year for him to wear their clothing and represent their brand.
Team and facility	Financial institution JPMorgan Chase has paid the Golden State Warriors basketball team a sum thought to be hundreds of millions of dollars to name the team's new arena in San Francisco. When it opens (in around 2019), it will be called the 'Chase Center'.
Event	Sponsorship money can even be paid to a competition for the right to be affiliated to it, such as Slazenger which has sponsored Wimbledon since 1902.

1 Often sportspeople or competitions become closely linked with particular sponsors if they are involved with each other for a long period. Below are some examples of associations between sports and sponsors that are well known. Can you name a further example for each of the five areas?

- **Individual:** Usain Bolt and Puma
- **Team:** New Zealand and Adidas
- **Sport:** Cricket in the UK and Waitrose (up to 2016)
- **Competition:** Olympic Games and Coca Cola
- **Facility:** Arsenal Football Club in the Emirates Stadium

Sponsorship can take three main forms:

- Finance – funding from the sponsor can help pay for the daily living and training costs of performers. In return, the performers will need to promote the business by wearing branded sportswear during competitions or at public functions.

- Clothing, footwear and equipment – for example, Nike provides Barcelona with all their best kit and equipment. The team does not pay for any of this. In return, Nike will receive huge public exposure and support from the club players and officials at events.

- Facilities – during the 2012 Olympics the O2 Arena in London was renamed the North Greenwich Arena to host the tennis competition. It has now returned to the O2 brand and will continue to gain further finance from other competitions.

2 Next time you are at a sporting event or fixture, make a list of all the different sponsors that you can see around the stadium during the fixture. Answer the following questions as you complete the task:

a) How many are there?

b) Do any of them look to be more prominent or important than others? If so, why might they have a greater importance to the fixture/competition?

c) Are there any sponsors that seem to contradict the activity they are associated with? For instance, many campaigners regard the sponsorship of the Olympic Games by fast food companies (such as McDonald's) as contradictory, because fast foods are often regarded as unhealthy, whereas sport should be promoting healthy lifestyles.

Developing the skills

Sponsorship can affect many sports in many ways. It can help to improve the profile of the sport and provide more opportunities for participation at different levels. However, what are the benefits for the sponsor and why would they want to be affiliated to a certain team or player?

The table outlines the benefits of sponsorship to the different parties involved.

Who benefits	Benefits obtained	Example
Sponsor	Being linked to success and glamour can raise their profile and status and increase the sales of their products.	Richard Branson and his Virgin Money Group sponsorship (partnership) deal with Manchester United.
Performer	They receive free clothing, equipment and a payment. Athletes can concentrate on training and playing and not have to worry about money.	Roger Federer now has his own line of Nike clothing.
Sport	The sport receives additional funding on top of admission and competition entries, which allows them to develop coaching and community schemes.	The Rugby Football Union promotes its sport in the community, involving players and even royalty to help publicise its projects.
Audience and spectators	They benefit when sponsors' money is used to improve spectator facilities. There may be direct benefits in terms of more access to watching sport (see example).	When BT Sport won the contract to show the Champion's League, all of British Telecom's customers (phone and internet) were given free access to watching the football games.

3. Create your own version of the table, with a different example for each of the four groups listed in the left-hand column. Use the internet to research different sports and performers to identify how sponsorship has benefited them. Compare your examples with those of your classmates.

Applying the skills

As the Wimbledon/Slazenger association shows, the use of sponsorship has been around for a long time. For just as long, sponsorship has also created problems and had more negative effects. For example:

- There have been occasions of sponsors going bankrupt and those who were sponsored suffering financially (e.g. after the collapse of ITV Digital in 2002, many lower-division football clubs experienced financial difficulties).

- Pressure from sponsors can lead to changes in the rules of the sport (e.g. the introduction of rugby and cricket video referees) to provide additional entertainment and increase the audience viewing figures. These can benefit the sport, but many people think they interfere with the flow of the game.

- The supporters may not benefit if the timing of events is changed to fit in with a TV schedule or if ticket prices increase due to the club's success and higher profile.

- Sponsorship deals with media companies may also mean that sports coverage changes from being free-to-view to pay-per-view.

4 Take a look at the questions in the table below, and the disadvantages of sponsorship in sport. Link the disadvantages to the questions.

    a) For each disadvantage describe why you think that this has happened. Could it be changed?

    b) Discuss each of the questions in column one.

Question	Disadvantages of sponsorship
1 Archery is not a major sport, and receives minimal TV coverage. What could sports like archery do to attract more sponsorship?	**a)** Sponsors can exert a strong influence on a sport, e.g. by dictating rule changes, clothing requirements and timings of events.
2 Maria Sharapova and Lance Armstrong are high-profile stars who have been banned from their sports after failing drugs tests. How does this damage the sponsor and the star?	**b)** Sponsors tend to prefer high-profile, televised sports with charismatic stars. Minority sports find it much more difficult to attract sponsors.
3 Rugby League officials now have microphones and video camera. Why has this become commonplace?	**c)** Sponsors can withdraw support if a performer's image is damaged.
4 In return for the support of the sponsorship, funding and benefits she receives, athletes such as Simone Biles are obliged to take part in her sponsor's events as part of their contract. What are the benefits and drawbacks of this arrangement?	**d)** Performers are often required to spend time at a sponsor's event instead of resting or training for the next game/competition.

5 Create a mind map to summarise the disadvantages of sponsorship. Use separate branches for each of the parties affected by sponsorship deals.

REFLECTIVE LOG

Imagine that you are working for a major soft drinks company and you have been put in charge of the sponsorship budget for the coming year. Make a pitch to the company directors by producing a presentation or report on a female athlete or sportswoman.

- Why have you decided that you think she would be the best choice for the company to sponsor?
- What are the positives and negatives to the company for choosing this athlete?
- What are the benefits to the athlete of your company sponsoring her?

Checklist for success

✔ List examples of the main types of sponsorship, with real-life examples.

✔ Draw up case studies of sponsorship of different kinds (different types of sponsor, whether team/sport/individual, form of sponsorship).

✔ Create separate mind maps to summarise the benefits and possible drawbacks of sponsorship for the various parties affected. Add examples.

Sound progress

- I can identify the different types of sponsorship in sport: financial, clothing and facilities.
- I understand the role sponsorship plays for the performer, club and audience.
- I can list some problems with sponsorship.

Excellent progress

- I can describe the different forms that sponsorship can take, with examples.
- I can explain the advantages and disadvantages for sponsorship for the performer/team sponsor/event and audience.

Media

LEARNING OBJECTIVES
- Identify the different types of media coverage.
- Explain how the media function in sport.
- Describe the advantages and disadvantages of media coverage of sport.

How do the media cover sport? What are the benefits and drawbacks of media coverage of sport?

Starting point

The **coverage** of sport through the **media** has changed over the years. Originally, sport was provided through newspaper reports once a week. It was the development of outside broadcasting in the middle of the 20th century that made live coverage and commentary possible. This has given both television and radio a new dimension in reporting sport. Nowadays, with satellite television, internet, online services, social media and apps, the media have become a hugely influential part of sport.

1 Discuss how you find out about sport or watch/listen to sporting activities in the media. Make a list of all the different types of media you use. Which do you use most regularly? Which do you prefer?

Key terms

coverage: the ways in which the media present information (e.g. as news, entertainment)

media: the means or variety of forms of communicating information to an audience

Exploring the skills

The media have an important role within society and with that comes a responsibility to the audience. This is shown by the four functions illustrated in the chart.

Some people would argue that the media are too influential, but at other times the effect of the media can be exceptionally positive, as you will explore later in this topic.

2 What do you think is the most important role of the media? Discuss this question with classmates.

Sports coverage through the media is now accessible 24 hours a day, seven days a week. This progress has led to the introduction of different forms of media alongside the traditional forms of newspaper, radio and television. The types of coverage offered by the different media are summarised here.

Inform
Giving news that tells people what is currently happening in sport

Educate
Providing knowledge to the audience, e.g. through statistics, pundits' analysis of events

The role of the media

Entertain
Allowing the audience to enjoy their leisure time and offering entertainment without the need to take part

Advertise
Publicising and advertising the sport, products and athletes, which brings money into sport for development

Print media

Newspapers:

- Published daily or weekly with sports sections
- Sports-focused newspapers such as the *Racing Post* or *The Non-League Paper* in football

Magazines:

- General and specific information or articles on sport
- Interviews, advice and insight into sport
- Different ranges of audience targeted, e.g. running, cycling, fishing, golf

Broadcast media

Radio:

- Offers live coverage and bulletins with up-to-date information
- Sports-specific stations, e.g. BBC Radio 5 live and talkSPORT, as well as sports bulletins on other stations
- Can be listened to while on the move
- Allows people to interact and share opinions through phone-ins and interviews

Television:

- Non-subscription channels (e.g. BBC, ITV, Channel 4 and Channel 5) deliver sports to the audience.
- Funding for the BBC is via the licence fee and for other channels is via advertisement money.
- Channels can bid to show sports or those the government has **ring-fenced**.
- Subscription channels such as satellite/cable services and pay-to-view channels have led to improved broadcasting.
- Pay-to-view channels such as Sky Sports and BT Sports deliver channels with 24-hour coverage.

Internet and social media:

- The internet allows access to both broadcast and print media.
- It offers the audience up-to-date, accessible and varied information, as well as the means to look up past events and statistics.
- Websites provide information about athletes, sporting events and ticketing.
- Social media give fans access to information and video footage from individual athletes, team and sports events.
- Facebook, Twitter, Instagram, LinkedIn invite people to share and connect with their idols.

Sport	Ring-fenced events
Football	FIFA World Cup finals
	UEFA Euro Championships
	The FA Cup Final (also the Scottish Cup Final in Scotland)
Rugby Union	The Rugby World Cup Final
Rugby League	The Challenge Cup Final
Tennis	Wimbledon Tennis Finals
Multi-sport events	Summer and Winter Olympic Games

Key term

ring-fenced sports events: sports events that the government prevents the television companies from charging to watch, so that everyone can watch for free

3. Try to remember two or three sports stories from the last week. How did you find about them: via newspaper, internet, radio? How were they reported: in detail or with small amounts of information? What makes you remember these stories?

4. Over the course of a week make a record of the different types of sports media you are exposed to. Use a table similar to the one here to record the number of times or the amount of time you see each form of media and analyse which form of sports media you are exposed to the most.

Media	Form	Total time	Rank order
Print	Newspapers	2 hours	5
	Magazines	1 hour	7
	Books	3 hour	4
Broadcast	Radio	10 hours	2
	Television	14 hours	1
Internet and social media	Websites	2 hours	5
	Apps	10 hours	2

Developing the skills

The commercial and other benefits that the media bring have had a huge influence on sport. This can be positive or negative, depending on the perspective of those involved. For those sports that get wide coverage, there are many benefits from raising the profile of the sport through increased sponsorship (see Topic 10.4). However, media influence can also have negative consequences for the performers, the officials, the sport and the audience. The table summarises some of the positive and negative effects of the media's involvement in sport.

Positive effects of the media	Negative effects of the media
• Media coverage makes it easier to attract sponsorship. • Viewers can get a better view of the action. • Supporters gain more knowledge from media experts/analysis. • Media have influenced rule changes to the benefit of the sport, e.g. use of the Hawk-Eye tracking system in tennis and cricket. • Attendances increase as people want to watch their favourite athletes/team. • Increased money for pay, prizes, equipment and coaching. • Performers can become role models and personalities, develop their reputation, promote themselves and the products. • Media coverage can increase participation levels and interest in sports.	• Some sports get more exposure than others; minority sports lose out. • Media feeds an obsession with statistics, beating records, etc., rather than the skills of the sport. • Media influence is large, with sports changing formats to suit media needs (e.g. tennis tie break, cricket T20 format). • Attendances can drop as people stay at home to watch on TV or if entry to events becomes too expensive. • Pay-to-view television channels mean many people can't access certain events. • Changes to the event timings to suit the media not the players or the fans (Friday Night Football on Sky Sports). • Increased exposure can lead to a loss of privacy, even attacks on performers and their families. • Performers can abuse their status, e.g. through offensive comments or behaviour, leading to fines and loss of sponsors. • Changes to the playing season such as with Rugby League becoming a summer sport. • **Sensationalisation** by the media to promote events can affect people's views of sports and individuals. • Over-exposure can lead to loss of interest in the sport. • Sports may become dependent on the money brought in by the media.

5 Using the information in the table, create a mind map to summarise the positive and negative effects of the media on sport. Create separate branches for:

a) performers

b) the sport in general

c) individual sports events

d) the audience/spectators.

6 Another group of people involved in sport that has felt the effect of media influence are people such as coaches, trainers and match officials, all of whom can come under the glare of the media spotlight.

Choose one of the groups below and do some internet research to investigate what effects the media can have on the person and their role:

Key term

sensationalisation: the reporting of something in a way that intentionally arouses curiosity by exaggerating a story or situation or focusing on certain details

a) officials – e.g. football referee Mark Clattenburg

b) coaches/trainers – e.g. Manchester United boss Sir Alex Ferguson

c) sports governors – e.g. former UEFA boss Sepp Blatter.

Applying the skills

The media coverage through television is still the most influential for sport. In 2016, Sky paid £4.81 billion for the TV rights to show the English Premier Football League and Fox Networks paid the NFL (the National Football League) $1.1 billion per year to show American Football on their channel and other platforms such as applications (apps) and website. Deals such as these certainly appear lucrative for the clubs, owners and players, as well as generating enormous publicity for the media companies. However, these developments also present challenges, as the competition for media attention and revenue can affect other parts of the sport or the audience.

Televised sports event	Date and time	Broadcaster	Viewing figures (millions)
UEFA Champions League Final Real Madrid vs Atlético Madrid	Saturday 28 May, 7.45pm	BT Showcase free view	1.28
Premier League Presentation Game West Ham Utd vs Manchester Utd	Tuesday 10 May, 7.45pm	Sky Sports	1.18
EUOPA League Final Liverpool vs Sevilla	Wednesday 18 May, 7.45pm	BT Sport Subscription only	1.65
UEFA Champions League Semi Final Manchester City vs Real Madrid	Tuesday 26th April, 7.45pm	BT Sport Subscription only	0.89
FA Cup Final Manchester Utd vs Crystal Palace	Saturday 21 May, 5.30pm	BBC 1 free to air channel	6.49
Olympic Games Rio 2016 Swimming, Rugby 7s, Cycling	Sunday 7 August, 7.30pm	BBC free to air channel	5.47
Euro 2016 Final Portugal vs France	Sunday 10 July 8.00pm	BBC free to air	12.27
Wimbledon Men Singles Tennis Final Andy Murray vs Milos Raonic	Sunday 10 July 1.50pm	BBC free to air	9.26

Viewing figures: (Source www.BARB.co.uk)

7 The table summarises viewing figures for a range of events in 2016. Using the knowledge you have gained of the media, try to interpret the data in the table by answering the following questions:

a) Which events had the highest viewing figures? Why do you think they were most popular?

b) Which events had the lowest viewing figures? Why do you think they were least popular?

c) Which broadcasters transmitted the most popular events?

d) What influence do you think date and time of broadcast had?

e) What issues can you identify in these figures and implications for sports, broadcasters and audience?

8 Write a short report discussing the issues surrounding the role of the television in sport. Use the figures in the table and any other information from this topic.

REFLECTIVE LOG

Produce a blog or podcast looking at the functions of the media, the different types of media and the advantages and disadvantages of the media in sport.

Checklist for success

✔ Sketch a diagram illustrating the roles of the media in relation to sport.

✔ Make a list of different forms of media and the kind of coverage they provide.

✔ Draw a mind map summarising the advantages and disadvantages of media coverage for all those affected: audience/spectators, performers, officials, the sport itself and individual sports events.

Sound progress

• I can identify the different types of media coverage used in sport.

• I can outline the advantages and disadvantages of the media in sport.

Excellent progress

• I can explain the role of the media in sport and describe the ways in which different types of media provide coverage.

• I can describe the advantages and disadvantages of the media as they affect the audience/spectators, performers, the sport and sports events.

Global events

LEARNING OBJECTIVES
- Identify the advantages and disadvantages of hosting global sports events.
- Understand how global sports events can affect areas of sport and society.
- Describe the effects of global sports events on different host cities/countries.

What are the effects upon sport and society of hosting global sports events?

Starting point

Hosting major global sports events has become a very sought-after prize for cities and countries. When London hosted the Olympics Games in 1948 after World War 2, very few cities wanted to host the games, and it became known as the 'austerity games', as it cost very little to put on: just £730,000. Today the process of becoming a **host city** or **host nation** is long and expensive, with the bidding process taking years and costing vast sums of money.

In September 2013, Tokyo was awarded the 2020 Olympic Games, ahead of rival Istanbul. When the decision was announced, the contrast in emotions between the delegates from the two countries was enormous, as can be seen in the photo.

The stakes seem to be very high, so why do countries and cities do battle over hosting these global events? The benefits of hosting these major sporting events must be huge. We will explore these in this topic.

> **Key term**
>
> **host city/nation:** a place that provides the space and other necessary things for a special event such as the Olympic Games

Exploring the skills

What kind of events do nations and cities bid to host? They tend to be global sports events, which could be either single-sport or multi-sports events.

- Multi-sports events are competitions that involve many different sports, bringing together athletes from different disciplines to live and compete in an environment of mixed sports. For example, the Olympic Games has many different sports that go on throughout two weeks of competition.

- Single-sport events have only one sport as the focus for competition, e.g. the World Badminton Championships. Within the championships, there may be different categories of competition, such as singles and doubles, separate men's and women's events, mixed events and events for disabled competitors.

1 Identify the event. Can you group the logos of these competitions into two lists of global sporting events: single-sport and multi-sports events?

Can you think of more examples in each category?

So, what are the benefits for these cities/countries in hosting these global competitions? Over the years many cities/countries have managed to organise successful and spectacular events that have proved beneficial to both the sport and the society. These benefits have come in a wide range of areas, as diverse as a general lift in national morale to a massive boost to the country's economy. The table lists some of the major benefits of hosting.

2 Read through the table and think of examples of countries that have hosted sporting events in recent years where that benefit has occurred.

Area	Advantages of hosting a global competition
Stadia and training facilities	Improved sports facilities are built that can be used both before and after the competition.
Home advantage	Hosting an event can give a country home advantage, with more spectators cheering home performers on. Performers also benefit from competing in a familiar environment and climate.
National pride	Can create a buzz for the country's residents, improving optimism and a sense of national pride.
Tourism	Increase in tourism with more visitors to the country, spending money on hotels, food, souvenirs and so on. This can lead to improved status and awareness of the city/country.
Economy and employment	Good for the economy with financial benefits from visitors at the time of the competition and from those who visit afterwards. Increased employment during the event.
Legacy implications	Event offers a legacy, in terms of better facilities available both for elite training and community use. Increased interest can lead to more participation in sports.
Infrastructure	Improved infrastructure around the venues and main cities such as road, rail and accommodation, offering longer-term benefits to the local society.

We have looked at what the countries, cities and the citizens have to gain from major global events, but what about the athletes taking part in these competitions? What is in it for them?

By competing at these global events, they gain a platform to compete against the best in the world. This can lead to further rewards and benefits that allow them to develop their careers. It can result in financial security through sponsorship and contracts. They become role models and an inspiration for others to achieve the same level of success.

Competing at global events can also bring pressures that affect performance negatively, causing athletes to make poor decisions. Examples of this are those who have cheated to reach the top, such as US cyclist Lance Armstrong and UK athlete Dwain Chambers.

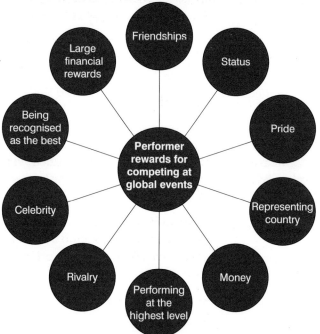

Developing the skills

Hosting a major sporting event can also have its drawbacks, as many host cities and nations have discovered over the years. The table lists some of the downsides to being the host.

Area	Disadvantages of hosting a global competition
Stadia and training facilities	Sports facilities can be a potential target of terrorists or those seeking to make their political views known.
Home advantage	Added pressure on performers from home nations to do well.
National pride	If the home team does not perform well, that can lead to a lowering of morale and feelings of negativity or pessimism.
Tourism	Increased tourism can put pressure on facilities (e.g. traffic jams, transport problems). Tourists' experience can also be negative and create bad publicity for the host nation.
Economy and employment	Risk of the competition being poorly organised or not run efficiently, which gives the country a poor image.
Legacy implications	If not managed properly, legacy benefits can quickly disappear.
Infrastructure	Huge financial cost of investing in infrastructure and sports facilities. Security concerns and the cost of added security.

3 Read through the table and think of examples of these problems or disadvantages to hosting a global event. What other disadvantages can you think of?

Applying the skills

In the next table, you will read about two global events, both of which presented the hosts with major issues to overcome and left substantial legacies in different ways.

	Montreal Olympic Games 1976	South Africa Rugby World Cup 1995
Cost	Estimated cost was $310 million Actual cost was $1.5–2 billion (paid off 30 years later thanks to a specific tax on tobacco)	Relatively low as it was a single-sport event and most stadia used were already used for club rugby
Background	Issues of **corruption**, mismanagement, labour disputes and high security costs	South Africa (SA) had missed the first two World Cup rugby competitions because of its policy of **apartheid**
Political and other issues	Huge debt for the city's tax payers, the Olympic stadia not all finished and costs mounted Political **boycotts** by 22 African states because of New Zealand's presence at Games (NZ had competed in South Africa during apartheid) Boycott by Taiwan because of Canada's links with China Premier of Quebec tried to stop Queen Elizabeth II coming to the games	Post-apartheid SA criticised by some for hosting 'white elite' sporting event President Nelson Mandela also criticised for his support of the event and for reaching across the 'great divide'
Positives from the games	6000 athletes from 88 countries Romanian gymnast Nadia Comaneci scoring seven perfect 10s on her way to winning three gold medals Bruce Jenner winning the decathlon Facilities still in use today to develop talented athletes all in very close proximity	Opportunity to show the new SA post-apartheid and bridge cultures Mandela in his SA shirt greeting the white SA team captain on the pitch prior to the opening game Chester Williams, the only black member of the SA squad, scoring a number of tries during the tournament South Africa winning the tournament Marked a positive future for SA: 'One team, one nation'

4 Find out more about the two events by researching on the internet.

5 An event may be seen at the time to be positive, but as time passes by then the true impact of the event might be felt.

a) Research at least two events from the list here, focusing on the issues mentioned. What benefits did hosting the events bring to the host cities/nations? What problems or negative issues impacted on the event and the hosts?

(If you prefer, choose other events in sports you are especially keen on.)

Los Angeles 1984 Olympic Games	(Commercialisation)
Barcelona 1992 Olympic Games	(No boycotts)
Athens 2004 Olympic Games	(After-effects of the Games)
Beijing 2008 Olympic Games	(Human rights)
South Africa 2010 FIFA World Cup	(First World Cup on African soil)
London 2012 Olympic Games	(Legacy and sustainability)
London 2012 Paralympic Games	(Legacy and sustainability)
Brazil 2014 FIFA World Cup	(Social inequality)

b) Produce a PowerPoint presentation that highlights the positives and negatives of the event. Give your opinion as to whether the event was, or wasn't, a success.

Key terms

corruption: dishonest behaviour by people with power, e.g. bribery or altering information for their own gain

apartheid: official policy of racial segregation formerly practised in the Republic of South Africa, involving political, legal, and economic discrimination against non-white people

boycott: refusing to take part in an event as a protest against a particular issue (whether sports-related or political)

REFLECTIVE LOG

What do you think about hosting global events? Is it something you think your city/country should become involved in? What would be the benefits for your city/country? What possible drawbacks can you see? What kind of events could your city/country host?

Reflect on the issues you have explored in this unit and present your arguments in favour of/against hosting a global event: for example, as a written report or a presentation.

Checklist for success

✔ Learn the list of the advantages of hosting global sports events, giving examples from actual events.

✔ For each advantage, suggest a corresponding disadvantage and think of a real-life example.

Sound progress

• I can identify the advantages of hosting a global event for a host city/nation, with examples.

• I can list some disadvantages of hosting a global event giving case study examples.

Excellent progress

• I can explain the positive effects of hosting global events for the societies and economies of host cities/nations.

• I can describe the pitfalls and problems of hosting and the negative effects it can have.

Professional and amateur performers

LEARNING OBJECTIVES
- Identify the differences between professional and amateur performers.
- Explain the blurred lines between professional and amateur status.
- Describe how sportsmanship and gamesmanship are displayed in physical activities.

What is the difference between professional and amateur performers?

Starting point

Most people that take part in sport are **amateur**, as they do so for the enjoyment of performing and being in the social environment that sport can offer. Over the years, commercialisation crept into sport through the involvement of sponsorship and media deals, and almost all top-level sport is now organised on a **professional** basis.

The professionalisation of sport has been happening for a very long time, but was not always seen as a positive step. The origins and rules of many modern sports can be traced back to British schools in the 1800s attended by members of the upper classes. For example, the game of rugby originated at Rugby School. In these schools it was believed that that the purest form of sport was amateur (without payment or reward).

On the other hand, professional athletes tended to come from the lower classes, because they competed for money, often from bets. Among amateurs, it was felt that competing for money was not 'gentlemanly'.

 Sports such as athletics, tennis, rugby and squash have clear links to this period in sports history. Do some research into one or more of these sports to learn more about their amateur origins.

> ### Key terms
>
> **amateur:** engaging in a sports pursuit, on an unpaid basis
>
> **professional:** performing a sports activity as one's main paid occupation, rather than a pastime

Exploring the skills

So what does it mean to be amateur or professional? The following table compares the two.

Amateur	Professional
Sport is a leisure activity.	Sport is their job.
Amateurs take part for the enjoyment.	Professionals take part for money.
Taking part is more important than the result.	Winning is the main aim, as they can often receive more money when they win more.
Training is done during their spare time, fitted in around other commitments such as work and family.	Training and playing is their job. This is a full-time occupation to be ready to perform and be in prime condition to do so.
They choose when and where to take part.	They perform where and when they are told to (by clubs, managers, sponsors, etc.).

2 Looking at these differences, consider the positives and negatives of becoming a professional. Imagine you are about to make the decision to become a professional or stay as an amateur. You play at a high level of amateur hockey and have a job that you enjoy. (Instead of hockey, you could think of a sport you play regularly.)

Produce a table similar to the one here to weigh up the factors influencing in your decision.

Amateur	Professional
I might not like training all the time and not enjoy the sport any more.	I can give up my job and focus on training to be a better at my sport.
	If I concentrate on my sport more I am more likely to ...

Professionalism became a major issue in sports in the 19th century, with different sports handling the issue in very different ways. Football and Rugby League went professional early on, but athletics and Rugby Union tried to keep their sports predominately for the 'gentleman amateur', the term given to upper-class individuals playing sport at the highest level.

Two members of the 1991 England Rugby Team and the jobs they held when they played rugby for England	British athletes who have had to make a living while competing for their country and collecting international honours

Brian Moore – solicitor

Rory Underwood – RAF pilot

Linford Christie – unemployed

Kelly Holmes – Army PT instructor

- In athletics, the Amateur Athletic Association was set up in 1880; no professional athletes were allowed to join.

- In 1997, the IAAF (International Amateur Athletic Federation) began to give out prize money to successful athletes at IAAF competitions for the first time.

- In football, professionalism was formally legalised in England in 1885 (1893 in Scotland).

- In 1895, rugby was split into league and union, with union remaining amateur until 1995.

Some of the last sports to become professional include Rugby Union and those that now allow 'open' competition, such as tennis.

The reason for these changes was the desire to improve levels of performance, alongside the increasing commercialisation of the sport.

Linford Christie retired as athletics became a 'professional' sport. He was unemployed when he won his first international event in 1986. So how did he and many other athletes mange to be amateur, but also follow a professional approach at the same time?

Key term

open: sports in which both professionals and amateurs can compete together (e.g. tennis and golf)

3 The table lists some of the ways in which amateur performers could fund their training and compete without being strictly professional.

a) Complete the 'Professional funding' column to indicate how professionals could receiving funding to be a professional athlete. Areas to consider include the following: government funding, media, sponsorship and competition fees.

b) Give examples of professional sportspeople being funded in this way.

Amateur funding	Professional funding
Sponsorships – these pay the expenses of the athlete in return for their endorsement of clothing or services.	
Trust funds – prize money is paid into a trust fund for the athlete to take expenses and have the rest on retirement.	
Scholarships – universities offer places for talented athletes to study, train and represent the university.	
Gifts – gifts are given by businesses or friends that could be used or sold on for money.	
Token jobs – the athlete is employed by a company but the work involved is nominal.	

The example of athletics highlights the increased blurring between amateur and professional status that occurred in the late 20th century. The restriction of the sport to amateur athletes was being worked around, with most competitors effectively being professionals. As the distinction was so hard to enforce, it made sense for the sport's governing bodies to change the rules and allow professionals to compete.

Developing the skills

The Olympic Games is an example of changes in attitudes towards professional and amateur sport. At the 2016 Olympic Games in Rio there were 42 different sporting events. The vast majority of the competitors were professional. Once, however, the Olympic Games was only for amateur performers, but increasingly it become harder and harder to distinguish between amateur and professional:

- In the 1960s and 70s, some countries' competitors were effectively sponsored by their government to train and represent their nation (e.g. the former East Germany).

- Some athletes were being paid secretly so that they could compete.

- In 1971, The International Olympic Committee (IOC) changed the rules to allow athletes to receive compensation for missing work or funding, but only in certain sports.

- In 1986, permission was given for professionals to compete in each sport at the Olympic Games. The US basketball team lined up with world famous stars such as Michael Jordan.

4 Why is it in the interests of the IOC and the hosts of the Olympic Games to have professional sports stars at the games?

Although now a largely professional event, the Olympics does also provide the opportunity for amateur performers to compete. Over recent years some amateur athletes have become famous through determination rather than domination.

CASE STUDY: Eric Moussambani, swimmer

- Eric Moussambani or 'Eric the Eel' represented Equatorial Guinea at the 2000 Olympic Games in Sydney.

- He had learnt to swim only 8 months before the Games and had never swum in a 50 m pool before the Olympics.

- He won his heat in the 100 m freestyle as the other two swimmers were disqualified for false starts.

- In the semi-final he finished more than a minute behind the winner Pieter van den Hoogenband, who set a new world record.

- His time was 1:52.72. He eventually brought his personal best down to under 57 seconds.

Applying the skills

The view of what it means to be either amateur or professional over time has changed. This is clearly seen in the modern-day use of the terms, where 'amateurish' means clumsy or mediocre, whereas 'professional' means thorough and disciplined in your approach.

The distinction between amateur and professional also extends to ideas about the way in which sports should be played. For the 'gentleman amateur', it was essential to be seen to act as a gentleman and to behave in a sportsmanlike manor. Abiding by the rules and upholding the spirit of the game were priorities.

In many ways, this contrasts with what we often see in modern professional sport, where **sportsmanship** is often abandoned in favour of **gamesmanship** – the attempt to use any means possible to gain an advantage over your opponent. This involves behaviour such as time-wasting, appealing for decisions when you know that the decision should go against you, distracting your opponent, 'diving' in football (pretending you have been fouled when you have not been).

Gamesmanship is unfortunately commonplace in sport. Moments like the ones in the pictures show examples of athletes/coaches trying to exert influence on the official or opponent. These examples are not against the rules of the sport, but the question is whether they are against the spirit.

Key terms

sportsmanship: upholding the spirit of the game by being honest, playing by the rules and showing respect for your opponents

gamesmanship: seeking to gain an advantage in any way you can that is not against the rules; at times this may be unfair to your opponents and treads a fine line between cheating and playing by the rules

'Fergie time': Football manager Sir Alex Ferguson was sometimes accused of trying to intimidate match officials

Mind games to affect the opponent's performance

Last-minute substitution to waste time

5 Think of other examples of 'gamesmanship' in sports you are familiar with. You might find it entertaining to look up 'football dives' on YouTube to see some spectacular examples of one particular kind of gamesmanship.

Having said that, there are plenty of examples to prove that sportsmanship is far from dead in modern sport:

- During a rugby test series in 2005, Colin Charvis of Wales was accidentally knocked unconscious by Jerry Collins of New Zealand. Collins' teammate Tana Umaga was concerned and ran over to put Charvis in the recovery position. In recognition of this act, Umaga was later awarded the Pierre de Coubertin medal for sportsmanship.

- In 2005, England cricketer Andrew (Freddie) Flintoff chose not to celebrate in front of Brett Lee after England defeated Australia in the Ashes Series.

- In a 5000 metres heat at the 2016 Rio Olympics, New Zealand athlete Nikki Hamblin tripped and fell, accidentally tripping up the USA's Abbey D'Agostino. The American got up and instead of running on, helped Hamblin up. D'Agostino herself later fell again and Hamblin helped her up and the two ran the race together. Both were handed places in the final, but the injury prevented the American taking part.

6 Produce an article on sportsmanship and gamesmanship that could be added to a website or a podcast. Include:

a) examples of both gamesmanship and sportsmanship

b) the principles of the gentleman amateur and the push for sportsmanship

c) whether professionalisation of sport has led to a greater acceptance of gamesmanship.

> **REFLECTIVE LOG**
>
> Reflect on what you have learned in this unit about amateurs and professionals, and sportsmanship and gamesmanship. Make a poster highlighting the four main areas you have studied:
>
> - what it means to be amateur and professional
> - how the lines between amateur and professional performers became blurred
> - professionals and amateurs at the Olympics
> - the effect of professionalisation on sportsmanship and gamesmanship.

Checklist for success

✔ Learn the definitions of amateur and professional and summarise the differences between the two statuses.

✔ Draw up a timeline marking key moments when sports became professional.

✔ Use examples and case studies to illustrate acts of sportsmanship and gamesmanship.

Sound progress

- I can identify the difference between a professional and an amateur performer.

- I can recognise the social and other changes that make it difficult to keep the amateur ideal.

- I can give examples of sportsmanship and gamesmanship.

Excellent progress

- I can describe the blurring of lines between professional and amateur sports with examples.

- I can describe the factors that changed the Olympic Games to an open competition.

- I can link the rise of professionalisation and commercialisation to changes in sporting behaviour, such as sportsmanship and gamesmanship.

Technology in sport

LEARNING OBJECTIVES
- Identify the different forms of technology used in sport.
- Understand how technology is used in sport by officials, improving performance, recording time and distance.
- Describe the positive and negative impact of technology on sport.

How does the use of technology affect performance and decision-making in sport?

Starting point

Technology has had a major impact in the world of sport, affecting almost every area:

- how officials organise events and make decisions
- how performers train for events and deliver their best performance
- how athletes' performances are measured and recorded
- how sports are enjoyed by spectators, whether in the venue or watching via the media.

Sports such as Formula 1 and cycling tend to be at the forefront of technology. The cars and bikes are developed to ensure maximum streamlining and efficiency. Every piece of equipment, from helmets to shoes, is tested and refined. The teams use science to make sure that their performers are able to achieve their quickest times, are at their optimal weight and strength, and are in perfect control of their equipment. If they do not continue to evolve their technology, they will be at a disadvantage compared with the other competitors.

New and innovative clothing, footwear, racquets, clubs and balls are developed through technological innovation. They all help improve the athlete's performance in accordance with the rules of their sport.

Here are two examples of how technology is used to help in training and preparation.

Altitude

Altitude tents are artificial environments used to recreate living and training at altitude (see Topic 7.2), in which athletes breathe in oxygen-reduced air for the purpose of improved performance.

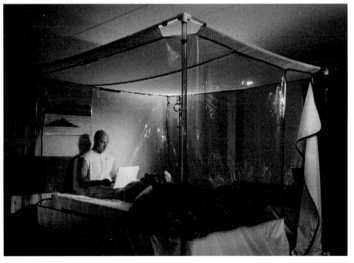

Multisensor monitoring (e.g. Viper Pod)

Placed into a holder on a vests it is used for data analysis of an athlete's physical performance, such as heart rate, movement around the field of play, speed, effort and intensity levels.

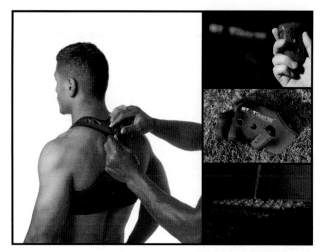

Exploring the skills

The types of technology available in each sport vary, but they tend to be found in areas such as protective equipment, training aids, stadia improvements, sports medicine and so on.

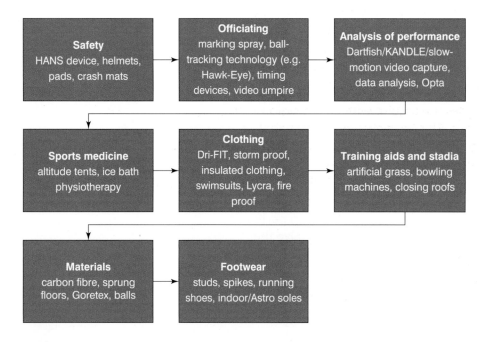

1. Read through the flow diagram of sports technology. Use the internet to find out more about any terms and references to technology that you are not familiar with. Discuss the examples listed with classmates. Which sports would they be used in?

2. Choose two different sports, such as a racket sport (e.g. tennis) and a team sport (e.g. cricket). Produce your own flow diagram like the one above. On it note down the technology used in each category by the two sports.

Making the correct decision in sport is vital, with the large sums of money involved and the investments of sponsors and the media. The use of technology in decision-making by officials has resulted in huge advances. Some of these are outlined here.

Ball-tracking (e.g. Hawk-Eye)	Hawk-Eye is a complex computer system used in sports such as cricket and tennis to visually track the trajectory of the ball and show its most likely path.
Infra-red imaging system (e.g. Hot Spot)	Infra-red imaging systems are used in cricket to determine whether the ball has struck the batsman, bat or pads; this helps the umpire to decide whether a batsman is in or out.
Fully automatic time (FAT)	FAT is a method of timing a race where the clock is activated by sensors in the starting blocks and stopped by line-scan cameras using a laser line at the finish.
Goal-line technology (GLT)	GLT is a used to determine whether the ball has crossed the goal line; a radio signal can be sent to the referee's *watch* within a second.
Laser measurement (e.g. LaserLynx)	Laser-based distance measurement devices can produces accurate, computer-generated measurements for field events.

In tennis, ball-tracking provides the umpire with an indication of whether the ball is in or out. This has now advanced so that players can request a replay of the shot on the screen. Similarly in athletics, officials use line-scan cameras to determine who has won the race and laser cameras to measure distances in field events: for example, how far a javelin has been thrown or a long-jumper has jumped.

 3 Think of more examples of how new technology is used to help decision-making in sport. How has it changed sports that you play regularly or are keen on? What might the future hold? Can you think of further developments that might occur?

Developing the skills

The introduction of new technology has had effects on all those involved: performers, officials, spectators and the sport itself. Not all of these effects have been positive. The table suggests some of the positive and the negative impacts new technology has had.

10.8

Effect on ...	Positive effects	Negative effects
Performer	• Improvements in training leading to improved performance. • Able to review decisions in competition that may go against them unfairly.	• Not all performers have access to the best technology. • Gives advantage to performers from wealthier countries. • Can interrupt or slow down the game.
Sport	• Fairer and more consistent decision-making. • Adds drama and suspense while the decision is made. • Brings in more investment.	• Can disrupt and slow play down if used too often. • Doesn't always give the correct decision. • Investors such as media companies may demand more influence in return for investment.
Audience/ spectators	• Better informed from expert analysis, replays, different camera angles. • Can see how decisions are made and trust that they are fair. • Added excitement in drama of waiting for the decision.	• May see errors or poor decisions if viewing on platforms with technology that the officials don't have, causing problems for the officials and sport. • To keep play fast only a few reviews are allowed, so mistakes are still made if the team/player has no reviews left.
Officials	• Help to make the correct decisions. • Improved communication with colleagues.	• Reversed decisions may lead to officials being undermined. • May become too reliant on the systems to make decisions.

4 Look at the equipment/technology that has been introduced to sport over recent years. Choose two from the list below to identify the effects of technology on the audience, performers, officials and sport. Present this as a poster, mind map or PowerPoint presentation:

a) ball-tracking in tennis (Hawk-Eye)

b) goal-line technology in football

c) the use of video referees in both codes of rugby

d) performance analysis aids such as Viper Pods or bike technology

e) the use of laser camera systems for recording time and distance.

Applying the skills

The introduction of some modern technology has been embraced by certain sports such as tennis, athletics and rugby. Other sports, such as football, have been slower to adopt it: in the UK goal-line technology has been permitted in matches since 2012, but is not required and is currently used only at the highest levels of the game. Other recent developments in football include:

- having a button on the flag so the referee knows his assistant has flagged
- the use of microphones allowing officials to speak to each other about decisions
- the use of a spray marker to make sure the wall is the correct distance from the ball.

5 The next step for football could be to move towards using video referees or having 'open microphones', so that everyone can hear the conversations the referee has with his colleagues, or with players and managers.

a) Make the arguments for and against the introduction of either video referees or open microphones into football. Considerations include:

- how it would work practically
- how the method you have come up with will affect the game
- how it will affect the players, sport, official and audience
- what role the media will have to play
- the effect on those that play the sport outside top-level sport
- cost.

b) Make your recommendation as to whether or not to introduce the new technology, based on the arguments you have discussed.

> **REFLECTIVE LOG**
>
> For a sport of your choice produce an information sheet looking at the types of technology used and how technology has changed the sport. Explain the advantages and disadvantages of these technologies in this sport.
>
> Think about the aids that are used to help the officials. Why are they a benefit? If they don't have any technological aids for the official, then what might help them?

Checklist for success

✔ Create a dossier of examples of different forms of technology used in sport.

✔ List examples of how technology is used by the different people involved for different purposes.

✔ Draw up a table outlining the positive and negative impact of technology on sport.

Sound progress

• I can give examples of how technology is used in various ways in sport.

• I can suggest how this has had both a positive and a negative impact.

Excellent progress

• I can describe in detail the use of technology in all aspects of sport, from athletes' training to officials' decision-making.

• I can explain the positive and negative impacts of technology on sport on all those involved.

Check your progress

Use these statements as a way of evaluating your progress throughout this chapter.

Sound progress

- I can identify factors that influence which recreational activities people do in their leisure time.
- I can list the factors that influence the growth in leisure activities.
- I can identify the different stages of the sports development pyramid.
- I can outline the pathways performers must follow to progress up the pyramid.
- I know what is involved in the work of sports development officers.
- I can list the factors that affect people's access to physical activities.
- I can identify the factors that affect participation, with examples.
- I can suggest strategies for improving access and participation.
- I can identify the different types of sponsorship in sport: financial, clothing and facilities.
- I understand the role sponsorship plays for the performer, club and audience.
- I can list some problems with sponsorship.
- I can identify the different types of media coverage used in sport.
- I can outline the advantages and disadvantages of the media in sport.
- I can identify the advantages of hosting a global event for a host city/nation, with examples.
- I can list some disadvantages of hosting a global event giving case study examples.
- I can identify the difference between a professional and an amateur performer.
- I can recognise the social and other changes that make it difficult to keep the amateur ideal.
- I can give examples of sportsmanship and gamesmanship.
- I can give examples of how technology is used in various ways in sport.
- I can suggest how this has had both a positive and a negative impact.

Excellent progress

- I can explain with examples what factors influence people's choices of recreational activities.
- I can explain the effects of different factors on the growth of leisure activities.
- I can describe the four stages of the sports development pyramid and the characteristics of each stage.
- I can describe in detail what support performers need to progress through the pyramid.
- I can summarise the role of different people and organisations involved in sports development and the support they offer.

- I can describe how factors such as age and disability can affect people's access to physical activities in a wide range of ways.
- I can explain how various factors affect participation with a wide range of examples.
- I can describe a range of strategies for increasing access and participation, including more promotion, better provision and greater access.
- I can describe the different forms that sponsorship can take, with examples.
- I can explain the advantages and disadvantages for sponsorship for the performer/team sponsor/event and audience.
- I can explain the role of the media in sport and describe the ways in which different types of media provide coverage.
- I can describe the advantages and disadvantages of the media as they affect the audience/spectators, performers, the sport and sports events.
- I can explain the positive effects of hosting global events for the societies and economies of host cities/nations.
- I can describe the pitfalls and problems of hosting and the negative effects it can have.
- I can describe the blurring of lines between professional and amateur sports with examples.
- I can describe the factors that changed the Olympic Games to an open competition.
- I can link the rise of professionalisation and commercialisation to changes in sporting behaviour, such as sportsmanship and gamesmanship.
- I can describe in detail the use of technology in all aspects of sport.
- I can explain the positive and negative impacts of technology on sport on all those involved.

Chapter 11
Ethics and other issues

Starting points

In this topic, you will develop an understanding of the ethical influences on sport and performance. This includes the troubled topic of the use of drugs in sport to enhance performance. You will also explore how to assess and minimise the risks involved in physical activity. You will also learn how to treat common injuries, should they occur.

You will:

- investigate the reasons why some athletes use performance-enhancing drugs (PEDs)
- explain the disadvantages of using PEDs and the negative consequences of drug scandals
- examine the reasons why some performers use blood doping
- describe how blood doping is carried out, what its effects and potential side effects are

- identify different types of risk in sporting environments and assess them
- suggest strategies for reducing risk and injury in physical activities
- describe the causes of, and treatments for, minor injuries
- explain the causes of bruises, muscle, tendon and ligament injuries
- find out how to use the RICE method for treating injuries.

Chapter contents

The activities you complete will primarily relate to theoretical work, but you will also be exploring practical situations and your own experiences to understand the ethical issues in sport.

You will:

- create a mind map of reasons why performers turn to PEDs
- investigate the four main types of PEDs and their links to particular sports
- think of strong arguments to persuade people not to use PEDs
- outline the role of national and international bodies in combatting the use of PEDs
- learn about the main methods of blood doping: use of EPO and blood transfusions
- show how blood doping can have negative effects by annotating an outline of the human body

- give examples of real and perceived risks for particular physical activities
- create a mind map summarising the possible causes of risk
- draw up a risk assessment form for evaluating risks in sporting environments
- outline strategies for minimising risk and injury for particular physical activities
- suggest a cause of, and outline treatment for, minor injuries such as cuts or blisters
- give examples of physical activities or sports where particular injuries are likely to occur
- explain the four stages of treatment using the RICE method.

Some athletes choose to use performance-enhancing drugs.

Performance-enhancing drugs (PEDs)

LEARNING OBJECTIVES
- Describe the different types of PEDs and their effects on performance.
- Understand the reasons why some performers use prohibited PEDs.
- Explain the disadvantages of using PEDs.
- Describe the negative consequences of drug scandals.

What are performing-enhancing drugs (PEDs) and do performers use them?

Starting point

Over the years there have been many high-profile cases of sportsmen and women using **performance-enhancing drugs**. One of the most recent and widespread cases was that of the 68 Russian athletes banned from the Rio Olympics in 2016. There are athletes who will take extreme measures to achieve success. Although there are rigorous tests in place to check for use of drugs, some athletes consider it worth taking the risk, in order to improve their performance and have a higher chance of winning.

The use of drugs in this way is one of the major **ethical** issues affecting sport.

1 The reasons why some performers take PEDs are to gain an advantage and achieve success, although their reasons are not always so straightforward. Look at the pictures of the eight sports performers and identify:

a) what their sport is

b) what drugs they used and why

c) when they were banned and how long for.

Key terms

performance-enhancing drugs (PEDs): chemical substances that change the chemical balance of the body when taken, affecting the performer's ability and providing an unfair advantage when performing

doping: the use of illegal substances (PEDs) by athletes or sports performers in order to improve their performances

ethical: to do with morals or principles; ethical behaviour involves high moral standards, being honest and following the correct code of conduct

Exploring the skills

You have researched some of the high-profile cases of performers using PEDs and what happened to them, but the question still remains: why did they use PEDs? The mind map below shows some of the reasons often given.

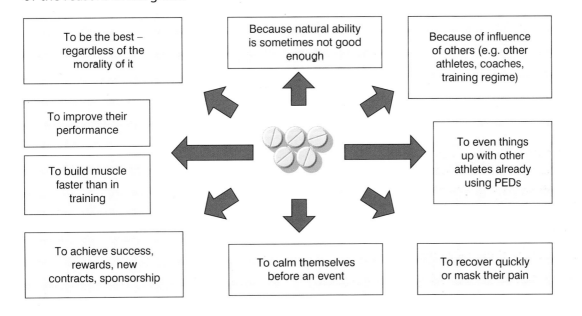

2 Looking at the statements in the mind map, identify three that you feel are clear reasons for *not* taking PEDs. Write a statement to present your opinions, showing your understanding of the reasons and the consequences of someone taking this action.

Performers who use drugs to improve their performance know the risks they are taking to achieve their goals. They risk being found out and banned from their sport, damaging their reputation and losing sponsorship. However, the consequences can go even further; using PEDs can affect their health.

The table includes information about four of the most common types of the PED: <u>b</u>eta blockers, <u>a</u>nabolic steroids, <u>d</u>iuretics and <u>s</u>timulants. (To remember these, take the first letter of each to create the mnemonic **BADS**.)

Type of PEDs	How they affect performance	Risks	Associated with
Beta blockers	• Prevent adrenaline in order to keep heart rate low • Calming and relaxing effect • Reduce anxiety	• Reduce blood pressure • Cause tiredness • Heart failure • Depression	• Archery • Diving • Shooting • Snooker
Anabolic steroids	• Increase muscle mass fast • Let athlete train harder for longer • Increase power and strength • Speed up recovery time	• Aggressive behaviour • Heart disease • High blood pressure • Liver problems • Effect on hormones	• Athletics • Baseball • Cycling • Football • Rugby
Diuretics	• Increase the amount of water passed out of the body • A way of reducing weight quickly • Mask other PEDs being used	• Dehydration • Weakening of the muscles • Kidney problems • Nausea	• Boxing • Equestrian • Gymnastics • Jockey
Stimulants	• Affect the central nervous system • Reduce pain • Increase alertness: mental and physical	• Addictive • High blood pressure • Strokes • Increased risk of injury as pain is suppressed	• Athletics • American football • Swimming

3 Choose one of the above PEDs and create a poster highlighting the following:

a) the sport(s) targeted

b) the reasons why someone doing that activity might take it

c) the risks involved.

Developing the skills

Sports performers at the highest level often experience pressure to be the greatest and achieve success in terms of victories and medals. The expectations of the fans, coaches and sponsors can be overwhelming. Many performers will take drugs in the full knowledge of the risks to their reputation, their health, their team and their sport. Nevertheless, they continue to take those risks in the search for fame, wealth and glory.

 4 What arguments can you use to try to stop someone taking drugs? For each of the reasons listed in the mind map earlier in this topic, suggest at least one strong argument to convince the person that it is not acceptable. Draw up a table listing your arguments, like the one here.

Reason for taking PEDs	Counter-argument: why the reason is not good enough
To be the best	Using PEDs means you do not have the natural ability or dedication to become the best without cheating.

Applying the skills

When a performer is caught using PEDs, the most immediate impact may be on them personally, through a ban or suspension, as well as loss of reputation. The effects can go wider, however. It can negatively affect the credibility of their sport. What drugs cheats don't consider is the direct impact it can have on their fellow competitors, teammates and country. For example:

British sprinter Dwain Chambers was banned for life in 2003 from the Olympic Games and stripped of all medals. Most notably was a European Gold medal for the 4 × 100 m relay, which meant his teammates (although they were clean) lost theirs too. He was later allowed back into athletics after winning an appeal.

The fight against use of PEDs is led by the **World Anti-Doping Agency (WADA)**. It was established in 1999 as an independent agency, funded equally by the sports movement and governments around the world. Its key activities include scientific research, education, development of anti-doping capacities and monitoring of the World Anti-Doping Code through structured and random testing doping across all sports.

Key term

World Anti-Doping Agency (WADA): an independent agency that monitors all sporting activities across the world, providing tests on performers and educating through scientific research

Each government that has athletes or performers competing at a national or international level must fund organisations called National Anti-Doping Organisations (NADOs). They are responsible for testing their own and any other athletes who compete inside their borders. There are also Regional Anti-Doping Organisations (RADOs), and testing regimes run by Olympic and Paralympic committees.

WADA and the other organisations have had a significant effect in the fight against doping through the use of the World Anti-Doping Code and its five standards:

- prohibited list – identifying all substances and methods whose use is banned

- testing investigations – establishing procedures for how samples will be collected and tested

- laboratories – set up by WADA to establish valid rest results and data

- therapeutic use exemptions (TUEs) – TUEs may be given if an athlete has valid medical reasons for taking a substance that could appear on the list

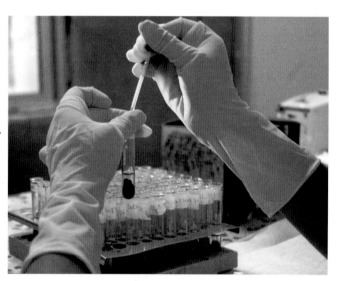

- protection of privacy and personal information – ensuring that all data that is gathered and analysed is kept confidential.

Of these standards the main focus now is on the testing of PEDs by the following methods:

- random selection – athletes can be called for drug testing at any time, in or out of competition

- blood testing – athletes are provided with a sealed kit in which to place two samples (A and B); if the kit has been tampered with, it must be returned

- urine sampling – similar to blood testing, although the sample must be given in view of an official of the same gender

- sample testing – samples are sent to a registered laboratory where sample A is tested; if a positive result is found, the athlete is notified before sample B is also tested

- sanctions – if both tests are positive, the relevant sporting organisations are notified; they decide what penalties or bans to impose.

5 Research the role of WADA in leading the fight against doping. Find examples of successes it has had in reducing the use of PEDs. Create a podcast or drama scene to raise awareness for young athletes and sports performers on 'the impact of taking PEDs' and promote the work that WADA does.

Despite WADA's high profile and many successes, the issues around using PEDs still continue as athletes and performers strive for success, financial gain and to be the best, whatever the cost.

 6 Create a campaign video or radio commercial to argue for the banning of PEDS and at the same time raise awareness of the organisations and mechanisms in place to help uncover and eradicate doping in sport. Focus on the three main reasons for banning PEDs:

a) health risks – the possible short- and long-term physical and mental health problems

b) unfair advantage – how PEDS provide an advantage in strength, power and recovery and how that undermines the notion of a 'level playing field'

c) morality – how use of PEDs goes against the ethics of being a sports performer and being a role model.

> **REFLECTIVE LOG**
> Reflect on what you have learned about performance-enhancing drugs. In your reflective log note down the top five reasons why you should never take PEDs.

Checklist for success

✔ Create a mind map of reasons why performers turn to PEDs.

✔ For every reason given for using drugs, suggest a strong counter-argument.

✔ Practise listing the effects and risks of the four main types of PED, identifying why they might be associated with particular sports.

✔ Summarise the role of national and international bodies in reducing and preventing drug use through testing, monitoring and education.

Sound progress

• I can identify what PEDs are and why some performers use them.

• I can describe the effects of PEDs and the risks involved in using them.

• I can outline the role of organising bodies in preventing the use of PEDs.

Excellent progress

• I can explain the impact that PEDs have upon a performer and why they would use them.

• I can explain the negative consequence of PEDs on both a performer and others.

• I can describe how national and international bodies help prevent drug use through testing, monitoring and education.

Blood doping

LEARNING OBJECTIVES
- Outline the reasons why some performers use blood doping.
- Describe how blood doping is carried out.
- Explain the effects and potential side effects of blood doping.

What is blood doping and why do people risk carrying it out?

Starting point

Blood doping is defined by WADA the (World Anti-Doping Agency) as the misuse of techniques and/or substances to increase a performer's red blood cell count. One of the most high-profile cases of blood doping involved the cyclist Lance Armstrong, who won the Tour de France seven times in a row.

We will discover the complexity of this illegal method of enhancing your performance that can also involve other PEDs.

Exploring the skills

Lance Armstrong admitted to using both EPO and blood transfusions as a way of enhancing his performance by increasing his aerobic fitness.

EPO, or **erythropoietin**, is a hormone naturally produced by human kidneys to stimulate red blood cell production. Cyclists and other athletes use EPO to increase their red blood cell counts. This allows more oxygen to be delivered to their muscles, improving recovery and endurance.

The presence of EPO can be detected through blood tests, which is why drugs cheats turned to using blood transfusions instead. However, this process is far more complicated and time consuming. It has to be carefully planned out by the athlete and requires the help of others. The timeline below shows the different stages involved in carrying out the doping.

A Blood is taken 3–4 weeks before a competition, usually at a point when haemoglobin levels are high (see Topic 3.1 to revise the role of haemoglobin in carrying oxygen).

B The blood is frozen to maintain the high haemoglobin levels that will produce more red blood cells.

C One or two days before the competition, the blood is thawed and then reintroduced to the performer via a blood transfusion.

Key terms

blood doping: the misuse of techniques and/or substances to increase a performer's red blood cell count, e.g. by using the hormone EPO or by injecting oxygenated blood into a performer before an event

EPO (erythropoietin): a hormone produced in the kidney that can also be artificially produced; it helps stimulate the production of red blood cells to carry more oxygen with haemoglobin to the muscles

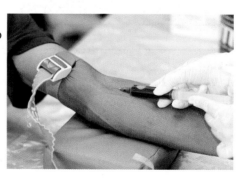

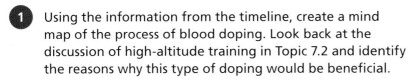

D This will increase the number of red blood cells in the body and the capacity to carry more oxygen.

E The performer's aerobic capacity is increased and they can perform for longer without fatigue.

The timeline shows the process of using the performer's own blood in doping. Transfusions can also be carried out using blood taken directly from another person. This carries a whole range of risks, as the blood may not be compatible between the two people.

1 Using the information from the timeline, create a mind map of the process of blood doping. Look back at the discussion of high-altitude training in Topic 7.2 and identify the reasons why this type of doping would be beneficial.

Developing the skills

Blood doping is used as a short-cut way of improving an athlete's aerobic fitness and allowing them to work harder and recover faster. However, these so-called benefits come at a cost. We are now aware of the many side effects that blood doping has.

Side effects include:

- blood becoming more viscous (thicker)
- increased chance of heart attacks, strokes pulmonary embolism (clot on the lung)
- risk of infection (when sharing blood)
- kidney disease (through EPO).

2 Carry out some research into athletes who have used blood doping and identify some of the health problems they experienced. Create a leaflet or poster warning potential cheats of the dangers they are putting themselves in.

3 Using a blank outline of the human body, summarise the risks and dangers of blood doping, by indicating the parts of the body affected and adding descriptions of the side effects.

Applying the skills

A screening test was introduced in the summer of 2000 for the Olympic Games in Sydney. First the blood was screened and this was followed up with a urine sample to detect synthetic EPO in the performer's blood.

Tests were then introduced in 2004 that can detect the use of blood transfusions involving a second person's blood. However, reliable tests have not yet been developed to detect transfusions of the athlete's own blood. WADA is funding research projects aimed at developing tests for these kinds of transfusion.

The authorities suspected Lance Armstrong of cheating, following his meteoric rise after recovering from cancer. He has since admitted taking steroids and using EPO and blood doping.

 4   Lance Armstrong was stripped of all his titles and prize money, which affected his 'Livestrong' brand. Which other sports have been affected by blood doping? What impact has it had on those sports? What has happened to the athletes/performers since?

REFLECTIVE LOG

Create a mind map that includes all information in the last two topics about PEDs and blood doping. Include the reasons for cheating in this way and the risks involved.

Checklist for success

✔ Summarise the main methods of blood doping: use of EPO and blood transfusions.

✔ Practise drawing the blood transfusion timeline to check your understanding of the process.

✔ Revise the side effects of blood doping by annotating a blank outline of the human body.

Sound progress

• I can identify reasons why performers would use blood doping to enhance their performance.

• I can describe the process that is used to undertake blood doping.

Excellent progress

• I can explain the reasons why people use blood doping and describe the side effects.

• I am aware of the impact that blood doping has upon a performer and the sport.

Risk and risk assessment

What are the risks involved in different physical activities and what can be done to minimise risks and injury?

Starting point

Participating in any physical activity has a risk involved. It is important to identify any potential or actual harm that might occur and to make the activity as safe as possible. Simple precautions taken before, during and after will reduce the likelihood of injury or fatality.

There are a number of different types of risks, including:

- **absolute risk** – the highest level of risk there could be before health and safety controls are identified and put in place
- **real risk** – the level of risk after taking into account safety controls and measures
- **perceived risk** – an individual's view of risk: what some people may think of as dangerous, others may not.

People's perception of a particular risk can often differ from the real risk (which can be statistically calculated).

Key terms

real risk: the amount of danger that actually exists in the activity

perceived risk: an individual's subjective or personal judgement about the dangers of an activity

risk assessment: a process used to evaluate the real risks involved in an activity

 Look at the following example that identifies real and perceived risks:

> A class is taking part in a session using an indoor climbing wall. The teacher has conducted a **risk assessment** and devised an action plan. For the students involved the perceived risk is low (they are secured to the wall by ropes). However, many of the parents will perceive the activity as high-risk (their children could fall off and injure themselves).

Write a similar paragraph, identifying the real and perceived risks involved in:

a) a javelin competition

b) a trampoline lesson

c) geocaching/orienteering around a local park.

Exploring the skills

To assess the risks involved in an activity you need to have a clear understanding of how they could be created. A real risk has a higher likelihood of happening than one merely perceived by another individual, as you have identified in task **1**, but you need to take account of both types of risk.

Risks may be caused by:

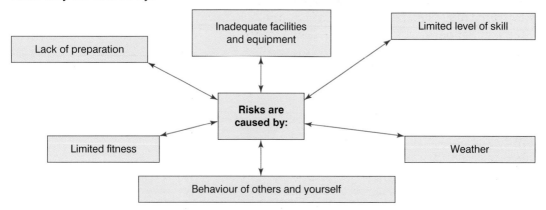

Conducting a thorough risk assessment will minimise the risk and help prevent accidents occurring. This involves the following steps:

- Identify the risks. What are the real risks? What are the perceived risks?
- Identify who is at risk. Who is at risk of harm and in what way?
- Evaluate the risks and decide on what to do next.
- Record your findings.
- Review your processes. What was a success? How could you improve it?

For example, in assessing the risks involved in squash, you would note these factors:

- The confined space restricts movement, with the potential for collision.
- Both players have racquets that can cause physical injuries.
- The ball is small and hard, and is the size of an eye socket.
- Although weather cannot contribute, the surface area of the court could become slippery.
- Those at risk are the players – they are also risk factors as behaviour can be unpredictable (e.g. if one player is losing).

2 Using the example for squash above, write a similar list of factors involved in one of the following sports:

a) judo in a sports hall

b) water polo in a swimming pool

c) hockey on an artificial pitch.

Developing the skills

An important stage is to assess the area that will be used for a particular activity. Your teachers, coaches and others have this duty of care and will do this before, during and after the activity. This is to make sure all real or potential risks are identified and measures put in place to minimise risks.

3 Look at the picture and identify which are real risks or what some people may perceive as risks. Indicate the level of potential danger – whether high or low. Provide a reason why you think this.

The table shows one method for assessing the level of risk involved in an activity. Each risk is given a rating (1–5) based on how severe it could be and a rating (1–5) based on the likelihood of it happening. The two ratings are multiplied using the equation:

Risk = Severity × Likelihood

The maximum rating will be 25 (5 × 5), while the minimum will be 1 (1 × 1).

Level	Severity	Example	Level	Likelihood	Example
1	Insignificant	Fall over	1	Rare	There will be a fire in a stadium.
2	Minor	Black eye	2	Unlikely	A player will suffer from heat exhaustion.
3	Moderate	Sprained ankle	3	Reasonable	A player will be hit by a ball.
4	Major	Dislocated shoulder	4	Likely	A skier will fall over.
5	Catastrophic	Death	5	Almost certain	A water skier will fall into the water.

4. Study the table and complete the examples.

Example	Severity (S)	Likelihood (L)	Risk (S × L)	Rating (1–25)
Collapse of a stadium	5	2	10	Low
Bruising in a boxing match				
Slipping on a wet floor in a badminton game				
Your own example				

5. In school there are many areas that are used for PE and sports where their use involves some risk, e.g. dance studio, cricket pitch or athletic track. Copy and complete the risk assessment table to provide details on what could be prevented and how.

Name of assessor	Date	Activity or Area	
Stage 1 What are the risks? Look around. Ask others. Identify: weather, equipment, facilities.	**Stage 2** Who is at risk? Players? Spectators?	**Stage 3** What is the level of risk? Which are low? Which are high? What are the perceived risks of those involved?	**Stage 4** What measures have been introduced to counter risks? Safety precautions? Instructions/rules? Demonstrations of good practice?

Applying the skills

There are many steps that can be taken to reduce risks:

- wearing protective clothing and footwear to prevent injuries
- lifting and carrying equipment safely and correctly
- maintaining a hydrated body during an activity
- using a warm-up to prepare and a cool-down to return body back to normal after an activity
- creating suitable levels of competition to make sure everyone can participate and not be at a disadvantage
- following rules and instructions to encourage fair play and prevent confrontation.

6 Look at these pictures of strategies used to reduce risk in different activities. Write down a description or verbally explain to a classmate (with the other person not looking at the book) what the image is without using the name of the object. To extend this task, think of other sports and how they have reduced risk through similar strategies.

REFLECTIVE LOG For a sport you take part in regularly, write a summary of the risks involved (both real and perceived). What is the level of risk? What strategies can be taken to minimise risk?

Checklist for success

✔ Give examples of real and perceived risks for particular physical activities.

✔ Create a mind map summarising the possible causes of risk.

✔ Draw up a risk assessment form for evaluating risks in sporting environments.

✔ Suggest strategies for minimising risk and injury for particular physical activities.

Sound progress

• I can describe what is meant by real and perceived risk.

• I can suggest ways of reducing the risks involved in physical activities.

Excellent progress

• I can give examples of real and perceived risks and describe the difference between them.

• I can assess the levels of risk involved in different activities.

• I can devise strategies for preventing risk or protecting against injury during physical activities.

Injuries

LEARNING OBJECTIVES
- Describe the causes of and treatments for minor injuries.
- Explain the causes of bruises, muscle, tendon and ligament injuries.
- Know how to use the RICE method for injuries.

What kind of injuries happen during physical activities and how should they be treated?

Starting point

Taking part in any physical activity or sport carries risks – one of the main risks is that you can get hurt or injured. Fortunately serious injuries are extremely rare; the majority of injuries suffered are **soft tissue** or **minor injuries**.

Whenever there is any injury to bones, joints, ligaments, muscles or tendons, blood vessels will be damaged. Broken blood vessels mean that blood leaks out – either through the skin or internally into tissues around the injury. As well as obvious external bleeding, this will lead to swelling, bruising and pain.

1 Have you ever been hurt or injured while taking part in a physical activity? What happened? How did you treat the injury, if at all? Share a few experiences with classmates.

Exploring the skills

Some of the most common minor injuries are described in the table, along with potential causes and simple treatments.

2 For each of the four types of injury listed in the table, think of situations when this might happen during physical activity or sport. What precautions can you take against each type of injury?

Key terms

soft tissue: soft parts of the body including tendons, ligaments, skin, fat, muscles, nerves and blood vessels; hard tissue is bones and teeth

minor injuries: injuries that can be dealt with at the scene of the incident by a first aider, such as cuts, bruises or grazes

Injury	Description	Cause	Treatment
Blisters	A small pocket of fluid that forms in the upper layers of skin after it has been damaged. Most blisters are filled with a clear fluid (serum), but may be filled with blood (blood blisters) or pus if inflamed or infected.	Repeated rubbing of the skin, e.g. on the foot where the shoe rubs against the heel Burning	Unbroken blisters: don't pierce the bubble. Cover with a plaster or a gauze pad or dressing. Burst blisters: don't peel off the dead skin on top of the blister. Allow the fluid inside to drain and wash it with mild soap and water. Cover the area with a dry, sterile dressing to protect it from infection until it heals.

Injury	Description	Cause	Treatment
Bruises	Bluish or purple-coloured patches that appear on the skin when capillaries break or burst underneath. Blood leaks into the soft tissue under the skin, causing the discolouration.	Impact with a hard object	Cold compressions such as a flannel or cloth soaked in cold water or an ice pack wrapped in a towel will help to reduce swelling and internal bleeding.
Cuts and grazes	Cuts: where the skin is broken causing damage to blood vessels beneath. Graze: where skin is rubbed off again causing damage to blood vessels.	Cuts: contact with a sharp object Graze: scraping or rubbing against a rough surface	Stop any bleeding by applying pressure to the area using a clean, dry absorbent material – such as a bandage, towel or handkerchief. When the bleeding has stopped, clean the wound and cover it with a dressing.
Winding	Difficulty in breathing because of exertion or a blow to the stomach.	A blow to the abdomen by a ball or hitting action, making the diaphragm go into spasm	Loosen the clothing. Sit in a crouched position as this helps the muscles to relax. Try to stay calm and take slow deep breaths.

3 Label the simple illustrations below to identify:

  a) the equipment

  b) the body part being protected – use the anatomical names for the bones and muscles (refer to Chapter 1)

  c) possible injuries that could be suffered if the protection were not worn.

Developing the skills

Sporting and physical activities can place great demands on the body and at times the body cannot cope, with the result being a more serious injury, such as a sprain or strain, or even dislocation of a joint.

The table describes injuries that can occur involving muscles, tendons, ligaments and joints.

Injury	Description	Treatment
Muscular injury	Muscle is overstretched or torn (also known as a strain). Caused when muscles are over-used, e.g. during a weight training session. Muscle strains are particularly common in the legs and back, such as hamstring and lumbar (lower back) strains.	Use of RICE method. Limited training.
Tendon injury	Tendons can also be overstretched or torn (strained). Inflamed tendons (tendonitis) occur through repeated actions (e.g. tennis elbow). Tendon injuries usually happen during activities that involve sudden, sharp movements, such as throwing or jumping, or after repeated overuse of the tendons, such as running.	Use of RICE method. Reduced and limited training. Rest and painkillers if needed.
Ligament injury	Also known as a sprain. Caused by the ligaments being twisted or pulled past their range of movement. A serious injury is the ACL (anterior cruciate ligament) in the knee, a common injury in football and basketball.	Use the RICE treatment in the first instance. Severe pain or a lack of movement could indicate a more serious injury, which might require an operation.
Disclocation	Caused by sudden force that moves the joint out of position (e.g. an arm lock in judo). A dislocated shoulder causes swelling and great discomfort.	Use the RICE method and go straight to the hospital. It is sometimes possible to relocate i.e. (put it back into the ball and socket joint). This could result in an operation depending depend upon the severity of the injury.

4 For each of the types of injury listed in the table, think of physical activities or sports where that kind of injury is a possibility or even likelihood.

The most effective treatment recommend for these kinds of injuries is that of the **RICE** method. This will provide a basic series of steps to support and relieve the injured player. It will ease their pain and decrease the time of recovery. If the injury appears severe, however, it is important to get the person to hospital so they can receive specialist treatment.

Key term

....

RICE: Rest–**I**ce–**C**ompression–**E**levation: the method of treatment after a minor injury

R	Rest	Stop the activity. Rest and protect the injured or sore area.
I	Ice	Apply an ice pack right away to reduce pain and minimise swelling. Then keep applying for 15–20 minutes every two to three hours. A bag of frozen peas, or similar, will also work well. Wrap the ice pack in a towel to avoid it directly touching the skin.
C	Compression	Wrap the area in an elastic bandage. This will help decrease swelling.
E	Elevation	Keep the injured body part raised above the level of the heart whenever possible. This may also help to reduce swelling.

Applying the skills

5 A player sprains their ankle in a football game. Place the following actions in the correct order.

A Apply an ice pack from the first aid box to narrow the blood vessels and reduce the blood flow.

B Stop the person from playing and sit them down, to prevent any further damage.

C Raise the ankle above the heart level to reduce the blood flow and minimise swelling.

D Bandage up the ankle to prevent any further build-up of blood in the injured area.

6 Your local sports club has asked you to make their coaches and players more aware of the different injuries that can happen. They have asked you to create a video they can put on the website to identify different types of injuries with examples. It should give advice on what you should – and should not – do if you see a person injured and how you would treat the injuries.

REFLECTIVE LOG

Research other sporting injuries and the methods that can be used to prevent and treat them. How do the injuries happen? Would the RICE method provide the correct treatment? What kind of protective clothing can be used? Focus on physical activities or sports you are particularly interested in or take part in regularly.

Checklist for success

✔ With a partner, quiz each other by naming an injury and asking the other person to give a description, suggest a cause and outline treatment.

✔ Think of examples of physical activities or sports where particular injuries are likely to occur.

✔ Remember the four stages of treatment using RICE.

Sound progress

• I understand the types of minor injury and can provide sporting examples for them.

• I can identify what RICE stands for and how to use it.

Excellent progress

• I can explain how minor injuries and injuries to muscles, ligaments and tendons happen.

• I can use the RICE method effectively to reduce pain and prevent further damage.

Check your progress

Use these statements as a way of evaluating your progress throughout this chapter.

Sound progress

- I can identify what PEDs are and why some performers use them.
- I can describe the effects of PEDs and the risks involved in using them.
- I can outline the role of organising bodies in preventing the use of PEDs.
- I can identify reasons why performers would use blood doping to enhance their performance.
- I can describe the process that is used to undertake blood doping.
- I can describe what is meant by real and perceived risk.
- I can suggest ways of reducing the risks involved in physical activities.
- I understand the types of minor injury and can provide sporting examples for them.
- I can identify what RICE stands for and how to use it.

Excellent progress

- I can explain the impact that PEDs have upon a performer and why they would use them.
- I can explain the negative consequence of PEDs on both a performer and others.
- I can describe how national and international bodies help prevent drug use through testing, monitoring and education.
- I can explain the reasons why people use blood doping and describe the side effects.
- I am aware of the impact that blood doping has upon a performer and the sport.
- I can give examples of real and perceived risks and describe the difference between them.
- I can assess the levels of risk involved in different activities.
- I can devise strategies for preventing risk or protecting against injury during physical activities.
- I can explain how minor injuries and injuries to muscles, ligaments and tendons happen.
- I can use the RICE method effectively to reduce pain and prevent further damage.

Acknowledgements

Photographs

The publishers wish to thank the following for permission to reproduce photographs. Every effort has been made to trace copyright holders and to obtain their permission for the use of copyright materials. The publishers will gladly receive any information enabling them to rectify any error or omission at the first opportunity.

(t = top, c = centre, b = bottom, r = right, l = left)

Cover & p 1 © Stefan Schurr/Shutterstock; p7 Wilson's Vision/Shutterstock; p11 Dennis Kuvaev/Shutterstock; p15 notarYes/Shutterstock; p17 Gwoeii/Shutterstock; p20(tl) Palych1378/Shutterstock; p20(r) Alan Edwards/Alamy; p20(bl) takoburito/Shutterstock; p24 ruigsantos/Shutterstock; p31(t) Marcos Mesa Sam Wordley/Shutterstock; p31(b) Wavebreakmedia/Shutterstock; p34 AkeSak/Shutterstock; p42 Rich Carey/Shutterstock; p45 Microgen/Shutterstock; p47 Dima Moroz/Shutterstock; p60 ostill/Shutterstock; p62 Maxisport/Shutterstock; p66 Zuma Press Inc/Alamy; p70 Rido/Shutterstock; p74 LeventeGyori/Shutterstock; p77 art_of_sun/Shutterstock; p78 Georgias Kollidas/Shutterstock; p79(ttr) smileus/Shutterstock; p79(tr) Wavebreakdmedia/Shutterstock; p79(c,br) BlueSkyImages/Shutterstock; p79(bbr) Chen Ws/Shutterstock; p80(l) patrimonio designs/Shutterstock; p80(r) Jasper Image/Shutterstock; p81(t) Herbert Kratky/Shutterstock; p81(r) mooinblack/Shutterstock; p81(b) Alfonso de Tomas/Shutterstock; p84 John Kropwricki/Shutterstock; p85 Radu Razvan/Shutterstock; p86(l) Joe McNally/Getty Images; p86(r) PCN Photography/Alamy; p89(t) Matthew Lewis/Getty Images; p89(b) Ken Cook/Shutterstock; p90(t) Aspen Photos/Shutterstock; p90(c) Stu Forester/Getty Images; p90(b) grant Pritchard/Alamy; p93 acceptphoto/Shutterstock; p96 Brois15/Shutterstock; p99 maxpro/Shutterstock; p104 National Health Service; p106 Shaun Finch/Alamy; p109 Alex Brylov/Shutterstock; p110(t) Steve Christo/Getty Images; p110(b) Lilyana Vynogradova/Shutterstock; p111 robert_s/Shutterstock; p112 Mitch Gunn/Shutterstock; p113 Lifetime Stock/Shutterstock; p116 Banks Photos/Getty Images; p120 BSIP/Getty Images; p126 photobyphotoboy/Shutterstock; p131 Wavebreakmedia/Shutterstock; p134 Inu/Shutterstock; p142 alphaspirit/Shutterstock; p143 Bettmann/Getty Images; p144(l) Roka Pics/Shutterstock; p144(c) dotshock/Shutterstock; p144(r) Jamie Roach/Shutterstock; p144(b) Nelosa/Shutterstock; p145(t) S Forster/Alamy; p145(b) Dennis Grombkowski/Getty Images; p147(t) Lilyana Vynogradova/Shutterstock; p147(tc) fizkes/Shutterstock; p147(bc) Mooinblack/Shutterstock; p147(b) Photoworks/Shutterstock; p147(l) Marco Govei/Shutterstock; p148(b) Matt King/Getty Images; p151(l) Oscar Max/Alamy; p151(r) Viktor Cap/Alamy; p152 Hamish Blair/Getty Images; p154 Aflo/Getty Images; p156(t) ostill/Shutterstock; p156(b) Matt King/Getty Images; p158(t) epa/Alamy; p158(b) lightbpoet/Shutterstock; p159(t) ARENA/Creative/Shutterstock; p159(c) Francesc Juan/Shutterstock; p159(b) valjakum/Shutterstock; p159(bb) Jasper Juinen/Getty Images; p166(l) GONAZLO/Bauer/Griffin/Getty Images; p166(cl) photogolfer/Shutterstock; p166(cr) Jurgen Hasenkopf/Alamy; p166(r) Bob Thomas/Getty Images; p173 Bruce Trolff/Shutterstock; p175(l) Wavebreakmedia/Shutterstock; p175(r) patpitchaya/Shutterstock; p177 Timothy A Clary/Getty Images; p178 tomertu/Shutterstock; p179 Gajus/Shutterstock; p181(l) Juice Images/Alamy; p181(c) Ian Walton/Getty Images; p181(r) Andrew Redington/Getty Images; p183 Paolo Bono/Shutterstock; p186(tl) Blend Images/Shutterstock; p186(tr) Andy Hooper/REX/Shutterstock; p186(b) Laurence Griffiths/Getty Images; p188 Nigel Roddis/Getty Images; p189(l) Matthew Stockman/Getty Images; p189(r) Gilbert Lund/Getty Images; p190(t) Gabriel Buoys/Getty Images; p190(b) Elnariz/Shutterstock; p192(tr) REUTERS/Alamy; p192(br) Jeff Haynes/Getty Images; p192(bl) Ian MacNichol/Getty Images; p194 Phovoir/Shutterstock; p198 freesoulproductions/Shutterstock; p200(tl) candyBox Images/Shutterstock; p200(tc) Syda Productions/Shutterstock; p200(tr) 2xSamara.com/Shutterstock; p209(cl) Pressmaster/Shutterstock; p200(cc) glenda/Shutterstock; p200(cr) Marcin Balcerzak/Shutterstock; p200(lb) Andrey_Popov/Shutterstock; p200(lc) Bojan Milinkov/Shutterstock; p200(lr) herbet Katky/Shutterstock; p206 Krilurk Warasup/Shutterstock; p207(t) Maxisport/Shutterstock; p207(b) Alex Goodlett/Getty Images; p210 James Brunker News/Alamy; p218(t) Spiber.com/Shutterstock; p218(b) Bucchi Francesco/Shutterstock; p223(t) Bigred/Alamy; p223(c) Blend Images/Alamy; p223(b) rvisoft/Alamy; p228 Natacha Pisarenko/Press Association; p230 Katatonia82/Shutterstock; p235(l) David Munden/Popperfoto/Getty Images; p235(cl) Mike Brett/Popperfot/Getty Images; p235(cr) INTERFOTO/Alamy; p235(r) Stu Forster/Getty Images; p237 Stu Forster/Getty Images; p238(l) John Peters/Getty Images; p238(c) Luca Bruno/Press Association; p238(r) Dan Mullan/Getty Images; p239(t) Ross Land/Getty Images; p239(b) Ian Walton/Getty Images; p241 Jonny Kuntz/Press Association; p242 Viper Spilt; p243 THE AGE/Getty Images; p249 Robert Kneschke/Shutterstock; p250 laztllama/Shutterstock; p251(tl) Jimmie 48 Photography/Shutterstock; p251(cl) Marc Pagani Photography/Shutterstock; p251(bl) Tom Duffy/Getty Images; p251(tc) BUGNUT23/Shutterstock; p251(bc) Robert Cianflone/Getty Images; p251(tr) Paoloa Bono/Shutterstock; p251(cr) Martin Bureau/Getty Images; p251(br) emipress/Shutterstock; p253 Stu Forster/Getty Images; p254 Noah Seelam/Getty Images; p256 BigManKn/Shutterstock; p257 Christos Geogriou/Shutterstock; p261 Evgenia Bolyukh/Shutterstock; p263(l) Paul Orr/Shutterstock; p263(c) dotschock/Shutterstock; p263(r) CROX/Shutterstock; p264 Wayne0216/Shutterstock.

Text and data

The publishers wish to thank the following for permission to reproduce text and data. Every effort has been made to trace copyright holders and to obtain their permission for the use of copyright materials. The publishers will gladly receive any information enabling them to rectify any error or omission at the first opportunity.

We are grateful to the following for permission to reproduce copyright material:

Oxford University Press for the definition of "health" on page 94 from Oxford English Dictionary Online. By permission of Oxford University Press; World Health Organization definition of "health" on page 94. Reprinted from the Preamble to the Constitution of the World Health Organization as adopted by the International Health Conference, New York, 19-22 June, 1946; signed 22 July 1946. http://www.who.int/about/definition/en/print.html; The Food Standards Agency for The Eatwell Plate on page 104. Source: http://collections.europarchive.org/tna/20100927130941/http://food.gov.uk/healthiereating/eatwellplate © Crown copyright 2010; Professor Mark Wahlqvist for the table on page 105 'Energy used in different physical Activities' adapted from Asia Pacific Journal of Clinical Nutrition, HEC Press, http://apjcn.nhri.org.tw/server/info/books-phds/books/foodfacts/html/maintext/fig12.html, copyright © 2010 National Health Research Institutes. All Rights Reserved; BARB for 2016 viewing figures on page 226, www.BARB.co.uk, copyright © BARB. Reproduced with permission; Gold Coast 2018 Commonwealth Games Corporation (GOLDOC) for the logo on page 229 from Gold Coast 2018, XXI Commonwealth Games, https://www.gc2018.com. Reproduced with permission; International Hockey Federation (FIH) for the logo on page 229 from FIH Hockey Champions London 2016, www.fih.ch. Reproduced with permission; Invictus Games Foundation for the logo on page 229 from Invictus Games London 2014, www.invictusgames.org. Reproduced with permission; and 13th FINA World Swimming Championships, Windsor for the logo on page 229 from Windsor 2016 Ontario Canada FINA World Swimming Championships (25m), http://www.fina.org/content/13th-fina-world-swimming-championships-25m-2016. Reproduced with permission.

Index

Note: page numbers in bold refer to key word definitions.